MIDLANDS

Jonny Steinberg is a journalist and a script-writer. In the mid-1990s he was awarded a Rhodes Scholarship and studied at Oxford University where he graduated with a doc-torate in political theory. He returned to South Africa in 1998 and worked for Business Day, *writing on the constitutional court and the police. He left* Business Day *to write* Midlands, *which he did while based at the Centre for the Study of Violence and Reconciliation in Johannesburg. Steinberg is currently working on his second book.*

MIDLANDS

JONNY STEINBERG

JONATHAN BALL PUBLISHERS
JOHANNESBURG & CAPE TOWN

Published in 2002 by
JONATHAN BALL PUBLISHERS (PTY) LTD
P O Box 33977
Jeppestown
2043

ISBN 1 86842 124 4

Design by Michael Barnett, Johannesburg
Computer enhanced image on front cover by Heather Gourlay-Conyngham
Typesetting and reproduction of text by Alinea Studio, Cape Town
Cover reproduction by TripleM Advertising & Design, Johannesburg
Printed and bound by Paarl Print, Oosterland Street, Paarl, South Africa

ACKNOWLEDGEMENTS

Some time during the autumn of 1999, I phoned Graeme Simpson, executive director of the Centre for the Study of Violence and Reconciliation in Johannesburg.

'Graeme,' I said, 'I want to resign from my job and write a book about the murders of white farmers. Would you be prepared to give me an office and a telephone at the Centre?'

'I can do a lot more than that,' Graeme replied, without a second thought. 'I can make you a full-time, salaried employee and we can raise some money to pay for your research and salary.'

I'm not sure if this book would ever have been written without that generosity. It has been a fraught and lonely enterprise in the best of circumstances; without the institutional and financial support I received, I would almost certainly have abandoned it.

Aside from Graeme Simpson, there are others at the Centre to thank. Writing about a murder is a dark business. Having the corridors filled with warm and witty people – like Sasha Gear, S'bu Ntuli, Brandon Hamber, Polly Dewhirst and Pule Rampa – made it that much easier.

Claire Wright went well beyond the call of a lawyer's duty and found her client a publisher. I am extremely grateful for that.

Just when I had convinced myself that researching this book was impossible, Mark Shaw showed me a way into Langeni. Many thanks.

Several people read early drafts of the manuscript. I wish to thank four in particular. Carol Steinberg, had she chosen to live another life, would have made a wise and perspicacious literary editor. A couple of chapters in, she knew exactly how this book ought to be written, and told me about it. I hope I managed to carry out her advice.

Antony Altbeker's sharp and quirky insights were as eccentric and refreshing as he is. He was unreservedly amused by the tics, hang-ups and angst which he spotted in the most unlikely places, and he got me to laugh along with him.

I met Ivan Vladislavić at the lowest of ebbs. 'Seems to me,' he said, a little sarcastically, 'that you don't so much need editing as literary therapy.' He gave me both – they kind of came together in one package – and they worked.

Mark Gevisser applied his considerable gifts as both a writer and a journalist to his reading of the manuscript. I fear there are times when I drove him insane with my incessant questions, fears and obsessions. Thanks for putting up with me.

I have been blessed with a wonderful publisher. Jonathan Ball's enthusiasm for this book has been manna from heaven. And Francine Blum, whose competence in the production of books is surely unrivalled, has been a delight to work with. Many thanks to Owen Hendry for his fine copy editing.

Finally, I owe a debt of gratitude to funders. This book was supported in part by a grant from the Individual Project Fellowships Program of the Open Society Institute. Thank you to Gail Goodman, the former Individual Project Fellowships Program Manager, who was wonderful to me. I am particularly indebted to Mike Savage for his backing.

This book was also funded in part by the Harry Frank Guggenheim Foundation. Many thanks to the Foundation's Karen Kolvard, who gave warm support at a critical juncture.

PREFACE

In the months after South Africa voted Nelson Mandela into power, disturbing reports began filtering in from across the countryside. In June 1994, police in a remote Free State village reported that a white farmer had been stabbed to death in his homestead garden. Workers on the farm reported seeing three young black men driving away from the scene in the dead man's jeep.

A few days later, a farmer and his wife were shot dead in their home 700 kilometres away in the citrus-growing region of the Western Cape. The intruders took a car, a shotgun and R600 in cash. The following week, two similar reports were received from a rural district close to the Zimbabwean border, 1 900 kilometres from the previous attack. By the beginning of 1997, violent assaults on farmers were being recorded at an average of three or four a week. They have remained at that level ever since.

The meaning of this violence has never been clear. On the one hand, the motive for the vast majority of attacks appears to be robbery; the perpetrators flee the scene of the crime with guns, cars and money. And yet, so many attacks are accompanied by seemingly gratuitous violence, the violence itself performed with such ceremony and drama, that the infliction of painful death appears to be the primary motive. 'Farm murders', as South Africans have come to call them, occupy a strange and ambiguous space; they tamper with the boundary between acquisitive crime and racial hatred.

These attacks are all the more puzzling for having escalated in the early days of Mandela's presidency. The old man was larger than life; his generosity and his humour lifted him above his times, and he appeared to be taking South Africa with him. There was a feeling of lightness on the streets of Johannesburg and Cape Town, a sense of a common humanity that had been absent for centuries.

So the news coming in from the hinterland was troubling. Urban South Africa has always found the countryside inscrutable. The occasional Sunday newspaper feature on a rural town seems fantastical and strange – like a poor imitation of a Marquez story. Now, the dispatches from farming districts appeared to be telling us something all too real. Perhaps the goodwill of the Mandela period was illusory? Perhaps there were a host of unsettled scores we had brushed under the carpet? Maybe, for once, the country-side was way ahead of us, bringing a grim portent of life after the honeymoon.

*

In the late 1990s, I worked for *Business Day* newspaper in Johannes-burg, reporting on constitutional law and policing. Farm murders featured occasionally among the stories I covered, and reporting on them was a frustrating business. I wrote the same distilled, for-mulaic reports everyone else based in the cities did, scratching the surface, understanding nothing. I raised some money, and in September 1999 resigned from my job and began scouting the countryside in search of some stories I could get my teeth into.

In November, I found myself in the beautiful town of Alanview, in the southern midlands of KwaZulu-Natal, observing a tense and uncomfortable meeting between farmers and provincial secu-rity force representatives. Peter Mitchell, a 28-year-old white man, had been shot dead on his father's farm a few weeks earlier. Arthur, the dead man's father, sat with his back to me, a silent, subdued figure.

By then, I had visited half a dozen farming districts around South Africa and had interviewed dozens of widows, orphans and childless parents. My intention at that stage was to record the sto-ries of four or five murders across the country, to use breadth and variety to capture the texture of the epidemic. But after a couple of months in the Alanview district, it became clear that it would require a book to do justice to the story of Peter Mitchell's murder. I either had to abandon it completely or forfeit the other stories I was working on.

Mitchell was killed, not just figuratively, but quite literally, on the southern midlands' racial frontier, the dust road on which he died a boundary between the white-owned commercial farmlands to the west and the derelict common land of a dying black peasantry to the east. Those who murdered Mitchell did so in order to push the boundary back, a campaign their forebears had begun in the closing years of the nineteenth century, and which their great-grandchildren believed it their destiny, as the generation to witness apartheid's demise, to finish.

For his part, the dead man's father knew the score, and resolved to defend his land and fight to the finish. Following his son's murder, Arthur Mitchell, his rage contained and guided, resumed his daily journey to his irrigation fields along the dirt road on which his son was killed, three bodyguards in tow, their automatic rifles scanning the bush. His daily farm work done, he would take up his second job – finding his son's killers.

I initially thought I was to write about an event from the recent past, but it soon became clear that much of the story lay in the immediate future, and that I would do well to hang around and record it. This was a silent frontier battle, the combatants groping hungrily for the whispers and lies that drifted in from the other side. It was clear from the start that Peter Mitchell would not be the only one to die on that border, that I had arrived at the beginning of a deadly endgame. And I knew that the story of his and subsequent deaths would illuminate a great deal about the early days of post-apartheid South Africa.

*

The murder that is the subject of this book took place in 1999, several kilometres from a small village in the southern midlands of KwaZulu-Natal. I have changed the name of that village, and indeed, of every southern midlands town, river and mountain that appears in this book. I have also changed the names of those who people these pages, both the living and the dead. The date on which the man I have called Peter Mitchell was murdered has been altered, as well as the dates of several other events that might reveal the identities of people who agreed to talk to me. This, I have come to see, is the consequence of writing about an unsolved murder.

Changing names was not an easy decision. Any journalist who endeavours to conceal must, if he is honest, admit to a defeat of sorts. A book that claims the status of a historical or documentary record surely loses some of its authority when the names scattered across that record are fictitious.

But there are many reasons why I was compelled to do this. During the course of my research, several people in this story made it clear that if I was to continue interviewing them, I must either remove them, or their names, from the record. By the time the research was done, the list had grown quite large. My choice was either to write a book that divided the names of people and places into the real and the fictitious, or to change all names.

One of those who asked me to conceal his identity was the father of the murdered man. I am not convinced that his reasons are sound. It is true, as you will soon see, that there are people living on his land who would like to kill him. At least once, a plot to assassinate him appears to have been planned. Yet it is also true that those who want him dead know who he is and where to find him, and that nothing recorded in this book will quicken their resolve. Everything he said to me he has said publicly, in contexts more immediate and damaging than the black-and-white of a distant book.

Nonetheless, I had no choice but to accede to his request, no matter his reasoning or his motives. This was not so much a legal, as an ethical consideration, one which stems from my understanding that every journalist hurts the person about whom he writes. It is not the sort of violation that can be captured in any sane law. The violation simply consists in the fact that the journalist, and not the subject, is the one who pens the book, and the subject, once he has read it, no matter how meticulously truthful the document, almost always wishes he had kept his mouth shut. Everybody who is written about has an image of what he will look like on the printed page. He is always disappointed. Mitchell cooperated with me because he believed, initially, that this book might bring him justice. I, on the other hand, approached him because I believed that his son's murder said something of extraordinary value about life on post-apartheid South Africa's racial frontier, something that had not been properly recorded before. In the gap between our respective motivations lies the violation.

A person who agrees to open his world to a journalist is not simply inviting a crowd of innumerable strangers into his life. A book's author, together with its readership, is a vicarious and hungry animal. It intrudes greedily, from the shelter of its own invisibility. However much the self-righteous journalist may protest, it remains true that his vocation is not a generous one. That is why the gap between a journalist's and his subject's motivations is troublesome. My task was not to protect Mitchell from his readership, still less to point out the poisonousness of having a readership at all. On the contrary, I was on the readers' side. My purpose was to tell a grander story, one that happened to implicate, and to reach into the life of, a man who had agreed to talk to me.

So, having rummaged through Mitchell's life for my own purposes, I felt that I owed something more to him than truthfulness. Rightly or wrongly, his request for concealment became that something. I did not ask him why he had become coy. Perhaps he realised, a little late in the day, what it means to have a stranger write a book about the murder of one's son. I decided that his motivations were no longer my business.

Then, there was the question of those who briefly stood charged with Peter Mitchell's murder. I tried on several occasions to make contact with the man I have called Mduduzi Cube, but each attempt, for reasons you will soon discover, failed. I was careful not to betray him or his family. Everything I have written about their lives I have checked and double-checked. Nonetheless, the point remains that I did not sit down with Cube, tell him my story and ask him for his. The prospect of using his name, without his knowledge, in a book that implicates him in so grave a matter, was deeply troubling.

*

There is one moment in this book where I have changed not just names but characters and identities. Two of the people I met while researching this book helped me on condition that they remain not just anonymous but invisible. This left me with a dilemma. My conversations with them had constituted one of the most formative aspects of my research. I felt that without their perspectives, and an account of the manner in which they were expressed, the book would be horribly incomplete.

So we struck a compromise. I took a fairly innocuous character in the book, whom I have called Elias Sithole; I altered his personal history to the extent that he became unidentifiable. And then I filled him up with the discourse of two people who refused to appear in this book. So, the words exchanged between Elias and me at the dinner in Izita and in the Pietermaritzburg pub are real enough: they are indeed verbatim transcripts of my discussions with the two men who demanded they remain invisible. All that has changed is that I have disguised the identities of those who uttered them.

*

Finally, the pages that follow are littered with historical episodes, some from as far back as the 1820s, others from as recent as 1994. I have changed the names of historical figures, institutions, tribes and clans. Where the specificity of an historical event threatened to reveal its location, I painted the episode in broad brushstrokes.

As with all Zulu families, the surnames of the Normandale tenants are not arbitary. Everybody's surname reveals something of his clan's history over the past 200 years; as you will soon see, the fate of the Normandale tenants' respective forebears has some bearing on the context of Peter Mitchell's murder. In choosing pseudonyms for the Normandale tenants, I have endeavoured, wherever possible, to keep their names consistent with their real clan histories. Where I have faltered in this task, students of Zulu history will probably grimace. I apologise in advance.

PART ONE

ONE

The Mitchell property lies on the slopes of one of the most beautiful valleys I have ever seen. It is in the heart of the southern midlands of KwaZulu-Natal, Alan Paton country, and it is true that '... from there, if there is no mist, you look down on one of the fairest scenes of Africa' Later I will tell you more about that landscape, and of how it changed during the course of my investigation; a spectacular backdrop of giant shapes and colours when I first saw it, a myriad dramas of human anger and violence when I left. But on my first journey out of that valley, what struck me was the peculiar position of the Mitchells' farmhouse. It offered only a miserly view of the visual feast beyond its doorstep. Instead, it faced the harsh bushveld on the slopes, and I wondered about the sensibility of the one who chose its location, many decades before the Mitchells settled there.

I arrived at the Mitchells' front gate at mid-morning on an unforgivingly hot day in the summer of 2000. Outside the fence, two brown men sat watching me from under the shade of a tree. They wore camouflage uniforms, their automatic rifles slung over their right shoulders. I nodded at them and they stared back expressionlessly. In front of me, the gate consisted of thick wrought-iron bars; a tall, forbidding fence stretched away from it on either side. Two young German Shepherds had trotted to the gate at the sound of my car. They paced there nervously, waiting for a signal from their master. Arthur Mitchell duly appeared and mumbled inaudibly to his dogs. They responded immediately, their sharp ears folding back over the sides of their skulls, their tails flicking, as the prospect of danger was transformed, at the sound of their master's voice, into an object of benign curiosity.

Mitchell was short, large-bellied and middle-aged, with the bright red neck that is a white farmer's signature. He greeted me with the studied civility I would come to know well, and ushered me into his home. There was something empty and abstract about its décor and I was struck immediately by its impersonality. Dark wood, subdued fabrics, everything impeccably neat and characterless. It was more an emblem of a middle-class home than the particular home of a particular family. Its decorator appeared to have had no particular taste, but had chosen the furniture only for the trappings of bourgeois respectability it signalled. For a strange moment, I imagined I was in a museum rather than a home, a distilled exhibition of a white middle-class lifestyle. Mitchell was its curator, ushering me through its silent rooms.

As I sat down to tea with my host, I suddenly realised what was troubling me. There were no pictures of Peter, Mitchell's dead son, and as I thought of him sitting in this very lounge just three-and-a-half months earlier, a young, strong man who had given little thought to his mortality, the absence of any signs of his existence appeared to haunt his father's house. It was impossible to absorb this home and its trappings without feeling the presence of the dead man who had recently lived there.

*

Peter Mitchell was 28 years old when he was shot and killed on the dirt track between his father's farmhouse and his irrigation fields. Farming tomatoes and cabbages requires a daily trip to the river bank to open the water pump, check the irrigation system for leaks, and monitor the workers who weed each vegetable one by one. Father and son took turns to do the daily trip and the assassins would not have known in advance whom they were going to kill. Peter had procrastinated that day, the entire morning filled up with a welding job that would not end. It was almost two in the afternoon before he set off for the irrigation fields.

Getting to the dirt track from the nearest public road is a four-kilometre journey on a narrow path that winds through dense bush, so the assassins must have started out by mid-morning at the latest. The maze of faint tracks that mark the bush is not navigable for anybody who has not spent a great deal of time there. Somebody among the party was able to navigate a brisk path from the public road to the dirt track, somebody who had spent a lot of his life on those farms and knew their labyrinths well.

4

The assassins seem to have thought that father or son had already made the journey to the irrigation fields, for it appears that the ambush was designed to stop a vehicle travelling towards the farmhouse. They chose a short, steep incline where the driver of a sluggish van or jeep would have no chance of racing away from danger. They must have been surprised to hear the noise of the jeep coming from the other direction.

Mitchell was shot neatly behind the left ear at short range with a shotgun. The entry wound suggests that he was looking to his right when he was shot. Somebody on the right-hand side of the road must have signalled to him to stop. He must have turned to talk when the bullet hit him from the other side of the jeep. Hugging the road to Mitchell's left is a thick bush with a deep hollow in the ground behind it. The assassin could have stood there at full height, two metres from Mitchell's vehicle, without being seen.

No cartridges were left at the scene, no fingerprints, no cigarette butts from which DNA evidence could be extracted – an unusually professional operation for a rural murder. Mitchell's pistol was taken from his hip, but his cellphone and his wallet were left behind.

A construction worker who was on the Mitchells' property to build a concrete weir found the body at 4:20 that afternoon, a little less than two hours after the killing. Seeing a stationary jeep with the engine idling he thought the driver had gone into the bushes to relieve himself. He waited about five minutes, then walked up to the vehicle and found Mitchell's body slumped over the driver's seat, his blood splattered on the windscreen.

By nightfall, most of the farmers in the district had visited the scene, stared at their neighbour's lifeless body, observed its stiffness as it was unfolded onto a stretcher and placed in the back of a police van. There was a bite to their horror that is absent from the horror of most murders. For white farmers were not killed under apartheid. Not like this, at any rate. They were killed by jealous spouses, by disturbed neighbours and by crazed children. But never like this.

A friend of mine who grew up on a massive maize farm in the Free State told me how, in the 1970s, his family used to leave the front door unlocked when they went away for a three-week holiday. Once, they came back to find their house had been looted;

5

everything was gone – the beds, the kitchen stove, the Persian rug that stretched across the living room floor. My friend remembers his father shaking his head. 'What is this country coming to? When you take your children on holiday, you have to lock your front door.'

But murder? Never. No black man entered the vast commercial farmlands to kill a member of a powerful white family. And on the handful of occasions when a crazy black man did kill a white, the police would comb the countryside with their fists and their electric shocks and they would get a confession.

So the horror of Mitchell's neighbours was starkly, inevitably political. The body before them was inscribed with the signs of the time, a time in which whites had lost institutional power and black men had become brave enough to walk onto a farm and kill its proprietor.

The morning after his son's death, Mitchell paid a visit to Langeni, the cluster of kraals at the bottom of Normandale from which he recruited about 40 women every morning to pick his tomatoes. He told the women waiting for him he knew that his son had been killed by people living in Langeni and that he would employ nobody from the kraals any longer. But the people whom he wanted to hear his message were not there. Usually, the unemployed men of Langeni would settle early into the Tearoom, a derelict shack at the side of the road that sells cheap beer, maize meal, tea and coffee. That morning, it was empty for the first time in months. The men of Langeni were nowhere to be seen. In the days that followed, several Langeni men were detained and questioned about the murder of Peter Mitchell. Each gave his alibi and each was released. After a couple of weeks, the police stopped coming. The Tearoom opened its doors and men began to sit there again.

*

We have taken our tea, I have filled a large notebook with Mitchell's words, and we are preparing for the trip down to the irrigation fields. The two brown men stand up when they hear the sound of Mitchell's jeep. He sticks his head out of the open window and addresses them in Afrikaans, his soft English accent smoothing out the rough consonants.

'Matthew, come with us. Hendrik, stay and watch the house.'

Turner, the smaller of Mitchell's dogs, climbs into the back of the jeep and settles on the right. Matthew gives the dog a wide berth and sits down on the left. Mitchell eyes Matthew in his rearview mirror. 'No,' he says. 'Sit right. Face left.'

Carved out of the wild midlands jungle, the four-kilometre track between the farmhouse and the irrigation fields is rutted and difficult and Matthew leans his back heavily against the sidewall of the jeep, the safety catch on his rifle unclipped, the barrel pointing searchingly into the bush. The vegetation on either side is thick and claustrophobic, the clearing through which we drive a narrow tunnel. Thorn-bush branches scrape against the windscreen and brush the side of my head. Turner's snout wanders too far out of the back of the jeep and he is caught on the nose by a passing branch. He sneezes fitfully then resumes his post.

You see nothing of the beautiful valley from the Mitchells' dirt track. A few metres beyond the side of the road, the landscape is swallowed up by the jungle. Sitting at my desk months later, I read over what I have written and the scenery is ominous in a kitsch and obvious way, as if this place was designed for a murder. I strain to remember the bush differently, and I wonder whether it would have been lighter and less suggestive if I had done that trip under different circumstances.

About two kilometres from his farmhouse Mitchell stops the jeep, pulls up the handbrake and reaches for a long canvas bag that has been lying between our two seats. He unzips it to reveal a short-barreled shotgun, loads it with bright red shells and places it on his lap. From his hip holster he takes a silver nine-mill. pistol, checks its magazine and tucks it under his right thigh.

He cuts the engine so I can hear him. 'See that narrow gap in the undergrowth on the right?'

I nod uncertainly. I would have missed it had he not pointed it out – a tiny tunnel winding into the bush, big enough for a rabbit or a baby duiker.

'If a stranger follows that path he will get lost in no time. He will walk all day, further and further into the bush and never come out. But if you have lived here all your life, that trail is a thoroughfare that links this farm, Derbytin, to the next one, Normandale. After Normandale, it leaves the bush and does a wide arc around Langeni, where the Cubes and the Mashabanas live, and then comes out directly onto the public road. It is the only way to reach this dirt track without walking through my farmyard. If there is going to be another ambush, it will be somewhere between here and the spot Peter was killed.'

'What makes you so certain?'

'Two weeks ago, Matthew and Hendrik called me out. There were faint tracks here, left by two pairs of sneakers. And a flattened-out patch of ground, under this bush, nice and snug, two metres from the centre of the road but buried deep in the undergrowth. They could settle there unseen, close enough to touch us. The Bushmen judged that they had sat there for three or four hours. We traced the spoor back into the bush. They went all the way across Normandale, right to the outskirts of Langeni.'

'Was it going to be an ambush? Did they want to kill you?'

'No, not with only two of them. They are too cowardly to kill in twos. They would have watched. Reconnaissance. They would have watched me come past with three armed men and wondered to themselves how on earth they could get enough advantage to kill all of us without being shot at themselves.'

Mitchell pauses and looks out into the bush. 'If they are good they could do it, easily. Look at the thick bush; they can crouch right next to you and you will not know they are there.'

We drive another 500 metres or so and Mitchell turns off the jeep again. He gets out, gestures for me to follow, and then stops halfway up a steep hill we have just descended.

'This is where my son was killed.'

He shows me the mechanics of the murder in fine detail – the bush where the killer must have stood, the precise position of Peter's car, the direction in which he was looking when he was killed. His exposition is dry and emotionless, as if he is demonstrating the workings of a machine. He turns his back to me and his voice is less certain now.

'You know his brains were splattered all over the windscreen. That is the only thing I am thankful for. He did not know a thing.'

*

Later in the day, Mitchell takes a call on his cellphone from the detective investigating his son's murder. We are in his tomato fields, close to the river bank. He starts wandering away as he listens to his phone, motions me to come with him, Matthew to stay. He does not trust his brown bodyguard to overhear conversations about the hunt for his son's killers. The white journalist he can trust; he wants me to know that I am on the inside. I decline his invitation and stay with Matthew. After a moment's silence I smile at him and offer him a cigarette.

He and Hendrik are Khoi-San, the descendants of hunter-gatherers. For generations, their ancestors wandered southern Africa with their bows and arrows, stalking the animals of the wild. By the time Matthew and Hendrik were born, their kind was on the brink of extinction. Modernity had squeezed them into a tiny corner of the Kalahari desert where they had become the props of a living museum: flesh-and-blood relics of a distant civilisation.

It is a credit to the ingenuity of apartheid South Africa's war-mongers that they found a practical use for the Khoi-San's most exotic skill: the capacity to track the faint spoor left on the Kalahari ground by any living creature. When South Africa went to war with the liberation movements on its borders, hundreds of young men of the Khoi-San were offered an escape from the death throes of their culture and hurled into the trenches of a war for which they little cared. They were ill-placed to grasp that they had attached themselves to another dying breed – white minority rule. By 1994 they were jobless outcasts, the army to which they had lent their skills defeated at the negotiating table, southern Africa's new rulers suspicious of their past allegiances.

Mitchell, who was himself once a soldier in apartheid's wars, found Matthew and Hendrik on the streets of the dry Karoo town of Kimberley, 600 kilometres south-east of the homes to which they will never return. The blood of Namibian freedom fighters on their hands, they have not set foot in their native land since democracy came to Namibia in 1990. When Mitchell found them, neither had worked in five years. They had spent their days in a makeshift camp of army tents, waiting for another war.

It is a strange irony that the lives of these marginal, forgotten men should follow the front line of the region's politics so closely. In the 1980s they found themselves fighting conventional warfare between black and white. Now they follow the racial frontier as it is displaced, silently and unannounced, into the gentle farmlands of KwaZulu-Natal. I wonder where white men will drag these people next. Were it possible to witness the next 20 years of their lives, would one see in their footsteps how the future of this region is to pan out?

'Who is the enemy here?' I ask Matthew.

'The enemy?'

'Who is Mitchell afraid of?'

'The people waiting for him in the bush.'

'Who are they?'

'The ones who killed his son. The ones who want to kill him.'

'Why do they want to kill him?'

The question appears to unsettle him. He shrugs, adjusts his rifle and stares into the bush. Several minutes of silence go by and I am deciding how to broach the issue from another angle, when Matthew suddenly answers, as if I have just asked the question.

'I am not from these parts. I do not know why people want to kill each other here.'

'But you must have given it some thought. You must wonder who it is waiting for Mitchell in the bush.'

Matthew adjusts his rifle again and looks me in the eye for the first time. His reply is surprisingly fluent and confident.

'They want the bush back. Like it was before the whites arrived.'

TWO

The first time I laid eyes on Arthur Mitchell, I sensed he was a near-defeated man. Three weeks had passed since his son's death, and I was observing a meeting between white farmers and representatives of the criminal justice system – prosecutors, detectives, soldiers. My research was in its infancy then; I did not know yet that I would be writing a book about the Mitchell murder. I had been commissioned by the government's Department of Safety and Security to assess its crime-fighting plan in the midlands, which is why I found myself in that meeting. While I did my work, I kept an eye out for a good story.

We were seated around a conference table at the Alanview golf club. Beyond a large bay window, elderly white men shuffled across the fairways on ageing legs, trailed by black caddies slouching under the weight of golf bags. The atmosphere was bitter and accusing. The farmers had before them a memorandum addressed to the provincial minister of safety and security. The first bullet stated that the security force presence in the district was so negligible as to be non-existent. The second argued that the farming community's own security organisation, Farm Watch, was fulfilling what should be government's primary obligation – the full-scale policing of the district. The third demanded that, since farmers were doing the state's duty, their work be subsidised by government.

The geography of the room was sharply adversarial. A long table stretching the length of the entire room, a line of stern-faced men in checked and khaki shirts on one side, on the other, a clumsy assortment of army and police uniforms, uncomfortable faces, wandering eyes, fidgeting hands.

This was my first taste of farmer politics in the district and I wondered, as I listened to the staccato delivery of demands, whether this community was hopelessly naïve, or whether a stud-

11

ied, tactical intelligence lay buried in the subtext of its accusations. For there was no way government was going to acknowledge that state security functions had ceased, less still that the work of a private police force, there to protect the landed from the poor, was going to be subsidised from state coffers.

Mitchell sat with his back to me and I did not notice his presence until his fate became the focal point of the meeting. The managing director of Farm Watch, Colin Waugh, gestured to Mitchell and began speaking casually, as if describing a mundane, commonplace occurrence.

'This is Arthur Mitchell. He used to farm a herd of more than 300 prime beef cattle until they were stolen, one by one.'

Waugh paused, cast a sharp gaze across the uniformed men along the other side of the table, and continued, his voice too casual, its lack of drama too studied. 'As you all know, his son was killed on his farm three weeks ago. The murderers are still at large. Maybe Arthur can say a few words on the subject.'

Mitchell was the only farmer seated on the security force side of the table, and the army colonels and police superintendents had to revolve in their seats and turn their heads out of respect for the one who was about to speak. The shifting flesh and creaking chairs sucked the room's tension into the moment, and Mitchell proceeded in a voice so quiet that the fidgeters and the wandering eyes had to stop to hear him.

'The day after my son was murdered, a reward of R20 000 was put out for information leading to the arrest of his killers. I'm sure I do not have to explain to you how much money that is for a poor rural person. And yet three weeks later, nobody has come forward. Nobody will say anything to the police because people who give information about criminals get killed around here. Everyone in Izita knows who murdered my son. Nobody will put himself on the line.'

Mitchell's face was turned from me and all I could see was the back of his head and the wobbling of his puffy red cheeks as he spoke. I felt great sadness for this man who did not yet have a face or a history. My imagination stirred by his not-yet-formed figure, I carelessly believed I could read his being from the parts of him I could see. His cheeks seemed those of a baby, plastered incongruously onto the head of a middle-aged man; the Farm Watch's mascot, brought out to draw and nourish the soldiers' guilt.

My first impression missed the mark by a long way. In the

months that followed, I discovered in Mitchell the fortitude of an ox and the courage of a maniacal man.

The day I rode next to him on his trip to his tomato fields, his dog and bodyguard in tow, Mitchell told me of a third bodyguard who had just left him, a young white man named Craig, a friend of his dead son and a national rifle-shooting champion. Mitchell spoke of Craig with lightness and affection, a man who had moved into his son's old house after his death and who, by his youth and his distance from the tragedy, had broken the ominous tension that brews between parents in mourning.

'First came news of a death threat against me,' Mitchell had said, 'then an actual assassination plan, and then Matthew and Hendrik found the tracks on my farm. Craig smelled death on me and it started eating at him. He was waiting for a bullet every morning when we set out, every time we turned our backs to the bush. He started getting horrible migraines, vomiting, insomnia. I sent him to the doctor.' Mitchell paused and smiled a strange smile, one that suggested some sort of complicity between us. 'Chronic stress and hypertension. That was the diagnosis. He was waiting and waiting and waiting – for the bullet.'

He shrugged expansively. 'And he cracked.'

He stared at me with a hint of that smile on the corners of his lips. I gave the moment sufficient time for its poignancy to linger, and then smiled back at him. He continued: 'But *I* am the old man. I will be 60 later this year and I am the one who goes to the irrigation fields like clockwork, day in and day out, like a sitting duck. I am not afraid of dying.'

It was the only sign of vanity I was ever to see in Mitchell. That non-smiling smile where everything in his face remained serious except the corners of his mouth and a hint of defiance in his eyes. He had taken a step out of himself and had become a spectator of his own courage. And he liked what he saw.

*

'The thing you have to understand about Arthur Mitchell,' Colin Waugh told me in his theatrical baritone, 'is that he is no ordinary farmer. For years he was a high-ranking member of the South African Defence Force. Intelligence was his forte. He is as tough as nails, and he knows how to gather information.'

13

It was a few weeks after the meeting at the golf club, and I was seated in Colin Waugh's lounge waiting to meet Mitchell for the first time. I had written to Waugh immediately after the golf club meeting and had told him of my plans to write a book. He had welcomed me at once, giving me unconditional access to Farm Watch and its members, a surprisingly trusting response to a journalist from out of town. Later I was to learn that none of the white farmers in the district had thought not to trust me. The murder victim and I were both white, and the killers were black; it was assumed that I would write a sympathetic account.

By now I had visited several homes and offices in the district and had filled half-a-dozen notebooks with interviews. Colin's home was subtly different from the others; it was immediately apparent from the way he filled the spaces around him that he was neither a native nor a farmer. Still lifes and landscapes, painted by his wife Lucy, covered the walls of the lounge. Outside, a meticulously sculpted garden, filled with local midlands flora, revealed how Colin spent the afternoon hours of his semi-retirement. Their home exuded a self-consciousness, a relationship between personality and objects, that I would not see again in the white homes of the midlands. They had settled in Alanview eight years previously, but they would always remain outsiders.

Colin's wife, Lucy, came into the room with a tray of neatly wedged sandwiches and a pot of tea. She smiled at me elegantly, put the tray on the coffee table that separated Colin and me, and began to leave the room.

Colin frowned and looked up at his wife. 'Lucy, my dearest, aren't you going to pour the tea?'

'No, my dear.'

Colin smirked at me and leaned back in his chair. 'Why not?'

'I'm sure you are perfectly capable of doing it,' she replied. 'And if you are too decrepit, this strong young man can do it for you.'

Colin feigned an accusing glare at his wife and spoke with exaggerated indignation. 'Are you flirting with my guest?'

'Not in the slightest, darling. I am merely explaining the options you have in regard to drinking your tea.'

That was the essence of Colin Waugh. He spent most of his time parodying his own prejudices, or scolding his prizewinning terriers, or teasing his earnest and self-important stepdaughter, all with camp theatricality. The first few times I met him, I kept blinking to convince myself he was real. His accent was more Eton than any self-respecting Etonian would tolerate, the commanding tone of his voice, even during the most relaxed and light-hearted conversations, unique to the wilting aristocracy of south-east England. He took great joy in playing out his eccentricities, a mirthful and mocking undertone always lurking beneath his confident discourse.

Like Mitchell, Colin was a former military man, a professional soldier in the British army. He insisted that he was being groomed for the highest office in the British military in the late 1970s, but did not have the stomach for the lonely, workaholic life of a general, and asked for a permanent assignment abroad.

'I was given to the South African Defence Force in the early 1980s, gift-wrapped, courtesy of the British army.'

'A gift?'

'Yes, a gift to South Africa's war. I came here to fight the ANC.'

Most of the white men I met in the ensuing weeks had, at some time and in some place, fought against an African liberation movement. At the time, I was a little shocked at the pride with which Colin announced his credentials. I soon discovered that for most of these men, the war had never ended. They took their imagery of manoeuvres, positions, flanks and enemies with them into the quiet hills of KwaZulu-Natal and painted it all over the countryside.

Around town and across the district, Colin was known as 'the colonel'.

'Why colonel?' I asked a colleague of Colin's.

'He had a senior rank in the British army and he calls himself colonel. It makes him happy, it makes the farmers happy, so why not?'

Beneath his self-parody, Colin really was a bigot – his banter about women and queers was too incessant to be fake. He was also a master of small-town gossip, and in his eight years in the district he had angered more people than he would care to count. But over the months I grew fond of him. This was a dark story, and his lightness was a welcome relief. He was sharp-witted and intelligent, and I would grill him for hours on end, trying to poke holes in his version of the Mitchell murder. At times, his carefully woven web of evidence gave way to his fierce imagination. Whenever I pointed out that he had strayed from what he knew for certain, he would look at me gloomily, a hint of distrust in his eyes. Colin had opened the door to the white farmers of the district for me, and if I was going to spray them with dirt, the blame would rest on his head.

Colin cleared his throat. 'We were talking about Arthur Mitchell, about his career in the military.' Lucy had gone and I had poured the tea in the face of great protest. One of Colin's pampered terriers lay sleeping at his feet. 'The interesting thing about the Mitchell case is that Arthur bought Normandale to protect his flank.'

'His flank?'

'Yes, his flank. His farm is a border territory. Beyond it is the opposition.'

It took me a moment to understand what he was saying. The area covered by Farm Watch, the security organisation that Colin managed, consisted of four districts of commercial farms, about 200 in total. Each district had a small midlands town at its epicentre: Alanview, Sarahdale, Athol and Foster's Rest. And the four districts had something else in common: each shared a border with what, under apartheid, had been KwaZulu homeland territory, vast expanses of derelict and broken countryside, home to a former black peasantry that is now for the most part unemployed, and nominally presided over by the amakhosi, the traditional leaders whose pedigree predates the arrival of whites on the subcontinent. It is from the 'traditional lands' – as they are now misleadingly known – that white farmers recruit their labour, and it is from there that people come in the night to steal white-owned cattle. Whites whose farms abut the 'traditional lands' refer to their properties as 'border farms'. Mitchell's newly acquired farm, Normandale, was such a property. It was situated in the last line of commercial farms before the entrance to Izita, a former church mission which had long become indistinguishable from the derelict communal land around it.

Colin's discourse was littered with references to 'the opposition'. Sometimes, he was talking of the loose network of thieves, politicians and businessmen whom he believed were behind the Mitchell murder. At other times he was referring to one man in particular – Paul Mlambo – whom Colin, in his less lucid moments, swore on his life was the angel of darkness responsible for all the treachery in the area. But mostly 'the opposition' for Colin, was the traditional lands in their entirety and all their inhabitants. He had

16

blurred the distinction between racial difference and a military frontier. Later, when I tried to enter Izita in my white skin, I discovered that his 'opposition' had done the same.

*

The doorbell rang, and a moment later Arthur Mitchell walked into the lounge. He wore a starched white shirt and formal black trousers, and his cheeks were a shade paler than at the moment at the golf club when the generals had shifted in their chairs. Mitchell shook my hand and greeted me with what I took to be cold reserve. I was a stranger, about to write about the moment that tore his life to pieces, and his wariness was appropriate and expected. I decided that this was not the time to engage with him. I would say as little as possible, just let him speak until he had had enough.

Mitchell spoke for more than two hours with little interruption. He stopped as suddenly as he had started, got up and walked out of the house. I did not see him again for another month.

'I guess you could say that Arthur found himself in the wrong place at the wrong time,' Colin said by way of introduction. 'He walked into a situation of blind racial hatred that had been instigated by another man.'

'What other man?' I asked Mitchell.

He eyed me suspiciously, then cast a querying glance at Colin.

'It is crucial that you speak openly, Arthur,' Colin said. 'Otherwise you are wasting your own time.'

Mitchell stared back at Colin a long time. Colin shrugged, gazed out of the window, looked at his watch, sighed irritably. A silent, tense communication to which I was not privy.

'His name is Lourie Steyn,' Colin said defiantly, breaking the stalemate. 'He bought Normandale in 1969 and farmed it for 30 years. His labourers lived in a cluster of kraals in a 100-hectare valley at the bottom of Normandale.'

'The blacks called it Langeni,' Mitchell interrupted. He pronounced Langeni with a crisp English accent, as if deliberately flattening the lyrical Zulu word.

Normandale is about 20 kilometres from the tiny farming town of Sarahdale. You can see Langeni from the dust road that stretches from Sarahdale to the regional thoroughfare that runs through the

17

southern midlands. At the point where the dust road comes to Langeni's kraals, it rises steeply. It is said that in the late nineteenth century, carts got stuck going up that hill. The animals couldn't take it and would have to be unharnessed, and the cart would start rolling down the hill. So the blacks said Langeni was the white man's devil.

'Steyn is a right-wing Afrikaner,' Colin continued, 'six-foot-two and much feared. He was very hard with labour, not fair, not honest. After 30 years of his presence, Normandale was fertile ground for racial hatred.'

Mitchell looked uncomfortable. He clearly did not like Colin's story about Steyn. Later I would discover that he had very different ideas about the events preceding his son's murder. The problem, for Mitchell, was not that Steyn was too strong; he was much too weak.

'We all had problems with crime,' Mitchell said, 'but there is no doubt that people were gunning for Steyn. In the dry season, his fields would start to burn in the middle of the night. His fence would go down, but it would not be taken away and used elsewhere. It would just lie there at the side of the road. His cattle started disappearing in big numbers. Some time before he left, his son heard a noise outside the farmhouse and went onto the veranda to investigate. He was greeted by a volley of gunfire. I don't know if they were just trying to scare him or whether it was poor marksmanship, but the bullets were sprayed all over the place and missed him. A little while later, Steyn started receiving anonymous death threats.

'Between 1996 and 1997 Steyn lost 100 head of cattle. Basically, he was ruined. You cannot farm under those conditions. They had pushed him off the land, they had won.

'Steyn put his farm on the market, packed his bags and left. He retired to a smallholding that his family owned, a little place way up on the Highveld, west of Johannesburg. And he left his son Lourans in charge of the farm while he looked for a buyer.

'Lourans was lazy and uninterested. He didn't look after the farm properly, and when you have the problems the Steyns have, that means you essentially give your land over to the blacks. After Lourans left, we picked up more than 200 snares on Normandale. The blacks had taken it over and were catching all Steyn's game.

'Nobody was going to buy Steyn's farm. You do not buy under

those conditions. The land is worthless. So Steyn started phoning me, begging me to buy his farm. By the end he was phoning me three times a week. It got to the point when I was reluctant to pick the phone up when I heard it ring.

'But I got to thinking. What's going to happen if nobody buys Normandale? It will become a squatter settlement, the Izita location will start spilling over. Because my farms, Eleanor and Derbytin, both share a boundary with Normandale. And you know what happens when you have a squatter settlement on the border of your farm? You lose control. They take down your fences and their cattle start wandering onto your property. A bull with venereal disease gets among your cows, and soon your whole herd starts dying off. These cattle have not been dipped; they have picked up hundreds of diseases to which they have become immune. They urinate on your grass and your cattle eat the grass. So when the blacks' cattle wander onto your land you have to seal it off for months until the disease is gone. You get to a point where you cannot farm.

'People who don't farm can't understand that. They think I am vindictive. They think I don't want the blacks to have land and cattle. But it is not that. It is a question of the viability of my farm. If I have a squatter settlement next door, I have to stop farming and start fighting with people. I have to impound their cattle, make them pay fines, become a policeman. And I become very unpopular in the process. I am not a policeman and I am not a vindictive bastard. I am a farmer, and a farmer cannot afford to have a situation like that on his doorstep.

'So I bought Steyn's farm, and I will tell you openly that I bought it to protect myself. I wanted a bit of distance between my farming operation and Izita. But once I had bought it, I also wanted to use it, to recoup what I had spent to buy it and maybe to make some money as well. It is beautiful land – wild indigenous bush. The neighbours in the valley had clubbed together and had a large piece of land declared a conservation area. Normandale fitted into that very nicely. It is perfect for game. Perfect for tourism.

'I bought the land at the beginning of 1999 and Steyn's son moved out. In February I called a meeting with the nine families that live at Langeni. By the time Steyn had left, things had soured so much between him and them that nobody at Langeni was

19

employed on Normandale. One or two of the men worked in Pinetown, 100 kilometres away, and came back from time to time. But most of the men were unemployed. They sat around Cube's Tearoom all day and they lived off crime. I know I can't prove it yet, but I also know it to be true. By then the biggest employer at Langeni was me. I used the women there as seasonal contract workers, to pick the tomatoes, take the weeds off the cabbages and all the other aspects of intensive farming that require a lot of labour-intensive work.

'We met on the side of the road. I brought a police sergeant with me to act as a translator. I speak Zulu but I am not fluent and the matters we had to discuss were very important. I wanted no misunderstanding. I told them what my rules were. I wanted to turn Normandale into a game farm and told them it was out of bounds. Their cattle could not graze there. I told them that Langeni, all 100 hectares of Langeni, was theirs. One hundred hectares is a lot of land for nine poor families. When the Department of Land Affairs buys land to redistribute, they do not give nine families 100 hectares. So I thought the families were getting a good deal.

'I had a few other rules, about what happens at Langeni itself. I told them they could build new huts, but only with my permission and only if the hut was for a daughter, someone close. I did not want outsiders coming onto the land, and I told them that. I told them I wanted a guarantee of this, so I asked that they draw up a list of the names of the people who lived at Langeni. I did not think that was unreasonable. It is my land. I am entitled to keep an eye on who goes in and out.

'This is when the trouble started. A member of the Mashabana family, a man who had worked for Steyn for many years, got up and started shouting. He said blacks do not give their names and identity numbers to *umlungu* – the white man – because *umlungu* cannot be trusted with such information. He will keep it innocently for a while and then turn it against you.

'You must understand how hostile and provocative that comment was. I came to them in my capacity as the owner of the land on which they lived. He responded by addressing me as *mlungu*. He was telling his neighbours that I was not an individual man but a member of a hostile race. He was saying that we are at war with each other.

'I did not shout back. I did not even show him I was offended.

My family and I are more enlightened than all the farmers in the district put together. When I was a senior manager at a large chemicals company, I learnt to negotiate. I sat opposite trade union representatives on the eve of strikes, when things are tense and tempers are flying. I do not lose my temper. I do not confront. I listen, then withdraw. I said, "Okay, there is clearly a problem here. Let us leave the issue of names and identity documents for another time." '

'There is a cottage on Normandale. Small and modest, but a thoroughly livable little place. A week after the meeting with the Langeni people it was burnt to the ground. Arson, absolutely no question about it. Then sections of Normandale started to burn. Then the burning spread to the lands I farm on Eleanor. They started doing to my fences what they had done when Steyn was around. They would take them down, but for no purpose, not to build wire enclosures around their chicken runs. They would leave the fences lying on the ground for me to see. They were talking to me. They were telling me to get out. Between February and the day in September when Peter was killed, I opened 21 criminal dockets with the police. That is four incidents a month, one a week. This was a silent war.

'Maybe I am stupid but I fought it. I was damned if these bastards were going to chase me out of the area, so I fought back. Some time between the February meeting and the second meeting in August, I don't remember quite when, I was driving past Langeni after picking up the women to take them to my farm. The three Cube brothers were standing at the side of the road with Magijima, a local ANC activist from Izita, a man who wears an ANC T-shirt all day every day. He is not the big ANC man in Izita; that is Paul Mlambo. Magijima is Mlambo's lieutenant.

'I pulled up, got out of my truck and went to speak to them. Magijima did the talking. He was like the shop steward. The Cubes did not say a word. Magijima said there was a problem. Langeni is situated right next to the district road, but there is no access road to the kraals. We want to build a road on your property.

'I was blunt. I wanted to make a point. I told them I would consider giving permission for the access road if they told me who had burnt down my cottage. I said there must be some exchange here. How can you expect me to co-operate with you when you are walking all over me?

'Magijima walked off in a huff, with the Cubes trailing him, shaking their heads. I got back in my truck and went away.

'You must understand that I was never going to give them permission for the road. My vegetables were being pilfered from the irrigation fields at Derbytin every night. It was a problem, but not a catastrophe. They were taking as much as they could carry, and you cannot lug tons of tomatoes around on foot. But if a road was built they could bring a vehicle in, a big truck. Put in a road and I would wake up one morning to find that my entire crop had been harvested in the night. My tomatoes would be on sale all over the townships of Durban and I would have to close shop.

'Later the same day, when I drove back to the farm, Magijima was standing very aggressively in the middle of the road. I had to brake to stop myself from running him down. He marched up to the window and started shouting at me. He said I was getting in the way of the government's Reconstruction and Development Programme. He said I was a stingy man and a negative influence in the area. I said what I had said earlier. If they could tell me who had burnt down my cottage, I would talk about an access road. Magijima carried on shouting. He said they would build the road and force me to accept it. If I tried to get in the way, there would be big trouble for me.

'I took that as a threat and went straight to the police station to lay charges of intimidation. We had both thrown down the gauntlet. Things were looking bad, but I was feeling determined.

'In August, I decided it was time to meet the families again. Same story. The meeting went fine until I told them I wanted names. And Mhila Mashabana got up again and spoke threateningly. No names. Not for the white man.

'A few weeks before Peter was killed, I drove down to Langeni to pick up the women early in the morning. The men were not gathered round the Tearoom as they usually are. They had come down to the edge of the road. They were sitting, waiting. As I drove by, Mhila Mashabana, the one who had told people not to give me their names, stood up, walked up to my fence on the side of the road and started to rip it out of the ground. I knew immediately what was happening. He wanted me to get out of the car and beat the shit out of him in front of his friends. Then there would be assault charges and 15 witnesses would file into court to testify how I got out of my vehicle and beat an innocent man to a pulp.

'I got out of the car and spoke to him quietly, calmly, from a distance.

"What are you doing?"

"I am tearing down your fence. I think you should call the police."

"Do you want me to go to the police station and lay charges against you?"

"If that is what you must do, then do it."

'So I walked straight back to my car. He wanted there to be a scene and I wasn't making one. So he upped the ante. He started screaming at me. He said I must watch out because I would soon be dead.

'I kept walking back to my car. I said nothing, did nothing, just drove to the police station, wrote a statement and filed charges against him.

'They didn't like the calm way I handled that one. What is this man doing? His cottage has been burnt down, his fields set alight, we refuse to co-operate when he comes to set the rules – but he doesn't crack. He stays calm. They didn't like that. They wanted to draw me into court. They wanted to be able to say: "He accuses us of this and that, but he is the one facing a list of criminal charges as long as your arm. So who is the problem here? Us or him?"

'Three weeks later, my son was slumped over his steering wheel with his brains splattered across the window. I have no proof of who did it. Nobody will stand up in court and say they witnessed my tenants plotting the murder of my son. Nobody will say they hired an assassin from Pinetown, told him of our daily routines and led him to my farm. But explain this to me. Since the day my son was killed, there has been no trouble on my farms. Not a stray, not a single fence torn down, no burnt fields, no poaching, not a single footprint. Why do you think that is so?'

The question was rhetorical but he wanted me to answer it.

'I guess they had won?'

'Won? They'd killed my son and they were getting away with it. The days and the weeks went by and no arrests, nothing. They could kill a white man and everything went on as normal. They had won the battle. If *umlungu* wants to farm, let him have it.'

In the months that followed, I found that Mitchell had not been entirely honest with me. His neighbours had indeed stopped raiding his farms, but not because they had won. They were scared. Mitchell was fighting back with every fibre in his soul, quietly, unobtrusively, in late-night phone calls, in secret exchanges of money and information. And he was getting close. They were keeping clear of his farms because they were frightened. And there were people plotting to kill him because he was not going to stop until he had won. There was hidden treachery in the closed and quiet networks of this countryside that I had yet to discover.

*

Mitchell had stopped talking. His story was told. He was getting ready to go.

Colin looked anxious. 'You haven't finished, Arthur.'

Mitchell slumped back in his chair and shrugged his shoulders irritably.

'You haven't given the broader picture. You have given the impression that the problem is just between you and two families. Like it is an isolated event.'

Mitchell was animated again. He stood up and started pacing round the room. 'No, no. This is no isolated event. There is a campaign in this district to drive whites off the boundary of Izita and there are ANC people behind it.'

I put down my pen and stared out of the window onto Colin's neat suburban lawn. Sweeping claims of conspiracy made me uneasy. Until now, Mitchell had told a careful tale. It was rich in the dozens of parochial threads that make a story believable – the intricacies of a microscopic geography, the texture of an argument on the side of a road. White farmers have a tendency to drift into a fanciful world in which 300 years of history can be swept into a single sentence. A trivial altercation is drawn into a wild universe of ancient tribes that battle across generations. Mitchell had avoided that nonsense until now. With talk of conspiracy I worried that he would descend into the mists of ethnic paranoia and that his story would sink with him.

Colin sensed my misgivings. 'I don't think that's very helpful, Arthur. Jonny is a journalist. Your story is useless without facts.'

Mitchell sat down again, rested his chin on his fist and frowned. 'Incident by incident. Okay, that's not too difficult. Let's leave aside cattle theft for the moment. We know that few people farm

24

beef anymore because theft has made it impossible. Let's just talk violence against people. The last attack was on Harry Withers. He's an old man, well into his 70s, owns a tiny store on the road between Izita and the farms.'

I had passed Withers's store on my first journey past Langeni. A ramshackle, homemade structure of wood, nails and roughly cut panes of glass, it spoke of the precarious respectability of white poverty. A massive advertisement, pinned lopsided on the front façade, provided a manic addition of primary colours. 'Enjoy Rama Soft.' The KwaZulu-Natal hinterland, with its innumerable villages and its scrawny cows, was divided into rival turfs by invisible corporations. The maze of roads between the N3 highway and Underberg was Yogisip country. The Greytown district was solidly CocaCola. Here, Rama Soft ruled.

'He was ambushed while making his weekly journey to town to bank his takings. Every Wednesday morning for years he has been doing the same trip. They knew he was coming and they knew he had hard cash. But he's a wise old soul and when two men tried to flag him down he put his foot on the accelerator. They took out an automatic rifle and started shooting. He managed to escape but by the time he got to town the floor of his car was soaked in blood. A whole volley of bullets went through him.

'That night, while he was lying in hospital, his shop was looted. Maybe it was the people who shot him. Maybe word got round that he was not there. Maybe you just can't leave anything valuable unguarded in the vicinity of Izita. The next morning, I went to his shop, packed everything that remained into boxes and took them to my house.

'Then there was young Davis. I'm jumping around now. I'm talking off the top of my head. The Davis incident was some time ago, 1996 maybe. Davis managed Edenridge, a farm adjacent to Normandale. Absentee owner. Davis managed the place.

'One night, Davis was alone in his house and heard a noise outside. When he went to investigate, he found one of the Mashabana brothers standing on the front lawn, gesturing for him to follow.'

By now I had lost count of how many Cubes and Mashabanas there were. They cropped up everywhere. They were indistinguishable in the stories told by white men. Some said there were five Mashabana brothers and three Cubes. Others said there were three Mashabanas and five Cubes. Few people gave their first

25

names or personal histories. It didn't seem to matter much to the storytellers. They were bad men; that is what counted.

'This was one of the Mashabanas who does not live at Langeni. Three of them live in a little settlement across the road, on the border of Edenridge. Mashabana took Davis further and further from his homestead. He enticed him right into the settlement where the Mashabanas live. When he got there he was mobbed by three or four men who attacked him with bush knives.

'A young woman who lives in the settlement saved his life. She fled into the darkness and came back with a policeman, a young sergeant. The policeman drew his gun and dragged Davis away. Three Mashabanas were arrested and charged with assault with intent to do grievous bodily harm. The policeman and Davis both testified at the trial and the three of them all got a few years each. They are due to come out in a few months' time, and then there will be trouble. They are a wild bunch.'

The story was an odd one, and I interrupted Mitchell to get a better handle on it.

'The young woman. There are no telephones in the settlement. How did she get the policeman?'

'I don't know. But she got him.'

'Could he have been passing in his patrol vehicle, or visiting somebody in the settlement?'

'Probably. That's probably it. Just fortunate that he was passing by.'

'Where is Davis now? Does he still live in the district?'

Colin butted in. I found during the following months that he had claimed ownership of the Davis story. Whenever it was mentioned, he became alert, listened carefully and spoke with reserve.

'No, no. Davis does not live here anymore. He has gone mad.'

Colin loved to trot out shocking phrases and then wait for their effects to settle. I felt a little irritated and didn't beg for him to continue, just stared at him impassively and waited.

'When he was attacked, he raised his arms to protect his face and body. That probably saved his life, but his arms and hands were torn to shreds. It took hours of surgery to get the tendons back together and he is still not right. He can't use his hands much now and may never be able to use them again.

'But those are just his physical symptoms. There are severe psychological symptoms as well. He is immobilised. He cannot do anything. He lives somewhere on the coast and is looked after by his fiancée's parents.'

Every murder of or attack on a white person in the district left behind it a trail of rival tales. The Davis case was no exception.

Adjacent to Edenridge, where Davis lived, is a wild and beautiful stretch of land, which, until recently, was owned by a prominent Pretoria family, the Krieks. When the architects of apartheid settled into office in the late 1940s, the Krieks found themselves close to the levers of state power. It is rumoured in the Sarahdale district that some time in the fifties the Krieks got wind that a dam was to be built in the midlands and that the government would buy the land it had earmarked well above market price. So they bought it all, thousands of hectares of it, and waited. Nothing happened. The government abandoned its plans and this wealthy urban family, who wouldn't know an irrigation field from a bog, found themselves the proprietor of one of the largest properties in Natal.

I am told that by the time Davis moved in next door, almost four decades later, one of the Kriek descendents had turned his land into a massive marijuana plantation. This is one of the few stories that is common cause in the district – almost everyone I met, from white farmers to black tenants, spoke of the Kriek dagga plantation. It was placed with great care and discretion. From the district road one saw indigenous bush stretching to the horizon. But fly over the land in a helicopter and you can see the neat rows of plants, nestled snuggly into the sides of a shallow canyon that cuts the Kriek property in half.

Kriek seldom set foot on his farms. They were occupied by a handful of black families, members of the Macaba chieftancy who could not believe their luck: a massive chunk of white-owned farm, slap bang in the middle of the landscape their ancestors had traipsed since the 1840s, and nobody there to throw them off. It seems that the Kriek family and its tenants had instituted a delicate quid pro quo. The tenants would discreetly harvest the marijuana, pack it and have it ready for a helicopter that would descend into the canyon in the early hours of the morning. In return, the rest of the land was theirs.

Davis was not the sort of man the whites of the district took to. Young, long hair, baggy clothes, he was a city boy who hooked into the Woodstock generation two decades late. According to the banter of clubhouse change rooms and supermarket queues, Davis had seen too much. The Mashabanas had their own dagga racket going and they did not like having Davis under their noses – so they got rid of him.

There was another account of the Davis incident. A few weeks before he was attacked, it was said, Davis stumbled on a scene somewhere in the depths of the vast Kriek property. A line of tin targets, a row of young black men snaked on the ground, each clutching an AK 47, and an ANC activist standing behind them, shouting orders, military style, three belts of ammunition slung over his shoulders.

'He saw something he should not have,' it was whispered to me one afternoon in a bar on the town's main road. 'The heavies in the area were worried that he would blabber.'

In the coming months, I made a hobby of collecting the competing stories that wove themselves around attacks on white people. In two cases I got to the truth, and in the gap between myth and reality I found greater insight into the whites of the district than hours of interviews would ever elicit. But the Davis case remained a mystery. I never visited him or Kriek, and I never fed questions about him into the Izita network I eventually accessed.

Mitchell was not finished. There were more grim tales to tell about the fate of his neighbours.

'There was a man called Lottering who lived and worked on the Steyn property for years,' Mitchell said. 'He lived in an old caravan on Normandale. It was a rickety old thing, badly put together and crumbling with age. It had a bed and a tiny dining-room table, and it was linked to a generator, so it also had a television set and a fridge.'

The Lottering story is a common South African tale. In every farming district throughout the country you will find a handful of white men and women who have become lost and unhinged. No family, no land, their lives clouded in a fog of solitude, they are picked up and cared for by a commercial farmer who cannot stand to see a member of his race at the border of indigence. The gesture itself is never named as charity. The indigent is called a 'manager' or 'assistant' and is put on the payroll, several scales above the salary of the black foreman.

'There was a crack running down the middle of the caravan,' Mitchell continued. 'Nothing too dramatic, but big enough to hold the barrel of a gun. One night while Lottering was lying on his bed watching TV, somebody took a shot at him through the crack in his caravan and hit him in the ribcage. He managed to stumble out and get to the main house, and an ambulance was called. He survived.'

Mitchell leaned back in his chair, composed, at ease, a man who had unburdened himself of some weighty evidence.

'So, you see, the death of my son was not an isolated incident. This is a terrorist war. Mao said that when you kill one, you terrorise ten thousand. Lots of farmers were at the scene. They saw the blood. This was not just a strike on one farm. The killers knew that the blow dealt to my family could cause the entire area to collapse.

'There are nine farms on the border of Izita. Six of us have been attacked in the last three years. And that is just to talk of violence against people. There is also the relentless encroachment. Two families have stopped farming altogether. Their fences no longer exist. Black cattle graze all over their land, and they live in the confines of their homesteads, surrounded by electric fencing. And the other seven fight daily to keep our land. Because there is no such thing as title deed here. If I were to drop dead tomorrow, Eleanor would be theirs. They would just move in and take it over.'

Despite Mitchell's gruesome tales, I had heard little evidence of the conspiracy he so confidently proclaimed. An isolated outpost of privilege in a sea of poverty, yes. The silent encroachment of the poor, certainly. Racial hatred, probably. But where was the conspiracy? It was too early to tell Mitchell that I doubted his tale.

There was something Mitchell was not telling me. Every conspiracy has a chief conspirator and the bogeyman who fuelled the imagination of the district's white farmers had a name and a face. In the coming months, many farmers would talk to me in hushed tones about Paul Mlambo, the man who the whites believed ruled Izita. He was the chief's induna, the chair of the local branch of the ANC, he owned the taxis, the liquor stores and the people themselves.

Whenever I asked a white farmer about Mlambo, I got the same response.

'Before this country's first democratic election in 1994, Mlambo stood up at rally. He said: "All this land, everything you can see, everything from the river to the trees, will be yours again. So you

29

must vote ANC." And people did vote ANC, and then one year came and went, then two, then three, and still everyone was living in poverty and the whites still owned the land. People started to put pressure on Mlambo. "Where is this land you promised? Why do the whites still own it?" So Mlambo replied: "Who says they still own it? Why don't you go and take it?"'

THREE

Johannesburg rain showers are brief and spectacular. In the morning, the sky is blue, the city covered in hard light. By lunch time, incipient storm clouds are gathering over the mine dumps on the southern horizon and flashes of lightning strike the Free State's vast plateau, out of sight, beyond the banks of the Vaal River. The storm gathers its magic slowly, leisurely, its preparations stretching through the course of the afternoon. By four o'clock, the city is wild. Sharp gusts of wind sweep the litter down the streets of the central business district. Banks of heavy cloud block out the sun, and the downtown skyscrapers stretch up like angry colossi, their steel frames blackened by shadow. The clouds empty their bellies, sending sheets of water across the city. The noise of rain smacking streets and windows and roofs is deafening. By early evening it is quiet, scrawny spirals of mist rising from the streets, armies of flying ants squeezing their way through the crevices under doors and the tiny holes of air vents.

In January 2000, something went crazy in the skies over Johannesburg, and the taps forgot to close. It bucketed down for days on end, unrelenting, drowning the city in torrents of fast-flowing water. Intermittently, the skies would clear, but no sooner had the sun given evidence that it was still around than the clouds would form again as if from nowhere and the sound of water hitting the city would resume. In the slums of Alexandra, squatters who had built below the flood line hastily gathered their belongings as their tin shacks were swept into the violent tides of the Jukskei River. Some who stayed behind, standing forlornly on tin roofs to guard their worldly possessions, were held up at gunpoint and robbed, as the chaos of the floods let loose Johanesburg's predators and scavengers.

The morning I left the city to visit Lourie Steyn, the rain was

31

smashing down on the grey asphalt, and traffic jams snaked across the urban thoroughfares, locking me into the city for more than an hour. Out in the countryside, visibility was close to zero and the farmlands on either side of the road had vanished, a violent fog of driving rain in their place. Steyn lived on a smallholding about 30 kilometres outside Adristad, a small rural town in the North-West Province. He had told me on the phone to call him when I got to the outskirts of town for further directions.

The phone rang for a long time. I hung up and tried again, and heard the voice of a middle-aged woman at the other end.

'Môre tannie. Kan ek asseblief met Mnr Steyn praat.'

My accent must have been awful, for the woman replied in English. 'He's not here.'

'When are you expecting him back?'

'I don't know. Not for a while.'

'I have an appointment with him. He was expecting me. Did he leave a message?'

'Yes, yes. He told me you would call. He went to town, to the hotel in the middle of town. He won a free holiday on a TV show, and he's gone there to meet with the TV people. Just go there and you'll find him.'

Adristad is one of those rural towns to which city boys like me are banished in our nightmares. A grid of 20 suburban streets, low fences, dull, square houses, one after the other, rollout plastic awnings to shade the verandas. The place was so small it wasn't even necessary to ask directions. I pulled into the parking lot of the only hotel in town, a one-storey building resembling a cheap American motel, gray cardboard knitted together with bright red trimmings.

A tall and substantial middle-aged man leaned against the door-post at the front entrance. He wore faded blue jeans, gashed at the knee to reveal a hint of pink skin, the bottoms turned up over a disheveled pair of trainers. His shoulders hunched lazily into an old blue sweater, the shirt underneath untucked, its creased ends dangling in front of his crotch. His face placed him somewhere in his early sixties – sun-beaten and leathery, but animated; the marks of a mischievous sense of humour around his lively eyes.

The man stooped to look into my face under the enormous umbrella I was carrying. He smiled courteously. 'You're the man writing the book.'

'And you're the man who won a free holiday on a TV show.'

Steyn laughed: 'I've been waiting for these assholes for nearly two hours. They told me they would be here ten o'clock sharp. Maybe the rain stopped them,' he mused, still leaning against the doorpost. He nodded at the street in front of him. 'You won't get far in a sedan.' He unhinged himself from the doorpost and gestured extravagantly for me to come in from the rain, as if he were inviting me into his own home.

On the road an hour or two earlier, I had spoken to Arthur Mitchell. 'Be cautious with him,' Mitchell had said. 'He is very suspicious of you.'

'What sort of suspicious?'

'He phoned to ask me whether I had checked you out. Thought you might be working for the CIA.'

I laughed. 'Does he have that much to hide?'

Mitchell chuckled and cleared his throat. 'We're all a little nervous. When things around you start going insane, your imagination lights up.'

In fact, Steyn had had intelligence agents on his trail in recent years. In the early 1990s, he had tried to start a branch of the AWB, the neo-fascist Afrikaner movement that came of age in the mid-1980s. Steyn had fumbled around for a few months, but after its second meeting, his AWB branch hiccupped and died. The majority of farmers in KwaZulu-Natal are English-speakers, and those with a bent for trouble would not openly join the black-shirted brigades of Eugene Terre'Blanche. The movement was doomed anyway, and would wane overnight on the brink of democracy, when three of its members were executed on the side of the road during an abortive right-wing invasion of Bophuthatswana. For his troubles, Steyn earned himself a slim dossier in the files of the National Intelligence Service, the old intelligence agency of the apartheid state. It must have been one of the last dossiers the Old Guard filed before their organisation merged with ANC intelligence.

The foyer of the hotel was too big for its furniture. A gloomy dungeon of a room, a jet-black lounge suite, designed for a cramped family living room, trying in vain to fill it. A young white man sat at reception playing solitaire. Three black bellboys, their postures rigidly ceremonious, stood behind him.

Steyn led me to an austere black couch and dragged a coffee

table across the floor. Aside from the four bored men behind the desk, we were the only people in the room. He reached for a pack of Chesterfield Filters, offered me one and lit another for himself. The ashtray on the coffee table was littered with six or seven Chesterfield stubs.

We made small talk for a couple of minutes, exchanging niceties about the pleasures of retirement and the task of writing a book. Then I took out my notepad and asked Steyn what he knew of the Cube and Mashabana families.

'The Cubes have been on Normandale since I bought the farm in 1969,' he replied. 'Old man Cube was there when I moved in. He already had two or three little children. They grew up on my farm. One of them was my son's age. They played together after school. The Mashabanas arrived a little later, also with small kids. Must have been 1972, old man Mashabana came. No, maybe '73 or '4. We got on very well, no problems between us.'

Steyn's eyes wandered incessantly around the room while we spoke. Aside from our first encounter in the doorway, he had not made eye contact with me.

'I don't know what happened between Mitchell and the Cubes and the Mashabanas. I don't know what his attitude was towards them. Maybe he upset them. Maybe he got too heavy about cattle theft. I don't know. Maybe it wasn't even them who killed Peter. Mitchell is only guessing. He could be wrong.'

'Who else might have killed him?'

Behind my back, somebody walked into the lobby, and Steyn jumped up and went briskly to reception.

'Are you the TV people?'

The man looked back at Steyn incredulously. 'The what?'

'Sorry, man, sorry,' Steyn said, holding up his hands in a gesture of apology. 'I won a free holiday on a TV show and I was meant to meet the bastards here at ten o'clock. They still haven't arrived.'

The stranger stepped past Steyn, and all four men behind the counter switched to bright and attentive mode.

Steyn didn't come straight back. He walked slowly round the edge of the room, stopping to examine each print that hung on the wall, as if he was thinking of buying one and wanted to check out its authenticity. His cigarette dangling in his mouth, both hands sunk deep in his pockets, he stepped into the doorway, looked out into the street, turned and walked back to the couch, stopping briefly to peer down an empty passage. I got the distinct impression he wanted to wish my presence away.

'Where were we?' he asked, sinking back into his place on the black couch.

'Who else might have killed Peter Mitchell?'

Steyn shrugged. 'You're asking the wrong person. I haven't lived in the district for a long time. You should go back and speak to the farmers who still live there. Porter, Jakobs, Draker, Cummings. They'll have a better idea than me.'

'Why did you stop farming and come here?'

'I'm getting old. It was time to put my feet up. I'd worked hard.'

Steyn paused, straightened and looked at me for the first time in a while. 'I was the first farmer in the district to start growing tomatoes. People said I was crazy, growing tomatoes on cattle farms. Now everyone wants to grow tomatoes. I started it.'

I should have followed his digression. Absorbed in self-affirming memories of his prowess as a farmer, he might have relaxed and spoken of other matters more freely. Instead I brought the discussion straight back to the place from which he was trying to escape, like I was a piranha on prime-time television, trying to catch him out. 'But there has been trouble in the district,' I said. 'A hundred head of your cattle were stolen. You received several death threats.'

'Ja, there was trouble.' He sniggered and shook his head at the mention of death threats. 'Things started going haywire in the early 1990s. Some Soviet-trained guerillas started coming back into the country, and they made big trouble.'

'Guerillas in your district?'

'Well, I don't know whether they were in the district as such. But the trouble started after the ANC was unbanned. It seems a hell of a coincidence that that's when things started going berserk.'

'So who was creating trouble in the district?'

'It wasn't the Cubes or the Mashabanas or anyone who lived on my property. We were at peace with them. It was this group of ruffians who lived in the valley about 10 kilometres from my farm. I had been the head of the civilian commando in the area for years and we used to raid them all the time. We'd find cattle carcasses, unlicensed firearms. Once I found my neighbour's hi-fi there. They were bad bastards. You had to go in there armed and heavy.'

'It was these people who wrote the death threats?'

'I don't know. I received three death threats. They were all anonymous, so I don't know who sent them. They were all in the form of letters delivered to my postbox in town. I don't know how they got my box number. One of them didn't even have a stamp. Somebody dropped it in personally.'

Steyn stared impassively over my shoulder, watching the front entrance.

'But I can tell you it had nothing to do with Normandale. It was because I was head of the commando. Because I was clearing crime out of the area. No, I was good to the people of Normandale. Old man Cube died in 1992. When he fell ill, I took him to the hospital. I bought a coffin for the family, organised the funeral. He is buried on my farm.'

I asked Steyn dozens of questions about the Cubes, the Mashabanas and his other tenants, and his replies were all lifeless and predictable. What little imagination he did invest in his answers painted him the orthodox paternalist farmer; tough but fair, a taskmaster but a man with a soul. Bad eggs get thrown out, but a funeral gets a free coffin, illness in the family a free trip to the doctor. His replies about the lives of his tenants were equally sparse. There were five Cube brothers on Steyn's count, and four Mashabana brothers. Two of the Cubes worked for Steyn, while the other three migrated to Clermont, a township on the outskirts of Durban, where they worked in a butchery. Two of the Mashabanas had also spent their working lives in Pinetown. The other two had stayed in the district and worked for Steyn.

Bar the details, these were things I could have guessed for myself. Most black rural men of the Cubes' and Mashabanas' generation, men in their thirties and early forties, had migrated to the cities at the beginning of adulthood. Most lived dual lives, one foot in their ancestral districts, the other in the urban ghettos. What I wanted from Steyn was the texture of intimacy, his impressions of men he had known and dealt with for three decades. He was going through the motions, waiting for this unwanted interview to end.

Just as I was about to admit defeat and go home, Steyn, unsolicited, dropped a small nugget. He must have been boring himself. It takes effort to present yourself as a cardboard character.

'I should tell you about one of the two Mashabana brothers who worked for me,' he said. 'Strange man. Very stubborn, very short-

36

tempered. Smoked dagga all the time. But he would give me information. So we got on okay.'

'What sort of information?'

'Well, at some stage there was a clash between the Cube and the Mashabana families. Intermarriage problems. One of the Cubes had married one of the Mashabanas and there were problems with lobola. An amount of cattle had been agreed to – I don't remember now which family was which, I mean, which was the daughter's family and which the son's – but anyway, there was this dispute, so there was no love lost between the two families. They used to play each other off on me. Mashabana would give me information about the Cubes. If they had stolen cattle, or had a gun, he would tell me and I would pay him for the information if it turned out to be true. Half the time, he was giving me bullshit. He just wanted me to storm into the Cubes' place to cause shit. But often his information was good.'

'So you used to raid the Cubes' kraal looking for stolen goods and firearms?'

'Oh ja. Quite often over the years. And I'd find things, too. They were not a bunch of innocents, the Cubes.'

'I thought you said you got on very well with the Cubes?'

'Ja, I did. They gave me information too, about the Mashabanas.'

'You raided the Mashabana kraal as well?'

'From time to time, when it was necessary.'

Another stranger walked in and Steyn got up to perform his ritual. This stranger had watched the same TV show and had also tried to win a free holiday, and he slapped Steyn on the back and congratulated him. Steyn offered the man a cigarette and they stood at the front desk smoking and talking for about ten minutes. The stranger moved on, and again Steyn walked slowly round the room, this time stopping to examine a large crack in the wall. He put his finger in it to check its depth, then crouched and peered into it as if it were a keyhole.

'You were saying the Cubes sometimes gave you information on the Mashabanas.'

'Ja, from time to time.'

'And was the information useful?'

'One time, it was very useful. My son was out on the farm in his bakkie carrying workers. They arrived at the fields they were going to reap, they all got out, and my son left his pistol on the passenger seat. When he got back five minutes later, it was gone. He rounded them all up, searched them, but found nothing.

'That night, my son got a phone call from one of the Cubes. Said he had some information. Said if we went to the Mashabana kraal we would find the gun in a plastic bag under the water pump. So my son went later that night and there it was, exactly as Cube had said. Lourans called the police. Two of the Mashabanas were arrested: one who worked for me, one who did not.'

'Did the case go to trial?'

'Ja, there was a court case, a trial, my son gave evidence. This was in 1996 or 1997. They got six months to a year each.'

I toyed with the idea of telling Steyn that his story was untrue. The previous day, I had spoken to the prosecutor who would have argued the case had it ever made it to court. The part about the gun going missing was true. Cube did phone Steyn's son, the gun was found in a plastic bag under the water pump, and the police were called. But the case had been thrown out before it got to court. There was no evidence linking the gun to the Mashabanas. The whole thing smelled of a set-up, of the Cubes using Steyn's ruthlessness to hit at the Mashabanas.

Later, I discovered what had actually happened. When the Mashabanas who lived across the road from Steyn's farm, at Edenridge, were convicted for attacking Davis, Steyn tried to evict the Mashabanas who lived on Normandale. It was an old and insidious practice in the area that when a black tenant was convicted of a crime, his entire family was evicted from the white-owned property on which they lived. Steyn must have been too embarrassed to tell me this. So he embellished on the stolen gun story instead.

The gun story intrigued me as much for what it said about the Cubes as for what it said about Steyn. This was not the only time a black family had hijacked white violence for its own purposes. One night in June 1998, the inhabitants of a kraal in the valley below Arthur Mitchell's farm were woken by a fist hammering on their door. The kraal was hidden deep in the recesses of the valley, miles from any public road, and no stranger would have found his way there in the middle of the night.

'I am Sergeant Manamela from the police station,' a voice shouted to them in Zulu. 'I am here with Arthur Mitchell. We believe you have stolen his cattle and we have come to take a look.'

The victims dressed hurriedly and opened the door to find four men in balaclavas pointing guns in their faces. The men took what they could carry and walked out into the night to raid the next kraal. By dawn, they had covered the entire valley. Four kraals in all. Each time they stopped to rob, they announced themselves as Arthur Mitchell.

Early the next morning, Mitchell got a call from the commander in charge of the police station. 'You are a suspect in a series of armed robberies that took place in your valley last night.'

'I was asleep in my bed.'

'Ja, you were asleep in your bed, but maybe you paid others to do it. We got a tip-off this morning. You want the people in those kraals to leave the valley, don't you? You want them to leave so badly that you are prepared to scare them away.'

When I heard the story, I marvelled at the robbers' sardonic humour. The politics of racial dominance had become their plaything. They stole their neighbours' life savings and toyed with the history of their own oppression in one gesture. And they left behind them a subtle taste of ambiguity. For who is to say that Mitchell is not a madman who pays thugs to control his valley? Somebody was toying with Mitchell.

So the Cubes had come to know Steyn well over the years, and they were using his quick temper to make life tough for the Mashabanas.

When I talked to Lourie Steyn in the Adristad hotel, I did not realise what an extraordinary story was unfolding before me. It was early in my research, the Izita/Sarahdale border was still new to me, and, in retrospect, I realise that I messed up the interview pretty badly. I did not know what I was looking for, and was oblivious to the fact that I had just found what I would have been seeking had I known better.

The truth is, I had stepped in on the 30-year relationship between Steyn and his tenants at its most interesting time. Both sides were behaving in ways that their forebears would have found unnerving and peculiar. Talking in shorthand, they were acting oddly because of South Africa's transition to democracy. The full tale is far more complex, and I hope to have told you a great deal of it by the time this book is done. For the moment, let me simply say that in the early 1990s, Steyn, the old paternalist who understood his tenants as natural and eternal serfs, greeted the prospect

39

of universal suffrage with horror. That he flirted with Eugene Terre'Blanche's neo-fascist movement at that time is an index of the turmoil he was suffering. His dossier in the files of the old intelligence service says he attended meetings at which the disruption of South Africa's first democratic elections was discussed. That is a desperate and panic-stricken way for a farmer in the Natal hinterland to spend his Sundays.

The Cubes and the Mashabanas, too, were acting in ways that would have sent cold shivers down their fathers' spines. It is true that their forebears would have done their fair share of tugging and prodding in their relationships with the white men who controlled the countryside. But their tactics would have been passive and subtle. Their goal would always have been to carve out just a little more room to breathe. The young men who came of age in the 1980s were a different breed altogether. The Cube and Mashabana men of this generation had all found themselves behind makeshift barricades in South Africa's urban insurrections. And they had witnessed something of the new interface between politics and crime, where young men chose whether to join a youth organisation or a car theft racket. They took these experiences back with them to the countryside, to their relationship with their white landlords.

In my meeting with Lourie Steyn, all I saw of this new sensibility was the story of the Cubes whispering tales about the Mashabanas into the farmer's ear. There is something funny and insouciant about using the white man's fists to make grief for a black neighbour. It is as if white supremacy had become something light, something one played with and manipulated to one's own ends. It spoke of a confidence and an arrogance that was new to the peasants of the KwaZulu-Natal countryside, as I was soon to learn.

The truth is that by the time I met Steyn, his family had been routed by their black neighbours. The arson, the burning fields, the unprecedented cattle theft, the gunshots in the night, these were vicious and brutal tactics, and Steyn, for all his right-wing posturing, never stood a chance. The man I met was trying lazily to cover the tracks of his retreat. His relationship with his tenants was fine, he told me. He had left with dignity, to retire. 'It was time to put my feet up.'

I would discover that the terms of Steyn's departure from

40

Normandale shaped in no small part the tragic string of events that unfolded after Mitchell bought the property. If you do not understand why Steyn left Normandale, it will be impossible to grasp why Mitchell's new tenants interpreted his words the way they did, when he met with them in February 1999.

*

The television man finally arrived, a short, nervous little fellow with a Hitler moustache, a creased black suit and a bright rainbow tie. Steyn towered over him, put his arm across his shoulders and squeezed his hand until he grimaced. Steyn was so pleased he could barely contain himself. In his excitement, he made me a promise he had no intention of keeping.

'I won't be long. Go and chill out at the restaurant across the road and I'll meet you there as soon as I'm done.'

After a massive steak and a close reading of every word in the local newspaper, it was apparent that Steyn was not coming. I got into the car, accelerated back into the rain and called Steyn on his cellphone. His voice was even and expressionless.

'Ja, I said everything I know, really. You must go and talk to the farmers who still live in the district. Get them to draw you a map. Then you'll see what's what.'

*

A few weeks later, I drove to Penville, a tiny town on the south-western edge of the midlands. I had an appointment there with a retired priest named Ernest Miller, who had run the church mission in Izita in the 1970s and 80s. Judging from his house, the pension of a mission priest is not for those who wish to grace old age with the trimmings of middle-class dignity. It was a sweet little box, topped with an ageing tin roof, so small I felt I could have put it on my back seat and driven off, Miller and his wife watching the countryside go by from their living room window.

I sat on a long, rust-coloured couch, the old man and his wife on stiff wooden chairs on either side of me. A massive dog, as tall as my waist, stuck her friendly head in my face and sniffed me enquiringly, then collapsed onto the floor and fell asleep. Miller's bran muffins were awful, and I estimated that there was space enough in the dog's mouth to hide two of them there without waking her.

Miller was an irritable old man with an unkempt beard and a wild look in his eyes. He answered each question in a lifeless monotone, and reserved his years of pent-up anger for his wife, whom he would contradict every time she opened her mouth. The old woman was not one to take his bullying lying down, and soon the two of them were absorbed in internecine warfare, while I tried to nudge the dog awake to keep me company.

Nearly an hour went by, and I'd written just half a page in my notebook. It seemed extraordinary that a couple could live in a place for more than a decade and have next to nothing to say about it. Perhaps the labyrinthine geography of black rural politics was impenetrable to these white people, and I decided to turn the conversation to the white farmers of the district.

I went through the names of all the farmers on the border of Izita, and the old couple bickered about who farmed well and who badly, who was strange and eccentric, and who was well liked. The priest had grown tired of arguing now, and his wife did most of the talking.

'Oh yes, I remember the Steyns well. They owned Normandale and used to employ Izita people at harvest time.'

The old man's contrariness had been whittled down to brief staccato sentences. 'Actually, we barely knew the Steyns,' he snapped. 'We had very little to do with them.'

She ignored her husband and looked at me intently. 'Not only did we know the Steyns, our children used to play with theirs after school. This was long ago, in the late 1970s.

'At some point, my children came home upset and disturbed, and said they did not want to play with the Steyns anymore. They did not like what the Steyn children were doing to the black kids who lived on Normandale. They would play a game called "ambush". The white boys would wait silently in the bushes for the black kids, and as they were walking past would hurl rocks and stones and pieces of timber and then rush out and storm them with sticks. My kids were upset. They said it was no game. There was real violence, real force.'

I chastised myself for the clumsy symbolism that came to mind, but it stuck throughout the two-hour drive back to Alanview. Could one of Peter Mitchell's killers have been one of the black kids coming home from school in the late 1970s? Was the military-style imagination that conjures a quiet dirt track as the site of an ambush learned from the games white supremacy's children used to play? So many of the games black people in the district played toyed with the past, mocked it, redeployed it for new ends. Maybe one of the killers, when he heard the sound of Mitchell's car, smiled to himself at the irony of the reversal.

FOUR

Hours and hours I spent with Mike Glossop on the dust roads that twist their way through the Alanview district. Glossop is a Yorkshireman with a thick north-England accent and the charm of a second-hand car dealer. Colin Waugh smiles mischievously when I mention Glossop's Yorkshire accent.

'Born two counties north of civilisation's frontier. That's deep in the savage lands. Too deep for my liking.'

Glossop carries a nine-mill. on the elastic strap of his short trousers, and the weight of the gun pulls the trousers down to expose an abundance of middle-aged flesh around his hip. Usually, it is impossible to shut him up, but when it comes to his past he speaks in vague, brief inferences: a policeman somewhere in Britain in the 1960s, a policeman in Rhodesia in the 1970s; then a salesman for a South African chemical company, and finally, five years of unemployment, during which he started a community crisis centre in one of Pietermaritzburg's townships. Waugh recruited him some time in 1999 as one of his Farm Watch co-ordinators. His history left me both suspicious and intrigued; a Brit who comes to Africa to do battle for a white minority regime and ends up as a township do-gooder? Many white men who chose to fight African liberation movements for a living have a fraught and ambivalent relationship with black people, a strange cocktail of anger and fascination. I was curious to get a glimpse at the soul that Glossop's relentless banter was hiding.

Glossop has been assigned a large chunk of the district to patrol. His job is essentially to conduct one end of an elaborate cat-and-mouse game between the farmers and the petty thieves in the black locations. Harvest time is not a good period for Glossop. Teenage children and middle-aged women steal out of the locations before dawn carrying large sacks. By sunrise, the sacks are full of tomatoes and potatoes, picked in the last hours of darkness on the perimeters of large commercial farms. By lunchtime, the stolen vegetables are neatly displayed in township street stalls, going for half the price of their supermarket equivalents.

During harvest time, Glossop hauls himself out of bed in the middle of the night to stalk tomato thieves. He has night-vision glasses with which to spot them and a massive spotlight with which to scare the shit out of them. Each tomato thief Glossop catches requires him to spend a day at the Alanview Magistrates Court some months later, waiting for hours to be called as a state witness.

'It's a not-in-my-backyard strategy,' Glossop explains, 'and it works. These poor buggers are not going to stop stealing tomatoes. The issue is where they are going to steal them. Put a patrol out for a few nights, catch one or two of them, and the rest won't be seen dead in the same neighbourhood. They'll get up a little earlier, walk a little further, and steal tomatoes in the next district where there is no Mike Glossop to catch them. The principle is: they can steal tomatoes wherever the bloody hell they like, except from our clients.'

Once, I set my alarm for 3 a.m. and joined Glossop on his ungodly patrol. It was near the end of the picking season, and he was flagging and worn out. He put his night-vision glasses and his spotlight away, sat on the bonnet of his bakkie, and began speaking in his baritone voice.

'Sometimes it is best just to let them know you're here.'

'How do you do that?'

'You do exactly what I'm doing, mate. You sit on the bonnet of your vehicle and you talk loud enough to wake people in Foster's Rest.'

If the folks of Foster's Rest were indeed woken by Glossop, they would have heard a home-brewed philosophy on how to deal with racial conflict out here in the hills of the midlands.

'There is one simple principle by which one must live,' Glossop said, the grey of pre-dawn making a silhouette of his chubby profile. 'There are 40 million of them out there and you're not going to drive them all away. You're not going to put up a fence between you and them and say, "Cross this fence and we'll beat the shit out of you," because they'll laugh in your face and tear down your fence in the night.'

Glossop was in pedagogic mode. He could have been on the stage at the town hall, hundreds of farmers in neat rows, heads tilted upwards, listening attentively.

'The name of the game is accommodation. You have to learn to live together somehow. Give a little, take a little: talk and listen. The white man has no political power in Africa anymore. It's gone. No use trying to get it back. But what he does have is money. This countryside is devastated, there are no jobs. Look at what we're doing out here at four in the bloody morning: stalking poor people who are scrounging around for a living.

'The white man has land and money: he has the capacity to employ people, and employment around here is gold. The workers on the farms don't want to go back to the violence and poverty of the location. They like it on the farms: they're something of an aristocracy in the midst of all this shit. So you make a point of looking after them. You investigate the theft of their cattle as carefully as you would the farmer's cattle. If one of them is assaulted, you find the perpetrator and you book him. Look after these people and they will look after you. Give them a bit and you can take a bit from them.'

Glossop usually spoke in code; he danced endlessly round the point he was making, drawing in anecdotes from the past, prognoses for the future. In short, he was telling me that he paid farm workers for information.

'Informer is an unfortunate word,' he frowned. 'Let us rather call them entrepreneurs: people who know which side their bread is buttered, and how to go about buttering it.'

'Entrepreneurs?' I laughed and shook my head. 'Call a spade a spade, Mike. You are talking about people who will put their neighbours in jail for a bit of extra cash.'

'No, no. The words you use are very important. You want to create a culture here, a culture that says theft is wrong and telling the authorities about it is right. Because that's the problem around here. Pilfering a farmer's cattle, one after the other until he has no cattle left, that's okay. Tell the police about it, that's not okay. That earns you a bullet between the eyes. You need to build a culture that says that's wrong. So when people give information for money, I call them entrepreneurs instead of informers. It means they are prepared to negotiate with the law, to put an extra buck in their pockets by doing something productive.'

I did not push Glossop on the sort of checks he set for his informers, how he tested the veracity of their information, but I would be surprised if he was not given the run around every now and then. In Cape Town, I had met Glossop's predecessor, an Indian man called Cuben, who had been pushed out of the district by a group of Sarahdale farmers who did not like the colour of his skin.

Some time in the late 1990s, a client of Cuben's on the border between Sarahdale and Izita had 15 head of cattle taken in one night. Cuben got hold of a police tracker dog and followed the cattle's trail through Izita, out the other side, and into the midlands bush. The trail headed deeper and deeper into uninhabited wilderness. There was nothing, not a single homestead, not a sign of a domestic animal. After more than 20 kilometres, he lost heart and turned back.

At dawn the following day, Cuben took a police helicopter over the area he had tracked. He flew for miles over dense bush until he reached the coast, turned around and followed the same route back: there was nothing, just empty vistas of wild bush jungle. Cuben became obsessed. That night, in the pitch black of the rural hinterland, he took two uniformed policemen and a detective from the Sarahdale station and retraced his steps of the previous day. The party walked for miles and miles, past midnight, through the early hours of morning, into the first sunlight. About 40 kilometres from Izita they began climbing a steep embankment. Near the summit, they heard a loud crack, like a gunshot. They hit the ground and leopard-crawled the remaining distance. At the top, in the dim 5 a.m. light, they found themselves on the edge of a steep ravine. In its basin, the 15 head of cattle stolen from Cuben's client drank quietly from a shallow stream.

The ravine was steep, too steep for a cow to climb out of, and Cuben immediately saw the cunning genius of the theft. If the cattle had been found behind a fence, it could reasonably be assumed that the owner of the property had herded them there. But the ravine was a natural enclosure and there was no need for a fence, and therefore no sign that a human being had had a hand in the cattle's destiny.

A cluster of mud huts stood on the plateau on the other side of the ravine. Cuben and the policemen had no search warrant, but they had come a long way, and they figured that a group of

47

peasants deep in the wilderness did not have instant access to a lawyer, so they marched in, asking questions, searching every hut. The detective with Cuben threw a volley of questions at an old man who had been drinking a cup of tea at the entrance to his hut when the party barged in.

'Who brought those cattle and herded them into the ravine?'

'That ravine does not belong to us,' the old man said with a shrug. 'Our property is this kraal, and the mealie field and grazing field next to it.'

'So these cattle, they broke down the fence at their farm in Sarahdale, walked 40 kilometres, climbed that steep embankment and settled into the ravine – just like that.'

'Stranger things have been known to happen,' the old man replied, deadpan and serious.

'But we heard the crack of a whip while we were climbing the embankment. One of your boys was herding these animals.'

'There are many noises out here in the bush. Where you are from, you are probably not used to them.'

'Why do you live here anyway?' The detective was at his wit's end. 'You are an eight-hour walk from the nearest shop. Why live somewhere where you can't even buy a loaf of bread?'

'I have lived here all my life,' the old man replied indignantly. 'And my father lived here before me. You think a black man can pick and choose where he lives?'

Searching through the family's meagre possessions, the policemen found a Durban phone number written into the identity document of one of the old man's sons.

'When we checked it out later,' Cuben told me, 'it emerged that it was the phone number of a well-known restaurant in Durban, one that prides itself on its fresh beefsteaks. The man with the number in his identity document insisted that it was the work number of a friend, but we didn't ever find this person. When the police visited the restaurant, the proprietor was outraged and told us not to come back without a judge's consent. But to my mind, there is no question that's where the meat was going. It was just impossible to prove.'

In one of the huts the party barged into, they found, fast asleep on a mat on the floor, a man the policemen instantly recognised as one of their most valued informers. Initially shocked to find his handlers in his bedroom, he quickly regained his composure, denied that he had anything to do with the cattle in the ravine below, and swore that every bit of information he had ever given to the police was honest.

During the following weeks, Cuben retrieved the dockets of the cases the informer had been involved in and tried to put together the pieces of the puzzle. There were times when his information had been correct and led to the recovery of stolen cattle. The function of this exercise was to keep himself useful, to gain trust, so that he could lead the police in circles when it really mattered. It seems that there were times when cattle had been stolen just so that they could be found. For the rest, the informer had sent the police on a wild goose chase, turning them in the wrong direction while his colleagues were quietly herding cattle out of the district, to butcheries in Richmond, Pietermaritzburg and Durban.

How far did this network of false information stretch? The cattle thieves up in the mountains could not have accomplished their task without some help from someone who knew the farm they robbed very well. Somebody was familiar enough with the terrain to herd 15 cattle in the middle of the night, cut fences and drive them in the right direction. And if the cattle thieves received help in taking the cattle, did the secret alliances they nourished include agreements to give false information? Could it be that some of Glossop's informers were paid to hoodwink him?

It should be said that this intriguing, labyrinthine operation was almost certainly unusual. Most cattle theft was small-time stuff. A worker would steal for his own pot. Neighbours would cut down fences and incorporate a few head of a farmer's cattle into their own herd. The Mashabanas, I learned later, had played a wily trick on Lourie Steyn. A few days after one of Lourie's cows had calved, the fragile little thing was carried across the Steyn farm in the arms of one of the Mashabanas and presented to a cow in the Mashabana herd, where he would begin to suckle, find a new mother and make a new home.

Indeed, a cursory glance at the endless piles of stock theft cases in the Farm Watch office in town made it clear that almost every case of cattle theft was an inside job. Glossop's spin about the blacks on white-owned farms being an aristocracy, protecting their privileged position against the blacks in the locations, his idea that workers can be used as a shield against the mass of the unemployed, was little more than a myth. It served as ideology, something to say to strangers who come to the district bearing notebooks and pencils. All it illustrated was his ignorance of the lives of the black people around him. When I got to know people in Izita, I found that they thought of the ones on white farms as unfortunate and inferior people. 'We were always free to move to the city and to run our homes as we wished,' an elderly man called Elias Sithole, whom you will get to know well, told me. 'These poor people were always forced to work on the land in order to keep their homes. And the white landlord controlled every corner of their lives. An aristocracy,' he laughed. 'No, they are serfs.'

In my experience, tenants on white-owned land did not feel privileged by their employment. Many whom I met would happily have stolen their employer's herd if they could get away with it. But perhaps that is too crude. Things are actually subtler than that. There are a host of unwritten rules. Stealing from a white land-owner is often a form of punishment, a signal sent across the racial frontier that the white boss has gone too far.

Driving with Glossop on the boundary between Izita and the Sarahdale border farms, we come across a cluster of huts with a diminutive mealie patch closed in by a sturdy wire fence.

'That fence came straight from Cummings's farm,' Glossop said. 'It came down about ten nights ago, about half a kilometre of it. During the next few days, beautiful new fences started going up around chicken runs and mealie fields. But you can't prove it. There is nothing to positively identify those chicken runs with the fence that came down on Cummings's farm.'

Usually, when a farmer talks about theft he adopts that awful tone one hears whites using on phone-in radio: passive hostility, dull, angry indignation. Not Glossop. He talks dispassionately about Cummings's fence. His tone is that of a tour guide. The subject matter evokes intellectual interest, rather than emotion.

'You'll think I'm daft, but it's quite gratifying to see Cummings's fence around this mealie patch. At least they're doing something productive with it. What scares me is when people take down a kilometre of fence and just dump it on the side of the road. That's trouble. That's sheer aggression, sheer destructiveness. That's when I start getting worried.'

I don't know if he knew it, but Glossop had just identified one of the rich permutations in the rules black peasants have made for white people. There are rules for those white farmers who defend their property too harshly, and for those who are not vigilant enough. There are rules for farmers who sink below a commonly held threshold of human decency, and there are rules for those who are considered kind. The bizarre thing, though, is that white farmers have absolutely no idea that these rules exist.

Shortly before I arrived in the district, a neighbour of Arthur Mitchell's woke one morning to find five of his cows lying dead in the field adjacent to his homestead, their throats slit from ear to ear. The farming community was enraged. There was talk that Paul Mlambo was behind it, that the ANC was launching a subtle campaign of terror, that the gauntlet had been thrown down.

Months after the incident, I met a man who had lived in one of the kraals on Mitchell's neighbour's property. Most black people in Izita and on the farms do not know the surnames of the farmers for whom they work. They christen each farmer with a Zulu name, and that is how he is known throughout Izita. The man I met, a policeman called S'bu, told me the story of 'Bebetu', Mitchell's neighbour, and why his cattle's throats had been slit.

'There was a tradition which Bebetu instituted many years ago,' S'bu told me. 'He has a maize grinder on his property. It has been there for years and years. Long ago, I think in the 1970s, some people from the boundary of Izita started coming onto Bebetu's property to grind their maize in his machine. Bebetu said it was okay, and it went on like that for 20, maybe 30 years.

'Then Bebetu fell ill, some time in 1999, and his son took over the farm. The first thing he did was to close access to the maize grinder. No warning, no negotiation. One morning, he was there, standing with his feet wide apart, his hands on his hips, shouting in broken Zulu. "That's it. No more maize grinder. I can't have strangers on my property, not with everything that is going on."

'So that is why his cattle were killed. To punish him. Because you cannot end a 30-year arrangement without an explanation or an apology, or even a sheepish smile.'

'Does everyone in Izita know why Bebetu's cattle were killed?' I asked.

'Everyone on that boundary. Everyone who was affected by Bebetu's action. And also his workers, who live on the farm. They all know why.'

'That is very ironic,' I commented. 'Because none of the white

51

farmers know why the cattle were killed. They think it was orchestrated by political activists.'

'He knows,' S'bu said, laughing through his teeth without pleasure. 'Maybe he does not know that he knows. But he knows.

'What he does not know, the son of Bebetu, is that he was nearly killed. Some time ago, maybe a year back, one of his workers had a stroke while working in the fields. Bebetu's son picked him up in his arms and put him in the back of his bakkie. But instead of driving him to the hospital, he took this ill man to his kraal, handed him to his family and drove off. The man died a few hours later.

'There were angry words at the funeral. Very angry words. There was talk of revenge. The dead man's sons said they knew of a hit man in Durban who would do the job for R1000. It took some older people to calm them down. But there is still anger.'

Talk of murder, of a group of tenants plotting the death of their landlord's son, brings Peter Mitchell into my head. I have no idea what he looked like. Someone once described him as tall and strong with thick blond hair, but that is not enough for a real image. Strangely, there isn't a single picture of him in the public parts of Mitchell's house. I did not have the heart to ask Mitchell or his wife for a photograph. I only met her once, fleetingly, but the façade she presented to the world seemed so strained, so difficult, I felt the walls that dammed in her pain were made of plastic, that a pinprick would destroy them.

The Mitchell situation was about unspoken rules. He bought a farm, marched into his tenants' space and laid down the law of his land. The way he recounts it, his law was decent and civilised. But the situation was by its very nature a precarious one. Mitchell had only bought the land so that his things should not circulate. He wanted a buffer between himself and his neighbours, and in the process of building his buffer, he had to negotiate with them. He was there, de facto, in their space.

Later, I would learn that the rules in the heads of the peasants on the Sarahdale/Izita border had changed dramatically in the course of a generation. I also discovered that Mitchell knew little of these rules, that he broke some sacred ones, ones that for his tenants were a matter of life and death. I spent a long time pondering whether Peter Mitchell would still be alive if his father had known his tenants and their rules a little better. Or whether, instead, the rules did not allow for another white proprietor on

Normandale at all, and blood would have been spilled no matter what Mitchell did or did not do. I never found out the answer to that question. Some say they know for sure, but they are not being honest with themselves.

Dawn breaks over the tomato fields Glossop and I have been guarding. His face is naked now, uncovered by the sun, and there is a subtle trace of depression about him. Glossop blusters a lot, but he also has the perceptive irony of one who is not from these parts. I think he senses something of the logic of these unspoken rules, and I think this knowledge is the cause of some loneliness. I stare at Glossop as he stares out over his client's fields, and I sense that he is watching himself from far away, wondering what on earth he is doing at this ungodly hour, stalking the destitute as they fill their sacks.

FIVE

Glossop and I are on a dust road that runs from Alanview into the wide valleys to the west of town. Glossop is my chaperone: Colin has given him strict instructions to show me the district inside out, to take me wherever I want to go, to wait for me in the car however long I take. I am a little embarrassed, but too grateful to say no. As a stranger, I can go knocking on people's doors, but they will not say much. Introduced by the Farm Watch, I am immediately a friend, and the words come pouring out.

We are going to see Jude Fowler, a leading figure in the Alanview farming community. When I mention his name people speak of him with respect. 'He talks straight,' they say, 'and he may offend you a little, but listen to him and you will learn a lot. He has his head screwed on properly and he has lived here his whole life. He knows this place like the back of his hand.'

Fowler is not home. He is somewhere on the spectacular fields that stretch away from his homestead, and we are given hasty directions. Glossop's bakkie is no match for the scarred tracks that cross Fowler's farm, and we are hammered around inside the cabin, our heads smacking the ceiling every couple of minutes. Eventually, the track ends and we find ourselves looking onto a ridiculously pastoral scene. 'These hills are grass-covered and rolling,' Alan Paton wrote of the southern midlands, 'and they are lovely beyond any singing of it.' Beyond any singing of it, indeed. Carved into the basin of these lovely hills is a rich, gold-coloured field, rows of beautifully manicured hay rolls stretching to the horizon. There is a tractor at the far end of the field, its progress so slow we are not sure whether it is moving toward or away from us. We sit and watch as the machine gradually gets bigger, and a red, sunburned face under a wide floppy hat becomes discernible above the steering wheel. Fowler is scooping his last hay roll for the day. He turns round, grips the joystick at his side and gently lays the hay roll on the ground. Satisfied, he cuts the engine, dismounts and slowly makes his way toward us. He is in his late fifties or early sixties. His face is hard and confident, his work clothes torn in places and soaked in sweat.

Glossop introduces me and Fowler smiles good-naturedly.

'I have the whole afternoon free. We can talk, I can drive you round the district and show you some things. Then I'll drop you at your car in town.'

'Before I leave,' Glossop butts in, 'Jude, you know that the goods stolen in the Van Vuuren burglary have been recovered. Koos should come and identify his television, his video.'

'Koos says he doesn't want to touch anything some kaffir has got his hands on,' Fowler replies, smiling an easy, affable smile. He looks at me and shrugs, as if to say, 'You can't help some people, that's the way they are.'

'Reading between the lines,' Glossop says, staring back at Fowler impassively, 'what Koos is saying is that he has a nice little insurance set-up which will get him lots of new goodies, and he doesn't want to see his old stuff again.'

'Reading between the lines,' Fowler replies, 'that's exactly what he's saying.'

*

Fowler and I are sitting in his living room. Beyond a large bay window, the fields of the Fowler farm stretch to the horizon. He is nibbling at a decrepit-looking sandwich. I am sipping lemonade.

'Peter's murder was political. There is absolutely no doubt about it.'

Fowler pauses at the end of each sentence to take another bite of his sandwich. He chews for ages before resuming his story.

'We get the sense that it is organised pressure. Where there is a border between a commercial farming district and a black area, and where the black area is controlled by the ANC, there is organised pressure. Each farm is slowly squeezed. Stock theft, vandalism, stolen fences, encroachment of black cattle. The weaker ones leave. They cannot farm and defend their properties at the same time. The stronger ones fight back. They must be taken out. That is what happened to Mitchell.'

55

Fowler's affable features belie an underlying intensity. His eyes are fixed on mine. He speaks with calm energy.

'Mitchell stood firm. He was a symbol of strength. So he was targeted. It is simply a political wheel that has to turn. When the ANC came to power, they said they would get the people land. And now they must deliver, by whatever means.'

When Fowler says 'political', does he mean that, at the highest level, the ANC has taken a decision to force white farmers off certain pieces of land, to make way for redistribution?

'It is difficult to know how high up it goes. But there has always been a close connection between ANC politics and crime. In the 1980s and early 1990s, when the ANC was fighting Inkatha, the ANC self-defence units collected funds by robbing banks. There are former MK soldiers who robbed banks and they are now high-ranking government officials.

'There is a sense in which it must go very high up. Take an example. The commando will do an operation in Athol on a Saturday morning – looking for stolen firearms, stolen cattle, that sort of thing. The operation will be handled impeccably. No nonsense. First thing Monday morning, the operation is known about in the highest government circles. And they are asking questions. They say there are allegations of bashing down doors, of thuggery. So, yes, there is something going on at the highest level. The blacks can rob us blind and there is little to be done. But we go in there and conduct an above-board operation, and they come down on us with the full might of the state.'

'So crime here has nothing to do with poverty, with unemployment, with land hunger. It's all politics?'

'It has nothing to do with poverty. It is about savagery. The Zulus are a savage nation. Theirs is a revenge culture. It is a crazily masculine society. It's the sort of culture where it's not good enough just to kill your enemy. You have to cut his balls out as well. In Zulu culture you can buy a wife. You buy a human being. She has fuck all say in the matter. She's your possession. Like a spade or a hoe.'

'Where did this savagery come from? Is it recent? Has something in the recent past aggravated it?'

Fowler thinks hard. He takes each question extremely seriously and answers with earnestness.

'The savagery has always been there, from long ago, from before the whites arrived in Africa. It was just suppressed by the apartheid regime. A lid was put on it, a white lid, for three generations. But it is back. It is just beginning to clear its throat.'

'How did apartheid put a lid on it?'

Fowler gives a wry, rich smile. 'The judicial process was quick and efficient under apartheid because the police used thumbscrews and racks. They did not need to piece evidence together. If there was a problem, they would blunder in, get what they wanted, haul their victim in front of a judge and slam him in jail.

'Now there is procedure, there are rules of evidence. They can't blunder in anymore. They need a search warrant. So the criminals can see them coming from a mile off. They go in with a search warrant and they find nothing.

'Simple things have ground to a halt. In the old days, you would catch somebody stealing potatoes, you'd take him and the potatoes to court the next day, and the matter was dealt with, there and then. Now, it takes two months. There are mounds of evidence. The suspect's lawyer wants to know that you have followed each letter of procedure. He drags it out to make some more money. By the end of it, you've lost three or four workdays sitting in court.'

'Yesterday I met Chief Zwanini, chief of the amaZwezwe,' I say. 'He showed me a map of the Alanview district drawn up in 1924. He claimed it shows that his people occupied much of the area that is now white farmland. This savagery – is it perhaps animated by a sense that there has been much injustice?'

Fowler brushes Chief Zwanini aside with an irritable wave of the hand.

'Chief Zwanini is talking crap. Go and read Allen Gardiner's diaries. He passed through this area in the 1830s. He did not see a single living soul. Between the reign of Shaka in 1824 and the migration of the Voortrekkers in 1837 there was not a single soul in this entire area. Gardiner found one human settlement between here and Durban. This whole stretch of the midlands was empty.'

Earlier in the day, I had driven along the boundary of Izita and Sarahdale with Mike Glossop. On our left, the land was pockmarked and scarred; on the right, manicured fields stretched into the distance.

'The two sides of this road tell you most of what you need to know about this district,' Glossop had said. He gestured to the right with his head and pointed his index finger at the richly matted grazing lands. 'These people have been here as long as the blacks, perhaps longer. They came up from the coast, their worldly possessions hauled up the mountains by carts. They took strain. It wasn't easy. And when they got here, they did not rest. They turned the soil with what implements they had. They were the first to turn the soil, no question about it.'

Glossop paused and pointed to the devastation on the left.

'They were not the first people to turn the soil. They followed the farmers up from the coast because the farmers had created something. White economic activity brought them here. They came as labour.'

This is the way white farmers across the district understand the past. A group of hardy pioneers came out from England in the mid-nineteenth century. They spent two months in the cramped bunks of filthy ships, they shat in buckets and threw their shit into the sea, and when they arrived in Durban they had nothing. They scraped together the last of their savings, bought carts, and when the carts broke on the unforgiving Natal terrain, they carried their meagre things on their backs. The land they found in the Natal interior was wild and harsh, but it was empty, abandoned a decade earlier by the Voortrekkers and never inhabited by the Zulus. ('It was too cold up here in the midlands for the Zulus,' an Alanview farmer told me. 'They stayed close to the coast.') So they took the land, and by the sweat of their labour they made a success of it. The Natal you see today, the beautiful, rolling hills covered with lush grazing grass and rich hay rolls, the valleys full of ripening vegetables – this is the legacy of the white pioneers.

And the Zulus? If their only role in this story was to provide menial labour, it was because they lacked initiative. Zulu men are lazy. They have a constitutional aversion to work. They drink beer while their women harvest their tiny crop and milk their scrawny goats. If the whites had never arrived, they would still be subsistence producers living in mud huts under warmongering tyrants, riddled with hatred and disease.

*

Like all myths of origin, there is a grain of truth in this one. The Voortrekkers did abandon the eastern Cape frontier to the British in the 1830s, and when they arrived in the midlands in 1837 they

58

found … Well, the land was not empty; there were thousands of people between the Umkomaas and Mzimkhulu rivers. But they were living strange and disturbed lives. The valleys and the grass-lands, where you would expect to find pastoral settlements, had been evacuated. There were skeletons of former villages there, recently abandoned. Their one-time occupants had scattered and fragmented into small groups; their cattle and often their leaders gone, they inhabited broken or forested country, living off edible roots and tiny patches of crops. They dared not rebuild permanent infrastructures or keep cattle in any numbers, because the mid-lands was a wild and violent place at the time, and anything one built would have to be defended with violence.

The truth is that the Voortrekkers had stumbled into the after-math of one of the most vicious episodes southern Africa has known. Historians once referred to the upheaval as the *mfecane* and attributed it to Shaka, the Zulu king, and his single-minded penchant for imperial expansion. More recently, a subtler picture has been painted. At the beginning of the nineteenth century, something unprecedented began happening in the myriad small chiefdoms that lay north of the Tugela river, about 250 kilometres from the ground on which Peter Mitchell was killed. The larger of the region's polities began building conscripted armies for the first time, their goal not just to subdue, but to plunder their neigh-bours. Some attribute this development to the incursion of European traders in the area, cattle traders in particular. Cattle were a staple in the region; if you trade your cattle, you must replace them. And so a premium was placed on domesticated beasts, and the ambitious and the acquisitive began to accumulate them by force. Weaker chiefdoms had a choice. They could stay north of the Tugela and pay burdensome tributes to the victors, or they could escape their fate and move south.

And that is what happened in the 1820s; the Thembu, the Chunu, the Macaba and dozens of other chiefdoms packed up and left; although 'packed up' is something of a misnomer, because they abandoned most of their valuables to those who had defeated them. The chiefdoms moving south had nothing, and they rebuilt by devastating the settlements they met on the way. They brought with them the violence and plunder from which they had escaped, and by the late 1820s, the southern midlands was in turmoil; it was not a place where anyone could safely put down roots.

Run through the surnames of Normandale's tenants and you will find that their forebears were in the thick of those ugly times. They were all refugees, moving southwards in haste. The Mashabanas were amaWushe, a chiefdom that claimed the area around present-day Howick 200 years ago. They were pushed south in the 1820s, as the Thembu and the Chunu forced their way through Wushe land. The Mabidas – whom I will tell you about a little later – fled south in a later migration in the 1830s, when the Zulu king Dingane killed their chief and drove them across the Umkomaas.

The Cubes, by contrast, have an unusual and uncertain story to tell, for it is odd to find people of that name as far south as Sarahdale. They are amaCubeni, a tribe that was never forced to flee south of the Tugela. Their forebears were ironworkers, a skill that became invaluable in the warlike era of the 1820s. Go to Inkandla, a few kilometres north of the Tugela, and you can still see the place – preserved across the generations by their descendents – where the Cubes made weapons of war. The powerful courted and shielded them; to drive them and their unique skills out would be to destroy the equivalent of modern armaments factories and their skilled personnel. So why the Cube family of Sarahdale left their heartland some time in the nineteenth century is a story that seems to have been lost forever. But it is by no means irrelevant to the relationship between Mitchell and his tenants. That the Cubes found themselves so far from their ancestral base may well explain why they were forced to live on white land for three generations, and why Mduduzi, Peter and Prince – the three Cubes who listened to Mitchell list his new rules at the roadside meeting back in February 1999 – inherited a stock of bitterness from which their more fortunate blood relatives were sheltered.

If this is what the Voortrekkers found in the southern midlands in 1837 – a scattered and nervous people, eking out a living in the forests – what happened next is uncertain. One side of the encounter was non-literate, the other was far from the literary centres of their grandfathers, so neither was much good at keeping records. What is known is that the Voortrekkers established a rudimentary government, a council of family fathers and elders, and portioned out the entire midlands into gigantic farms of 3 000 morgen each. A couple of thousand whites had stretched themselves across the breadth of the midlands and were preparing to farm it.

The trekkers had a pretty brutal plan for the blacks they encountered. They needed labour for their farms but they did not like the idea of thousands of potentially hostile people on their doorstep. So they passed a law stipulating that five black families could live on each trekker farm in exchange for providing labour. The remaining blacks, the unwanted surplus, were to be pushed over the Drakensberg mountain range and across the Mzimkhulu river.

In reality, the Voortrekkers' grim master plan was little more than wishful thinking. A few thousand trekkers in ox wagons do not make for much of a state, never mind a capacity to drive tens of thousands of people into the wilderness. The executive level of government, the Raad, only met every few weeks because its members had to travel miles on horseback to get to one central point. The fledgling state had no coercive arm to speak of; instead, the farmers of the hinterland were armed to the teeth and they came together, ad hoc, to avert danger whenever it arose. In far-flung districts like Alanview, the Voortrekker state had one representative, the magistrate or landdrost. He was judge, prosecutor, tax collector and law writer. In districts where the landdrost was a lazy man, or where his own business interests kept him occupied, the state had barely any presence at all.

So, in the far reaches of the white republic, the trekkers' relationship with their new neighbours was pretty tough. The blacks did not settle that quietly for the land-for-labour deal. And the whites were not gentle when the blacks refused to play ball. In 1843, less than 100 kilometres west of the site where Peter Mitchell was shot to death, members of the amaZwezwe made a night-time sortie onto four isolated trekker farms and stole more than 200 head of cattle. The following day, the trekkers in the district set off on horseback towards the foothills of the Drakensberg, where the amaZwezwe kept their cattle. A few days later, the commando returned with 'orphan children', who would work as slaves on the trekker farms, as well as 3 000 head of amaZwezwe cattle. The Mashabanas trace their pedigree to the Zwezwe; it is possible that their great-great-grandparents had first-hand experience of that nasty skirmish.

When the British arrived in the late 1840s, the trekkers left en masse, heading westwards over the Drakensberg. They had left the Cape in the 1830s to escape British rule and they were not about to submit to the moral codes of foreigners once again. Hence the resumption of the Great Trek, which was to become the founding myth of nascent Afrikaner nationalism more than half a century later.

The British were a little more sober than their Boer predecessors. Initially, at any rate, their plans were in keeping with the scant coercive machinery at their disposal. On paper, two-and-a-quarter million acres of land were set aside for purely black occupation in a specially constituted Trust. Blacks on these lands were grouped together under their hereditary chiefs, and were governed according to customary law. At the apex of this chiefly political system was the white Governor of the Natal colony, Theophilus Shepstone, who had the power, among many others, of dismissing chiefs, dissolving or inventing chieftaincies, or subdividing existent chieftaincies into parts.

In reality, this ghettoisation – so eerily anticipatory of the apartheid to come – was not quite as clean as that. In areas like Sarahdale and Alanview, vast stretches of Crown land, reserved for white farmers, were bought up by London-based land speculators, primarily by the Natal Land and Colonisation Company. Once British settlers began farming there in earnest, the speculators calculated, the value of their land would skyrocket, and they would make a handsome profit on their cheap investment. They waited a long time. By the 1880s – three decades after the initial purchases – only a handful of British settlers were farming in the area. In the meantime, African chiefdoms like the Macaba, the Mbo and the Zwezwe settled on many of these London-owned farms and began rebuilding the sort of lives they had once lived further north, before the disruptions of the 1820s. The forebears of the Mabidas, who were Mbo, and the Mashabanas, who were Zwezwe, would have been among these people.

Indeed, some present-day historians argue that these decades saw a fairly stable *modus vivendi* between black and white, in the southern midlands at any rate. The British were in part responsible for stabilising a violent and inhospitable place, and they did not appear, at least initially, to be acquisitive or land hungry. Although any proud Zulu nationalist who hails from south of the Tugela would dispute the fact today, when the British went to war with the Zulus in 1879, many black people in the southern reaches of Natal fought on the British side. As odd as it may seem now, for people like the Mabidas and the Mashabanas, the British were a benign force compared to the acquisitive and warlike Zulu. The latter were a distant and callous aristocracy. They gave the dialect spoken south of the Tugela the derogatory name 'lala' – which meant 'menial' – and exacted heavy tributes from the people on the periphery of their kingdom.

Two things began happening in the decade prior to the turn of the century that would change the relationship between black and white forever. I will tell you far richer and more evocative stories about these times when I introduce you to some Izita people and the memories they have inherited from their grandparents. For the moment, I will simply tell you in the most abstract terms that the British, following their victory over the Zulu, built a powerful coercive capacity, and that at the same time white agriculture became a formidable political force, its voice heard more and more frequently in the corridors of state power.

Say this to a white farmer like Jude Fowler today and he will laugh at you, but in the late nineteenth century it was black farmers, rather than whites, who fed Natal's towns. In the course of the 1880s, as white farmers began finding their feet and producing surpluses of their own, so they used their access to the white government to strangle their black competitors. Town markets closed their doors to black-produced crops. Black settlements were driven off land in places like Sarahdale as speculators like the Natal Land and Colonisation Company sold to aspirant white farmers. A barrage of new tax laws – on huts and livestock, wives and young unmarried men – forced black families to send their members into employment on white farms.

So the social landscape that is the backdrop to our tale – a white landlord and his black tenants – was shaped at this time and in this way, and if whites have forgotten that their forebears acquired their land by force, you will soon see that there isn't a single black person in the Sarahdale district who does not have memories of dispossession seared on his consciousness.

Which is not to say that the relationship between black and white in places like Sarahdale has been one of uninterrupted animosity. It is far more complicated than that. 'What analysts sometimes fail to understand,' the historian Charles van Onselen wrote recently, 'is that without prior compassion, dignity, love or a feeling of trust – no matter how small, poorly or unevenly developed – there could have been no anger, betrayal, hatred and humiliation.'

During the last hundred years, compassion and humiliation

have lived at close quarters in the southern midlands. Those blacks who found themselves living on white land entered a strange relationship with their landlords, one that shored up many conflicting emotions. Some of their wage would be paid in cash, some in kind. Farmers would underwrite the building and maintenance of a farm school for the sons and daughters of farm workers. Portions of farmland would be set aside for a rudimentary social infrastructure: soccer fields, crèches and the like. Farmers would pay a portion of hospital bills, they would subsidise the costs of a funeral, set aside land for a small cemetery, provide interest-free loans. And yet a farmer could also throw a worker off his land at a moment's notice, and he would lose not just his job, but his home, his children's schooling, his pension. The whole relationship was like a stylised drama; a set piece for betrayal.

Things get even more complicated. For blacks on white land never really accepted the paternalist relationship as a just and permanent one, and the white landlord who looked his tenant in the eyes saw a person with many conflicting identities and desires. Behind their landlords' backs, black tenants have always fought a scrappy, mischievous, ever-silent battle. It always concerned the minutest of details – the integrity of fences erected by white farmers, the field one chose to graze one's cattle, the keeping of hunting dogs and the killing of wild animals. None of these disruptive games has ever been simple. Each is deeply symbolic and laden with myths and memories; each encodes a message about the rival ways in which the countryside is used, about how things were in the fading, increasingly mythical times of the mid-nineteenth century, about what it might be like in the future.

'Stock theft,' the historian William Beinart wrote in an essay on the Umzimkhulu district of the 1890s, 'was a means of challenging European farm owners in the same way as letting stock wander, or letting dogs loose, could unsettle them. Strident demands for tighter policing and for heavier sentences on those convicted suggest that settlers lacked control over the African population as well as the environment. Thus their concern about the issue became something of a metaphor, deeply rooted in broader colonial society, for the desire to exercise tighter social controls.'

It is really quite extraordinary that these words describe Umzimkhulu in the 1890s, for you will see later that they describe the battle the Normandale tenants fought with Arthur Mitchell. So

64

much happened in the intervening century, and yet so much stayed the same. Or perhaps it is more accurate to say that the past returned after decades of slumber. For the tenants on Normandale not only used tactics reminiscent of the ones Beinart describes; their aims were remarkably regressive. They wanted to turn the clock back 100 years.

*

It is well that I give you this sketchy history now, in the middle of my conversation with Jude Fowler, for he is about to speak of the ways in which the demise of apartheid has affected his business, and it would be misleading to think of 1994 as a blank slate, a new beginning. The things on his mind are old and familiar – they concern a new twist in the three generations of compassionate and betraying relationships between landlords and tenants.

Fowler has finished his sandwich. We are sitting on bar stools, our elbows leaning against a high counter. He puts his plate down, swivels in his chair so that he is facing the stretch of his farm outside the window, and nods toward it with his head, as if it embodies the abstract themes he speaks of.

'There is a big problem in this province. Unemployment is rising. The population is growing. But commercial agriculture is shrinking. We no longer hire the great gangs we used to hire. In the 1970s, I employed 30 or 40 schoolchildren on a Saturday morning to run behind the combine and pick useable stuff from the ground. They would get paid on commission. The more they picked up, the more money they put in their pockets. It was a crucial part of family income. Now it is illegal to employ children; the tradition has died, and so has a valuable source of income.'

'You mean the illegality of child labour is why commercial farmers are employing fewer workers?'

'No, no, that was just an example. There are many others.

'Ten years ago, I would employ up to 60 contract workers in the harvesting season. Sixty contract workers. How many mouths does one of them feed – six, eight? Today I do not employ a single extra hand in the harvesting season. We have mechanised harvesting. One machine does the work of 60 pairs of hands.'

'Why? What's changed?'

For a second, Fowler looks at me as if I've dropped in from

65

another planet. He quickly recovers his impeccable composure and replies softly. 'Minimum wage. The spectre of it has been hanging over us since the early 1990s. You take out your calculator, you do your stats and you see that it is just not sustainable. We cannot afford to do it. It's cheaper to sink money into a machine and recoup it over the years.'

'Isn't the real spectre 60 newly unemployed people? Didn't you think of keeping them on just so their families could eat?'

'Of course I did. You don't stop contracting people lightly. But there was no choice. If the farms went under they would all be unemployed. And we are talking of farms going under. It's not easy out here. You have layers and layers of uncertainty: the weather, the market. Add inflated wages to that and you're fucked.'

There was something else I wanted to talk about. 'You've spoken about minimum wages,' I say, 'but there is something more important than that, isn't there? There are land and housing claims.'

'There is an old man who lives on this property,' Fowler says. He is smiling to himself now, tapping his fingers urgently against the counter. 'His father worked for my great-grandfather. Include my son in the picture and we are talking five generations of association between our two families.

'All his offspring live in Durban, children, grandchildren. They were brought up here on the farm, they went to the farm school the employers in the district provided. They drank milk from the feeding schemes we set up. When they were teenagers, they worked on the farms on weekends. But when they grew up, they all left. Big wages in the city. More than anything anyone here can pay. But the city was tougher than they imagined. Not all bright lights and dollar bills.

'The old man is retired now. He is very old. He can't work anymore. He needs to rest. And that is fine. He can stay here until he dies. That is his right. But the offspring – they are another story. About 18 months ago, they used the old man to lodge a claim on a piece of my land. And I did not like the way they went about it.'

Fowler is talking about a new piece of legislation that his worker's grandchildren have deployed. In the years after the ANC came to power, a number of laws were passed to rearrange access to land in the South African countryside. South Africa's new governors did not like the feudal echoes of the relationship between landlord and tenant – the serf who puts his well-being in the hands of a master in exchange for labour. The post-1994 lawmakers jumped into this complicated world and tried to make it simple. They wanted to reduce the relationship between farmer and worker to a wage relationship. However, they also wanted workers to keep the homes, fields and schools that came along with a job under apartheid, but this time, independent of the whims of farmers. So, the Labour Tenants Act immunised labour tenants from eviction, on condition that they performed their contractual obligations. It also gave labour tenants the opportunity to buy, with the help of a government subsidy, the piece of land they paid for with the labour of their children. The Extension of Security of Tenure Act recognised that farm workers have homes, not just jobs, on white farmland, and allowed for families to keep living on the farms, even after the family breadwinner has lost his job.

The descendants of Fowler's long-time employee used one of these Acts to claim a piece of Fowler's farm as their own. But Fowler was having none of it.

'Maybe I would have played ball if they had been decent folk, but they are an evil bunch. They would come out from Durban and they would assault the people who live on my land. They told the other families: "This land is ours. We are going to chase you off it, and when that is done, we will chase the white man off as well."'

'How seriously did you take that threat?'

'Seriously enough to oppose the youngsters coming here.'

'But you didn't fight the old man's right to stay?'

'Of course not. I have no axe to grind with the old man. It is the youngsters who are the problem around here. Their lives are fucked, they have no clue how to manage their lives, and then they flee behind the coat-tails of the older generation. This lot sponged off their grandparents their whole lives. It dawned on them that after the old man is gone, they will have to stand up to me alone. So they made a land claim. But they didn't abide by the code of the farm.'

'So they are not here? They did not win their claim?'

'No, we screwed them. Wasn't nice, but we had no choice.' Fowler betrays no pleasure in saying this. His demeanour is even.

He is confident, but warm. 'We let the assault cases quietly build up. Each time there was an incident, we called the police and made sure that records accumulated. And then we took this pile of police dockets to court. We said these people are criminals, they are a problem to their neighbours, it is here in the records. They are not the worthy beneficiaries of a land claim.'

'But if they had played their cards right, they could have had a piece of your land?'

'Maybe, maybe. I do not like the way they live their lives. The old man's granddaughter has children but no husband. They have the skills to work, but they refuse to do so. They want the land, but they want to give nothing in return. I don't like them.'

I was astonished at how closely Fowler's story resembled the stereotype. Across the South African countryside, the last generation of farm workers' children have shunned the farms and gone to the cities to look for new lives and new identities. Some find work, build city families and city homes, and seldom return to the farmlands of their childhoods. Some live in single-sex compounds in the cities 11 months of the year, and return home for Christmas and Easter.

But most find nothing in the cities. They live strange, transient lives, wandering between town and countryside, but they belong to neither. In the cities, they are jobless and live in the vast shanty-towns on the edges of the metropolis. In the countryside, they have lost both the wealth and the identities that would have them marry and continue old lineages in the traditional way. With the coming of democracy and the promulgation of land reform laws, many have taken the gap and claimed land: a small patch of turf they can call their own. Farmers don't like it. They do not want a generation of frustrated transients on their doorstep, people who came of age in the cut-throat world of urban shantytowns.

Fowler looks out over his farm for the hundredth time.

'We are not employing people any longer, not full-time employees. If you employ a man, you have to house his family as well, and he can leave, get another job, but still keep living on your land. And then another does the same, and then another and still another. Soon you have a vast community of strangers living on your farm. You don't know who they are. Some could be thugs. Some could make a living from robbery and theft. And they all pass by your farmhouse on their way home.'

Fowler has a habit of playing down his most important utterances. As if you have to earn access to their meaning, work for them. He fiddles with a hole in his torn work shirt and mumbles into his neck.

'Houses are being bulldozed across the countryside. As soon as they are empty, they are torn to the ground. And you know the interesting thing? Most times, the farmer does not have to do it himself. It takes just a nod and a wink, and his workers bash the house down. They do not want strange squatters moving into their kraals, and they know that the farmer will not be able to get rid of them. Across the midlands, more than a thousand houses have been demolished. And they will never be rebuilt. The long era of black families living on white-owned land is dying. In a generation, there will be no one left. We will all employ contract workers and we won't give a fuck what happens to them or their families when they walk off our farms in the evening. It will no longer be our business.'

I do not believe Fowler and I say so. 'Is this not just your propaganda against the new dispensation, the threat you wave in front of the new government? Employment in the agricultural sector is not shrinking nearly as fast as your stories suggest.'

'I will show you,' Fowler replies. He smiles good-naturedly. 'Let's drive around the district now and I will show you the bulldozed houses.'

We climb into Fowler's bakkie. The obligatory assortment of large farmyard dogs sniff the tyres with excitement and trot alongside us until we reach the gate. Once we get to the public road, they stop instinctively, at the border of their territory, and stand watching us disappear, tails wagging.

We take a series of dust roads that run through the countryside, roads I would not have found if I had driven around all day. After a few kilometres we are deep inside a massive pine plantation. Where the road runs across a valley, towering trees surround us and we can see nothing of the countryside. But the summits of hills open up wide vistas and there are rows of trees, carved into the rolling shapes of midlands, as far as the eye can see.

I turn to Fowler and gesture with my hand to the thousands of trees. 'They're beautiful.'

'Do you think so?' he replies, mouthing a brief, tolerant smile. 'No, they are very ugly. They were planted after the War. The big

69

forestry companies came here in the early 1950s and bought up thousands of acres of beautiful land. I can still picture vividly what these hills looked like when I was a boy. They were extraordinary.'

We drive in silence for a long time, and then Fowler begins to speak about the trees again.

'They were planted by people who do not know how to look after the land. The trees use too much water. And they are planted too close to the water-table. Look at the barren patch on your left. That land has been ruined by trees. You will not be able to grow anything there for years.'

I do not realise it at the time, but this is a classic exchange, repeated in many times and places, between a rural native and a visitor from the city. The visitor takes in the landscape as scenery, as a pleasing arrangement of colours and shapes. The native sees history, human history. It will take many months in the Alanview and Sarahdale districts before I begin to see the deeds of people written into the landscape.

We are driving through thick forest now; the neat plantation rows have given way to a wild, unkempt hybrid of indigenous growth and old pines. Fowler stops the car and points through a gap in the trees.

'Look, that is what I am talking about.'

Now I see it. The ghostly remains of a destroyed settlement surround us. In the undergrowth beneath the branches, the stumps of former houses rise no more than a metre from the ground.

Fowler points to a long stretch of crumbling wall. It is barely visible amid the wild shrubs that have strangled it.

'That was the kitchen. Meals for 100 workers were cooked there every evening.'

'What happened? Why was this settlement destroyed?'

'This land belongs to Sappi, the giant forestry company. Five years ago, they switched from permanent workers to contract. After they retrenched the workers, they smashed the compound to the ground so that vagrants would not move in. If they had left the buildings standing, there would be hundreds of squatters on this land now.

'Even these broken structures attract people. Every now and then, criminals move in. They use it as a base and make sorties onto the farms around here. Periodically, we come in and flush them out.'

'Where do the contract workers come from?'

'Sappi does not care about that. They hire a labour recruitment firm and it is the firm's responsibility to find workers, get them here in the morning, make them disappear in the evening.'

We drive on about 200 metres until we come to a heavily bolted gate. Behind it stand two long, forlorn buildings. They look like a high school: grey blocks of concrete, two storeys high, a row of wooden doors stretching along their facades. You can tell from the stillness that they have been empty for years.

'This is the compound where the contract workers used to live. A trade union got into the compound, organised the workers. They went on strike. Sappi fired the contractor immediately and ordered it to empty the compound. Nobody has lived there since. The new contractor employs day workers and takes them home in the evening.'

Driving through the remains of this ghost town, its rubble hemmed in by the forest, leaves a nasty feeling in the pit of my stomach. Back in the sunlight, up on the hills, the world returns to us, and we begin to chat again. I press Fowler about the labour market. He has told me that farmers will all switch to temporary workers. But that entails bringing strangers onto their farms. Don't you need familiarity to build trust?

'There is an element of truth in that,' Fowler nods. 'But in the long run, it won't matter. In the old days, we used to build labour accommodation as comfortable as possible. We built schools, we had feeding schemes, we helped out. Now, we make it as uncomfortable as possible. We try to make sure that they never bring their families – because if they do, they will never leave.

'The status quo is this: the nuclear family stays with the worker on the farm. But the extended family is not allowed to live on the property. They live in a location nearby. We go out of our way to keep the extended family comfortable where they are, so that when it is time for the worker to go, his whole family has somewhere to relocate.

'And I swear to you, when they go, the house they lived in will be torn down. Once this generation goes through natural attrition, it will not be replaced. Thirty years from now, no blacks will live on the farms.'

We are at the summit of a steep hill now, and the valley below us is beautiful. On the left, the honey-coloured fields of a commercial farm; directly below us, smaller, patchwork fields of maize, wandering goats, a cluster of whitewashed mud huts built gently into the hill face.

We climb out of the bakkie, walk to the verge of the road and gaze into the valley. Fowler nods in the direction of the mud huts.

'This is my neighbour's farm. Those huts form one of the kraals his workforce has built. It is difficult to keep track of who lives there now. Every once in a while, in the early hours of the morning, we come up here with night-vision glasses and watch. We wear dark clothes, and the hill behind us is black, so they cannot see us. But we can see them. Those white walls provide a wonderful backdrop. You can see anything that passes in front of them.'

'What do you watch for?'

'Who is coming in, who is going out. Movement. There is plenty of movement around here in the early hours of the morning. You cannot trust the people who live here. Take your eye off them and they will rob you blind.'

SIX

In early January 2000, almost three-and-a-half months after Peter was killed, an elderly black man rang the buzzer on Arthur Mitchell's gate. He had walked halfway across the district on tired, failing legs, and the sweat was pouring off his forehead. Mitchell recognised the old man when he saw him, although he had not thought about him in years. He had worked in Mitchell's garden in the 1980s and '90s before retiring to a village on the other side of Sarahdale.

Mitchell sat the old man down, gave him a drink and waited for him to recover from his journey. The longer he waited, the more nervous the old man became. His glass of water shook visibly as he put it to his lips. Eventually, Mitchell coaxed a reluctant story from him. They want to kill you, the old man said opaquely. When you pick up the women to take to your fields. In the morning. Outside the Ndunge store. Mitchell asked more questions – who? when? in what context did you hear this? But the old man had said all he was going to say. He finished his glass of water and left.

For Mitchell, the old man's unexpected visit was the most touching moment of his awful proprietorship at Normandale. It was the only time, before or after Peter's death, that a black worker came to warn him of harm.

A few days later, Mitchell received a visit from two policemen attached to the provincial crime intelligence division. They were rural villagers – members of a village elite, to be sure, given their policemen's salaries – and many of their neighbours would have worked on a farm like Mitchell's. They told Mitchell they had recently debriefed an informer from the Izita area. He had said that there was a plan to kill the father of the young man who was shot to death on his farm. The story was vague. When Mitchell pushed for details, they evaded him politely. They said they believed they had an obligation to inform him, in the broadest terms, of what they knew. Beyond that, they could not say much.

The following day, Mitchell and his bodyguards did not go down to the Ndunge store. They sent a message to the contract workers saying that work had been suspended indefinitely. For the next week, Mitchell's land lay idle. It was late summer, close to the picking season, a time of year when vegetables require careful attention. Mitchell visited his irrigation fields during that week. His crops were suffering. Weeds were growing fast around his cabbages. He had a choice to make. Either stop farming or go back to the Ndunge store to pick up the workers.

So a week later, Mitchell and Craig drove to the Ndunge store to greet the sunrise. They were back in a routine, back to the predictable rhythms of farm life that made the work of an assassin easy. It was now that Craig began to crack. Every morning they drove into a death trap. They had been told it was there, but had taken few precautions. They were armed, but their foes would have the advantage of surprise. If the operation was clean and well planned, they would not stand a chance. Craig drove to his death every morning, a death he had rehearsed in his sleep the night before, and the prospect was too much for him. His body took over, enveloping him in such awesome pain that he was immobilised, housebound, unable to go and face the danger.

Mitchell, on the other hand, lost no sleep. His body did not fail him. He had quietly steeled himself with testosterone and anger.

I told him that I thought he was insane. 'Why do you go through this? What is the point?'

He bowed his head slightly and smiled to himself. A wry smile? No, a pleased smile: he was taking his pleasure in eccentric ways since the death of his son. 'I am not a fool,' he told me. 'I do not believe I can win this battle. This is Africa. There is one of me and countless dozens of them. A few years from now, the border will have been pushed back a notch and the people who farm behind me will be suffering what I am suffering now. What does this farm mean to me anyhow? We were here to build a future for my son.'

Mitchell was finished. He seemed to have forgotten the question.

'So what are you doing here, surrounded by armed men? Why don't you just retire to Durban and be with your daughter?'

The answer was sharp and immediate, delivered through gritted teeth. 'Because I'll be damned if they'll walk all over me. I won't stand for it.'

Whenever Mitchell spoke of retribution, he shielded himself from the darkness of his thoughts by speaking of them as the work of divinity. 'The Lord will see that they pay for this,' he continued. 'I will not turn away from what is right.'

He was fearlessly, maniacally determined, and it was precisely because of his determination that his foes were plotting to kill him. The truth is that things had spiralled out of control. Mitchell and his enemies were caught up in an endgame, one neither had bargained for, one that was bound to end with the spilling of more blood on the border between Izita and the Sarahdale farms.

When Mitchell bought Normandale to buffer his farming operations behind the borderline, he did not bargain that his neighbours would defy his right to do so. And his enemies, in turn, did not bargain that he would fight back so hard: strings of criminal charges, foreboding meetings, and finally an eviction application. And so his son was killed, and those who planned the murder must have believed that their deed would end the matter once and for all. For Mitchell was white, wealthy and footloose. Defeated, he would surely retreat into the suburbs of Durban, where he came from. The peasants and the unemployed, on the other hand, had nowhere to go. They could sit it out because they had to. The shackles of their poverty were the sharpest weapons in their arsenal.

They were wrong. After his son's death, Mitchell ignored his family's pleas to abandon his farm and he went out to look for the killers. By the time whispers of death plots came to his door, he was getting a little too close.

*

A few days after Peter was killed, the Sarahdale Agricultural Association called a crisis meeting. It was held in a hastily erected tent in the middle of town. Most of the heavyweights were there: police provincial command, the provincial minister of agriculture and land affairs, the commissioner from the local police station, the army, the mayor, representatives from Izita. Angry words were spoken. Farmer after farmer fired volleys of accusations at the security forces. Policemen and soldiers responded with swallowed words and vague speeches.

75

Finally, Mitchell made his way to the microphone. He was characteristically soft-spoken and, as was the case when I first met him at the meeting at the golf club two weeks later, he must have evoked much sympathy from strangers, this quiet, humble man, fresh from his son's burial. What he had to say probably eluded those unfamiliar with the politics of the district, and besides, with his soft voice and his restraint, you had to be alert to understand that he was issuing a threat.

Mitchell spoke of the burning of his cottage, of the fences that came down during the night. He spoke of the threat against his life, and of the gunshots he would hear echoing through the bushveld on Normandale.

'Those gunshots are the sound of poachers, people who come onto my land to shoot my game. I want to issue a public warning here today. From now on, if I find an armed poacher on my property, I will arrest him.'

Mitchell's words were really aimed at two or three people in the audience: the Izita representatives, the ones who would go to Langeni and report what he had said. His words were chosen carefully. Why would he only arrest poachers, rather than those who stole his vegetables or rustled his cattle? Why did he narrow it down so finely? Essentially, he was telling the people of Langeni that his guns were drawn, that he would spill blood to defend his land. A farmer cannot kill an unarmed trespasser on his land and get away with it. But an armed poacher, a man shot to death with a gun in his hand on somebody else's property – that is a different story. Mitchell was saying that if he could kill someone on his land, lawfully, he would do it.

'They knew what "arrest" meant,' he told me. 'There was no need to spell it out.'

So his enemies knew from the start that he had dug in his heels. They had killed his son in order to drive him from his farm, and his first move was to tell them that they could not have it, that if they set foot on it, they might not walk out alive.

The performance at the meeting in the tent was only the start of things. Mitchell went home and got to work: he wanted to find the people who killed his son. In hushed tones, he let it be known that he wanted information, that he was prepared to pay handsomely for it. And slowly, information started coming in. A man had been seen walking the streets of Izita with a gun like Peter's on his hip. There were murmurings that plans had been hatched at the butchery in Clermont where the Cubes worked.

*

Some time in January 2000, a picture started coming together, and late one night in the new year, Mitchell found himself in the back of a police car driving through Izita, two white detectives from the Carton Bay Murder and Robbery Squad in the front of the car. The man in the passenger seat was Louis Wessels, a veteran detective and the investigating officer in the Mitchell murder. The one driving was David Uys, a 24-year-old rookie on one of his first murder cases. The three men were looking for the house of the person they believed had shot Peter Mitchell – a professional assassin, they had been told – and they were confident that by morning he would be behind bars.

You may find it strange that the complainant in a murder case accompanies the investigating officer and his assistant, late at night, on a journey to the home of the prime suspect. You will also want to know how the three white men came to believe that the person they were after had shot Mitchell's son. It is indeed a strange story, and a complicated one, and I want to break it down for you and tell it bit by bit.

To begin with, the two detectives would have needed to take a local with them because they had never been to Izita in their lives. They had the shooter's address, but an 'address' in Izita is not particularly useful. You either know where you are going from experience, or you ask people on the side of the road where so-and-so lives. The two detectives did not know where to go: they had barely heard of Izita until the Mitchell docket crossed their desk. And as for asking locals for directions: two white detectives wandering into Izita and asking to be led to the house of a murder suspect ... well, it would have made for entertaining comedy.

It was not unusual, in 2000, for the officers investigating a South African murder to be a little unfamiliar with the local terrain. A murder committed with a knife, or an axe, or with bare hands, was investigated by local detectives. Where there were witnesses to the murder and the suspect had a name and a face, local detectives also handled the case. But where the victim was shot and the suspect was unknown, local detectives were not allowed near the

77

case. The docket went straight to the offices of the nearest Murder and Robbery Squad, an elite unit that specialised in following the elusive traces left at the scene of the crime. Two years after Peter Mitchell's death, the police command decided to close down Murder and Robbery Squads and to distribute their personnel to local police stations. So, at another time, the investigation may have panned out very differently.

I say Murder and Robbery Squads were 'elite' units, but 'elite' is a bit of a misnomer. I need to tell you why, so that you will understand why our story ends the way it does, and to tell you why, I must start with a brief tour of the South African Police Services.

Policing in South Africa is not formally decentralised, as it is in most parts of the world. There is no Johannesburg or Cape Town police force. There is one national monster of an institution. It employs 120 000 people, making it the second-largest police force in the world, and it is chaotic and ungovernable. Head office is a wide grey building in the centre of Pretoria called Wachthuis – 'Guardhouse'. Two thousand people spend their working lives in its bowels, and a joke among policemen in units like the old Murder and Robbery Squads is that they never come out. I can believe it. I have been to Wachthuis dozens of times and have never been able to find my way out of the building without help. It is not so much tall as wide: dozens of labyrinthine corridors extend across each floor, and their geography is indecipherable. I once spent 45 minutes wandering around the sixth floor looking for room 624. Nobody I stopped to ask had heard of it or knew how to get there. You need to have been there many times; then the memory of 100 turns into 100 corridors will imprint itself on your memory, and you will sleepwalk your way.

Looking at Wachthuis from the outside, one wonders whether anyone is in there. From street level, its windows are dark, tinted slits. The building is like a giant mole, a blind beast standing in the middle of the city seeing nothing.

And in truth, Wachthuis is a blind animal. Its relationship with its 1 100 neighbourhood police stations, 42 area offices and nine provincial commands is a tenuous one to say the least. In six years of South African democracy, nobody in Wachthuis, including two successive Ministers of Safety and Security, has been brave enough to try to do anything too radical with the organisation. Commands, blueprints, restructuring plans, policy guidelines are

78

transmitted from Wachthuis to be sure, but they vanish into the ether. The concrete beast stands in the middle of Pretoria alone; the giant organisation to which it is ostensibly attached lives in another universe. Or perhaps I should say a thousand little universes, each hermetically sealed. For the South African Police Service is a myriad of tiny places, and each runs on the steam of its own legacy.

Memos are faxed from head office to provincial office, from provincial office to area office. Area office calls a workshop of all station commissioners and unit heads. The instructions from head office are represented as graphs and bullet-form text on overhead projectors. The area commissioner, who played no role in the countless Wachthuis meetings that preceded the drafting of the memo, has spent the last 48 hours trying to decipher it. He tries to look authoritative by clutching one of those red laser pointers, so that the overhead screen looks like it is about to be hit with a tracer bullet. And then everyone goes back to work and does what he has always done.

At the time of the Mitchell killing, Murder and Robbery Squads counted themselves among these micro-universes. It is crucial that we get inside our particular Murder and Robbery Squad, because its politics, and the politics of its relationship with other little universes in the police force, play no small part in determining the conclusion of our story.

'Elite' is an odd word to use when talking of a Murder and Robbery Squad because it did not employ anybody of senior rank. To earn money and prestige in the South African Police Service one needs to get promoted. And getting promoted means becoming a manager and sitting behind a desk, far away from the nuts and bolts of solving crimes. There is no other measure of success in the organisation. The ladders are all aimed at Wachthuis. To have made it is to have an office in the monstrous building in central Pretoria, to sit in countless meetings drafting policy, and to fax that policy into the ether once it is written.

The head of a Murder and Robbery Squad was usually a superintendent, a decidedly middle-rank position. A handful of Murder and Robbery Squads were run by senior superintendents; they were at the top of the middle, the last rank at which a policeman could still work at the coalface. If you were 28 and headed up a Murder and Robbery Squad, you were doing well. Chances were you were going places. If you were 35 and headed a Murder and Robbery Squad you were a little anxious. But once you hit 40 and were still at the coalface you were in trouble. You'd reached the end of the road in mid-career, and you were sentenced to sit out the remainder of your life in a junior rank.

And so middle-aged murder and robbery detectives began to stray. If they were good, they were offered well-paid jobs in the countless private security companies that service the South African middle class. If they were bad, they were stuck. Some paid doctors small fortunes to vouch that they were irreparably ill and thus qualified for early retirement on full pension. Some turned to alcohol and did indeed become irreparably ill. Others became corrupt. They sold murder dockets for thousands of rands, or found their way onto the payroll of a drug lord in return for keeping off his turf. It was possible to take this plunge without much fear of being caught. Formally, specialised detective units were accountable to their respective area commissioners. In reality, they were dark, secluded little places and nobody could see in from the outside. If everyone on the inside was disillusioned and had nowhere to go, nobody was going to spill the beans.

This story was true of many Murder and Robbery Squads, but not all. Some were very good. I once spent a week with a murder and robbery detective out on the dry plains of the North-West Province. We drove 250 kilometres north to south and then 150 kilometres east to west, and we never once left his jurisdiction. One-and-a-quarter million people lived on his turf, most of them in vast rural slums where no one has a job and the mortuaries are filled with young men every Monday morning. Despite the odds stacked against him, he had an extraordinary arrest rate under his belt. He was one of those detectives who love their work beyond reason. He had no desire to become a manager, he did not care about his poor pay and was sufficiently respected to get the infrastructure he needed. One of his secrets was the network of information he had built up. His Murder and Robbery Squad had more than 80 informers across its jurisdiction, all of whom were debriefed every week. Twelve out of 27 members of the squad had the sole task of recruiting and debriefing informers.

It was remarkable how many cases were solved this way. The trick, of course, was to recruit the right people. You need people whose drinking partners are worth betraying, people who know about crime because they earn a living off it themselves. An informer will tell a detective that somebody tried to sell him an antique revolver. A gun of that description would have been stolen in a fatal armed robbery the previous week, and the squad would have themselves a murder suspect.

Our Murder and Robbery Squad was not one of the good ones. It was one of the innumerable little places in the South African Police Service that had wandered far from the business of real policing.

In the late 1980s and early '90s, the Carton Bay Murder and Robbery Squad was reputed, among whites, to be pretty good. But a police unit on the Natal south coast at that time with a good reputation among whites was not necessarily a savoury place. There was a civil war raging then – between the Zulu nationalist movement, Inkatha, and the UDF, an alliance of organisations sympathetic to South Africa's exiled liberation movement – and the police force was in the thick of it. It is not just that due process was set aside when the stakes were high. It is not just that the murder suspect's confession was often signed in his own pain and blood. Things got a lot dirtier than that. Many an assassin in the ostensibly black-on-black war in Natal wore a balaclava to hide his white face, his police badge locked safely in his locker. Murder and Robbery Units would know not to investigate such cases too carefully.

Louis Wessels, the investigating officer in the Mitchell case, would have been a junior member of the Murder and Robbery Squad in the early 1990s. It was bad luck, really, an unfortunate time to be coming of age as a white South African detective, for squads like the one in Carton Bay were shattered by the demise of apartheid. The cause that animated the unit's work – already somewhat misty – was defeated, and vanished from the face of the earth. The men who inducted Wessels into his profession, and gave him pride in and knowledge of his work, drifted into the private sector or early retirement. The new order wrote a constitution so alien to the world of policing Wessels knew that he had to learn from scratch how to work cases that would stick. And if this were not enough, democratic South Africa was a rough country to police. There are towns on Wessels's turf where a detective who goes to interview a suspect is not sure whether he will come out alive. So much mortal danger, so much fear – in the service of a political order from which men like Wessels are so thoroughly estranged.

81

I was told that at one point in the mid-1990s, nearly half of the Carton Bay Murder and Robbery Squad was on 'stress leave'. 'Stress leave' is a euphemism for baling out. You pay a doctor to write a letter saying that you cannot eat or sleep – and more often than not, the doctor's words are true – and soon half your colleagues do the same. Before long, your squad room is empty. The dockets get delivered to the front door, but once inside they are sucked into the vacuum of depression and bitterness.

Later, I will tell you just how bad a detective Wessels was, or had become, and how utterly incapable the Carton Bay Murder and Robbery Squad proved to be. For the moment, let us just say that the two detectives barely knew the area, and that the address they had been given would not have been of much help unless somebody showed them where to go.

Under normal circumstances, the Carton Bay detectives would have elicited help from the local detectives based at the Sarahdale police station, rather than from the complainant himself. But they didn't, for two reasons.

A Sarahdale detective is less streetwise in the recesses of Izita than you might expect. He thinks twice before going into Izita to investigate a serious crime. And he never goes there alone. He goes with four armed men and two cars, and he keeps a distance of about 30 metres between the cars, so that he and his colleagues won't all be ambushed at once. Sixteen hours a day, the Sarahdale police station has only two patrol cars on the streets. And they must patrol a jurisdiction that spreads out from the centre of Sarahdale in a massive circle, covering Izita and two rural slums just like it. Going to Izita with back-up means leaving the rest of the jurisdiction unpoliced.

In mid-1998, Cuben, Mike Glossop's predecessor at Farm Watch, was looking for a stolen cow. He was told he would find it at an address in Izita. Cuben went in on foot, his pistol visible on his holster. He walked the three or four kilometres to the house, knocked on the door, and waited. A middle-aged man opened the door and looked at him enquiringly.

'That cow in your yard, it comes from Mrs Draker's farm, doesn't it?'

The man seemed to be in a trance. His answer appeared instinctual, involuntary.

'Yes.'

'And you stole it, didn't you?'

'Yes.'

Cuben cuffed his suspect and strolled back through the streets of Izita. It was mid-afternoon. People stopped what they were doing and stared.

After a long silence, the arrested man spoke.

'You do know that no policeman would ever do what you have just done?'

Now it was Cuben's turn to answer in monosyllables.

'Yes.'

'You do know that you are completely insane? You've just risked your life for somebody else's cow.'

'Yes.'

There was another reason the Carton Bay detectives did not consult their Sarahdale colleagues. They did not trust them. The Sarahdale police station was black, you see, entirely black: there was not a single white face in its ranks, from the station commissioner down, and the two Carton Bay detectives did not like that. When they began working the case, the first thing Mitchell told them about was the low-intensity war that had evolved between himself and his neighbours in the months preceding Peter's death. They would have sat in Mitchell's lounge, clutching cups of hot coffee, leaning forward in their chairs to show him that he had their attention. And Mitchell would have spoken through gritted teeth.

'In nine months I lodged 21 criminal complaints. Twenty-one. And do you know how many were solved? Do you know how many arrests were made?'

He would have paused a long time. The detectives would have leaned forward a little further to emphasise their concern.

'None. Not a single one.'

The detectives would have spoken to other white farmers in the area. They would have been told that the police's poor record in relation to the Mitchell issue could be put down to incompetence, at a push. But no, that is too generous an interpretation, the farmers would have said, it is more than incompetence. The local station commissioner is in the ANC's pocket. He is close to Paul Mlambo and, in truth, he has little desire to investigate crimes committed against Arthur Mitchell.

'That place leaks like a sieve,' Colin Waugh told me. 'Never tell them what you are doing. By the time you are in your car driving home, the information will be in the hands of the opposition.'

The opposition indeed. If there had been a single white face in the Sarahdale police station, the Carton Bay detectives would have checked out the farmers' story. They would have made contact with the one of their own, and they would have asked him a few gentle questions. They would have gauged his response – his body language, the expression on his face, his choice of words. They would have felt confident in their assessment of these things, in the subtle, intuitive literacy that cultural closeness brings.

But there was no white face at the Sarahdale police station, so they went a different route. They pulled rank. They petitioned the area commissioner and he, in turn, issued an order to the Sarahdale police station: every docket concerning Arthur Mitchell, not just the one recording the death of his son, but the cases of arson, of malicious damage to property, of intimidation, all these were to be taken away from Sarahdale and put in the care of the area office in Carton Bay.

Sarahdale is in the middle of nowhere. The presence of its station commissioner is seldom, if ever, felt at area office. It is one of those places where a policeman slowly rots. So the Sarahdale station commissioner would not have been pleased that the first mention of his name in Carton Bay concerned his inability to solve crimes. The detectives working the Mitchell case had sunk him and he was not going to do them any favours.

The Carton Bay detectives had an address, and the only person they trusted who could show them how to get there was Arthur Mitchell. So they set off into Izita in the middle of the night with the complainant in the back seat, giving directions. And when they reached the house, the complainant stuck close to the shadows so that nobody would know he was there.

The man they were looking for was named Ngwane Mabida. They had reason to believe that he was a professional predator who spent most of his time in the Durban township of Clermont. Word had it that he was a high-ranking member of a gang that dealt in armed robberies, hijackings and contracted assassinations. So in one sense, aside from the fact that the target was white, the commission to shoot one of the Mitchells would not have been too far from Mabida's regular line of business.

Yet there was one detail that did make Mabida's job an extremely unusual one. According to the information gathered by Mitchell and Wessels, the assassin had grown up on Normandale. Lourie Steyn had evicted his family some time in the late 1980s. Mabida would have been about 15 at the time. His family took their meagre belongings and retreated into Izita, finding refuge with relatives who had a modest house there. The assassin's mother still lived in the house in Izita. But her son … it was difficult to say where her son lived, as it is with countless of the young and the unemployed who grew up in rural South Africa in the last quarter of the twentieth century. Like the Cube and the Mashabana men, like the grandchildren of the old man who lived on Jude Fowler's farm, he migrated between city and countryside and he held on to what he could in both places. According to Wessels, he was a shooter in Claremont, and when his gun was smoking and he had to lie low, he retreated to his mother's house in Izita.

While hiding out in Izita, he caused trouble there too. Wessels was told that Mabida was widely feared in the Izita area. It was rumoured that he and his gang had been behind the shooting of Harry Withers, the man who ran the old store on the dust road that leads to Izita. He was said to have planned a robbery on the local bottle store and the hijacking of a car on the outskirts of Izita.

When the three white men arrived at his house, the shooter was not home. His mother and his uncle were there, drinking tea in the one-roomed house and listening to a wind-up radio. The detectives asked the woman where her son was and she shrugged. They asked the uncle and he shrugged too. So they set off for the Cube kraal at Langeni.

I never got to talk to Louis Wessels about what he thought when he finally met Ngwane Mabida. By the time I was making plans to interview him, Wessels had booked himself into a psychiatric clinic in Pretoria, a fraud charge hanging over his head. But that story is still to come. I did, however, get to speak to another detective who interrogated Mabida – a man by the name of Will Sullivan. I will introduce you to him later, for his story is also an interesting one. After a couple of minutes alone with Mabida in an interrogation room in Westville prison, Sullivan sensed that something was wrong. He had sufficient experience as a detective to know that a man who makes a living with a gun in his hand is as hard as nails in the interrogation room. He knows every trick and has no fear of pain, and the only way to get him to speak is to offer him something worth his while. Yet Mabida was visibly frightened and it was not long before he was blabbering away, throwing everything he knew, and many things he did not, at Sullivan.

'I sat there stunned, my mouth wide open,' Sullivan told me later. 'I looked under the table because I was sure he had pissed in his pants. It was as clear as daylight that this man was no more than a petty thief. He knew as much about contracts and assassinations as a small child.'

It appears that, like many white men before him who had gone into Izita looking for information, Wessels had ended up chasing his own tail. He had brought in his own informer, a sly black entrepreneur who was a stranger to Izita and made a living roaming the small towns of southern KwaZulu-Natal, snooping around on behalf of the police. Wessels had also befriended an estranged junior policeman at the Sarahdale police station, a man who would keep his knowledge close to his chest, if only because his colleagues at Sarahdale did not trust him. And, finally, Wessels had the information Mitchell had given him, whispers exchanged on the quiet for a wad of banknotes.

Between them, the men who went to Izita to find Peter's killer had been thoroughly outwitted. It seems there were people on the Sarahdale/Izita border who waited for them to come, and greeted them with a carefully prepared story. Ngwane Mabida, the small-time crook, was reinvented as a ruthless killer. The part about growing up on Normandale was true. The house in Izita did indeed belong to Mabida's mother, and it was also true that Mabida spent much of his time in Clermont and sometimes got into trouble there. But the anecdotes about armed robberies and professional assassinations were myths fabricated for Wessels's ears.

I never found out why Mabida, rather than someone else, was chosen as the culprit, but I did get enough experience of the Sarahdale/Izita border to know that Wessels's initial investigation must have been remarkable for its amateurism. That Wessels went straight to his puppet master and no further tells of a tired and depressed policeman, one who had lost his wits a long time before.

Of course, the three men in the car that night knew nothing of this at the time. As far as they were concerned, Mabida had pulled the trigger and the Cube family had paid him to do so. They drove away from the Mabida house, went to Langeni, and stopped outside the Cube kraal.

The detectives parked the car deep in the recesses of the kraal. It was late at night, and the darkness of the hinterland covered the car. Mitchell sat still in the back seat.

The two policeman looked for three Cube brothers – Prince, Peter and Mduduzi. Only Peter was home, and they asked him a few questions. After half an hour, they came back to the car and drove off.

*

The following day, Peter Cube walked into the Sarahdale police station and laid a charge against Arthur Mitchell. He said in his affidavit that Mitchell and two white men had come to his house late at night and kicked the door down. Since he did not know the two strangers, he could not lay charges against them. But he knew Mitchell and he wanted him charged with malicious damage to property.

The politics of Cube's move were subtle and layered. For a start, he had sent a message to Mitchell: I know you were in the back seat. I know these policemen are yours, and when they attack me I will attack you. Not once in his affidavit did he refer to the two men as policemen. In reality, he was saying, they are Mitchell's men. That they are policemen too is incidental. Cube had coded a second message into his affidavit: the Murder and Robbery Squad might be yours, but the police station is mine. You will use your policemen, I will use mine. We will both use the law; it does not belong to you alone.

Mitchell was stunned when he heard of the charge Cube had laid. When he recovered, his shock gave way to rage.

We were standing on the summit of a hill when he told me his side of the story. Langeni nestled beautifully in the valley below, and we both gazed at the mud huts. Mitchell pointed an accusing finger into the valley.

'That is what they do. They use the law and turn it against itself. They lay charge after charge after charge. When a police station is radically understaffed, like Sarahdale is, the system is soon clogged up. The police are investigating so many false charges that they cannot do their real work.'

Mitchell turned his back to the valley and faced me.

'The government talks of human rights. It is a joke. Where are my rights? My son is dead and nobody has been brought to book.

87

They are the ones with the rights. They can shoot down my son in cold blood and then lay charges against me. It's sick and rotten, isn't it? Something is rotten.'

That was how Arthur Mitchell, Jude Fowler and their kind understood South Africa's new constitutional dispensation. It was, for them, an edifice behind which the criminals, the savages and the killers of this country took refuge.

A few weeks earlier, Mitchell had told me the story of an armed robbery that took place in a kraal in the valley below his farmhouse. Two days after the robbery, an employee told Mitchell that the robbers were from one of the Langeni kraals. He had seen them stow stolen goods. He had seen strangers come into the kraal to buy them. Mitchell bypassed the Sarahdale police station and gave the information to a white detective in Alanview, 35 kilometres away. And then he waited – a day, two days, a week. He lost patience and phoned the detective again. The voice at the other end of the line sounded awkward and embarrassed.

'Well, Arthur, I'm actually not going to search the kraal. You see, there is a constitution now and you cannot just storm into somebody's home and rifle through his things. So I think I am going to leave it.'

I don't think it is too hard to guess what was going on. Mitchell had asked the white detective to stray onto his colleagues' turf and that was not a light thing to do, especially when he could not not be sure how sound the farmer's information was. The Sarahdale situation was fraught with the nastiest of politics, and the detective had decided to stay clear.

That was not how Mitchell understood things.

'So that is how things are now. The detective, you see, was in line for promotion. He knew that if he searched that kraal, the bastard would lay charges against him. Once that happens, he is automatically suspended pending the outcome of an investigation. And while the investigation is dragging on, somebody else gets the promotion. The wrong people are using the law in this country.'

There is little doubt that local policemen, like the white detective at Alanview, were fumbling clumsily with the rules of constitutional democracy and thus failing to do their jobs. I tried to tell Mitchell at the time that, for me, the problem was not the new rules, but a lacklustre police force's incapacity to work with them.

But Mitchell was having none of it. For him, his son's case had remained unsolved because of constitutional democracy.

He was right. If Peter Mitchell had been killed ten years earlier, somebody would have been hanged. The tenants at Langeni would have been dragged one by one into police vans and tortured. Their doors would have been kicked in, night after night. The ribs of their sons would have been broken. And when they could no longer take it, they would have given somebody up. Whether he was indeed the guilty one would have been decided by the politics of Langeni itself. A harsh and brutal Langeni would have sacrificed an unimportant family. A Langeni that frowned on the murder would have sacrificed the guilty one. He would have given a full confession and the case would have been solved. And the convict's family would have been evicted, and no black person in the area would have dared lay a hand on a farmer after that.

*

Mitchell and I sit on stiff chairs at opposite ends of his lounge. He is looking for a word and struggling to find it.

'I am responsible for stopping ...' He pauses, frowning. 'What is that word? I have stopped ... Help me here. When people take matters into their own hands. That word.'

'Vigilantism.'

'Yes. I am responsible for preventing vigilantism in this district. I have worked with the police all the way.' He pauses again, disengages from me and stares sideways out of the window, an uncomfortable posture. 'But sometimes I have my doubts.'

I ignore the last comment and the heaviness of what it implies. If Mitchell has something he wishes to share with me, he must volunteer it. I will not ask him about his doubts.

'How have you stopped vigilantism?'

'If I had killed a few people, I would have lost. They do not care about a few dead bodies. The tenants are just the pawns. All they would care about is that Arthur Mitchell is in jail, his land empty. If I kill my son's murderers, they will have won.'

'So you've prevented vigilantism by not killing anybody?'

'I have had phone calls. People have offered me money, favours. I have said no each time. This thing must be solved by the law. I

89

am throwing every ounce of my energy into assisting the police. Beyond that, I will do nothing.'

When he stops speaking, I keep my head down and write. I slow down to a snail's pace. The scratching of pen against paper is the only sound in the room. I want to make a point. I am telling Mitchell that he is always on the record when I am around. I feel great sympathy for his grief and his loss. I have told him that, and that the murder of his son was a terrible evil. But I do not want to get too close. I do not want him to believe that he can share dark secrets with me.

'But make no mistake, if I find them on my front lawn, armed, I will put a magazine in my rifle, I'll flip the switch to semi-automatic and I won't stop until they are filled with lead.'

A few hours later, Mitchell and I sit down to lunch. His wife, Linda, has prepared the meal, but has contrived not to be here to eat with us. In the morning, she greets me politely and vanishes. When it is time for me to leave, she reappears and says goodbye, her face all courtesy and warmth. But she wants no part of this. Mitchell has let me into his home because he believes the book I will write might play its part in bringing him justice. But Linda does not give his battle her blessing. She wants to get out of here. She is tired of wondering whether she will ever see her husband again every time he leaves for work. She is tired of living like a prisoner behind an electric fence, too afraid to take a stroll through her own land. Her daughter lives in Durban and has just married a good man. There is nothing left here for her. Sanity is in Durban.

Over lunch, Mitchell raises the vigilante question again.

'I tell you, my presence here is what is keeping the gunmen at home. If I leave, the people who killed my son will be taken out.'

'Why? Because you would no longer be implicated?'

'It would happen while I was away,' he replies, as if answering another question. 'Maybe in Durban.'

Mitchell slides ambivalently between two very different scenarios. Just when he seems to have settled on one, he switches to the other.

'Why are you telling me this?'

'Because you must know that my decision to keep within the law was a big one. I was presented with alternatives.'

SEVEN

Every relationship between a journalist and his subject has its unwritten code of rules. Ostensibly, the subject is the one who formulates the code. He marks out pieces of his life and his thoughts, and he guards them closely. The journalist, with his pen and his notebook, his silent judgments and his insatiable curiosity, is not allowed there. He hovers around the boundaries looking nonchalant, innocent. He nibbles and probes, and the moment the guard is let down, he darts into the forbidden zone and scavenges there like a vulture until the subject wakes from his reverie and drives him out. The journalist seldom waits long. For how can a subject – a human being, after all, who shares his pain and his laughter, who wants to appear as a sympathetic man in the pages the stranger is writing – keep up his guard forever?

Indeed, the subject is doomed to be a failed propagandist. He imagines the book before it is written, he sees himself in it, and when the journalist takes out his pen and paper, he thinks he is becoming the being he imagines. He is always wrong. The moment he sits down to read the book and imbibes the being the journalist has created, he realises that he never did have a say in writing the rules. To be sure, the journalist and his readers are interested in what the subject says. But what really keeps the scavengers scavenging are the things he does not say, the things he says by accident, the things he betrays in a laugh or a wince.

Arthur Mitchell leaves very little for a professional scavenger to work on. His emotions are lean, his demeanour finely guarded. He is not the sort of man who feels the need to lie on the analyst's couch, nor on any of its equivalents. And besides, he has been certain from the start that the book is not about him; it is about the murder of his son. He is the competent farmer and the fair employer, the man who has done nothing to provoke the bullets that killed his son. Beyond that, his life is none of my business, and he is seldom tempted to make it otherwise.

*

Mitchell and I are down in his irrigation fields in the blinding heat of a late summer morning. He has lent me a wide-brimmed hat – the city boy did not think that a day bareheaded in the heart of a midlands summer would be a slow and torturous death. Matthew lingers 50 metres behind us, discreet and invisible, his own cap knitted tightly to his skull.

Arthur Mitchell has brought me down here to fill my notebook with the man he sees in my pages. He wants me to watch him as he speaks to his workers, to show me that his relationship with them is good. And in the short and superficial time we spend with them, it does indeed appear to be a good relationship. In a large, open shed at the side of the river, six young black women are arranged in an assembly line. The first two wash tomatoes in a large trough, the second sorts them by size and ripeness, the third packs them into boxes. They glance at us casually as we enter, and then continue with their work. Mitchell greets them collectively in his calm, soft voice, and they return his greeting with equal soft-ness. We linger a few moments – long enough for the image of the good employer to engrave itself in my mind – and then we wander out into the scorching sun.

It is just Mitchell and me and the wide, beautiful valley, and I feel this is a good time to get something off my mind.

'I've been wondering these last few days, Arthur. I am a stranger. You don't know me from a bar of soap and you immediately let me in, to write about the most awful moment in your life.'

'Of course it has crossed my mind that you might have a nasty agenda,' he responds briskly and clearly. He seems to have given the matter a lot of thought. We are walking side by side, and Mitchell's eyes slant at me intermittently as he speaks. 'When you contacted Lourie Steyn, he phoned me and asked whether I was sure you don't work for the CIA.'

I try to remain deadpan, but I end up laughing a little uneasily and Mitchell joins me, generously, to keep me company in my awkwardness.

'For all I know, you do have something up your sleeve. But I went ahead anyway because I have nothing to hide. My story is a simple one. As long as you tell the truth, I can't possibly have a problem.'

I jolt awake for the first time since meeting Mitchell. It has been so long since I have spent time with a person who thinks that way that I have forgotten that his kind exists. I want to explain to him that there are many ways to tell a truthful story, some sympathetic, others cold and ungenerous. I want to tell him about feeling and tone, about the cruelty of silent observation. He has thought so little about books, about the making and the writing of them, I feel I must warn him about who I am.

'But Arthur,' I say, 'I can be completely truthful and still upset you.'

He nods and says nothing, waits for me to continue.

'For instance, my book is going to try to explain why your son was killed. And when you read the explanation, it will sound like I am condoning the murder. I will speak about apartheid, about how your tenants were humiliated by farmers and policemen and government officials for generations.'

Mitchell waits for me to continue, and when he realises I am done he is clearly puzzled.

'That will hardly make me angry. It has nothing to do with me. That is about Steyn and his friends, the Afrikaners.' He pauses for a long time, and then a new thought comes to him. 'That's interesting, isn't it? We're not just battling against generations of Zulu madness. We're also battling two generations of Afrikaner madness.' He looks at me and smiles wryly. 'I guess I'm between a rock and a hard place.'

A heavy dose of disdain fills me, and I am left feeling light-headed. How can a white South African living in this violated and broken countryside let himself off the hook so glibly? I have come out here with an open mind, assuming that everyone has a soul that is rich and worthy of respect. But how do I respect a person who lives off the fat of barbarism and does not begin to see it? We walk on in silence. I have nothing to say. Mitchell appears not to notice the tension, and he is soon chatting away about vegetable farming.

Later, when the heat of the day has passed and I am lying calmly in a cold bath, I scold myself for my moment of teenage indignation. Scorn and self-righteousness have nowhere to go. They can

93

produce a book that mocks its subject, that manipulates his igno-rance about the writing of books. But they certainly cannot pro-duce a decent book. In the coming months, I think a lot about the words Mitchell chose to use that day, and I begin to think about them with some empathy and some imagination. Armed with these seemingly blunt and benign weapons, I see for the first time that Mitchell has in fact left a great deal through which a scavenger might rummage.

*

Mitchell is a city boy, or at least he was one until he was almost as old as I am now. He grew up in the suburbs of Durban, and as a young man he bought a piece of land about 13 kilometres from Normandale. At first, beef farming was something of a hobby, something he did on weekends, the way other people mess about in boats or learn to water-ski. He started with a small piece of ground and a tiny capital base; he was good at it and he loved it, and within a decade he was a large and prosperous landowner. When he got a handle on running beef he bought a piece of land along the river and learned to grow vegetables.

'It's pretty unusual for a young man from the suburbs to become a farmer,' I say to him. 'What drew you? Is there a history of farm-ing in your family?'

He is the sort of man who is usually quick to talk, but now he is suddenly quite coy. He shrugs a little shyly, smiles at me and looks out over his valley, as if the landscape will answer my question better than he can.

'Who taught you to farm?' I continue.

He smiles again, this time with pride. 'Nobody. We taught our-selves.' He detects the self-congratulation in his own voice, checks himself and adds some words of modesty. 'Well, we read the right books – about grazing capacity, about the nature of the soil. The books taught us.'

The tone of his voice betrays a sliver of what he sees when he looks across the valley and up the bush-covered hill that leads to his house. In part, the land is an occasion for adventure, for a young man who leaves the city and discovers the logic of the sea-sons and the soil, of beasts and the diseases that kill them if you do not look after them properly. But it is an adventure of a particular kind, a moral and spiritual adventure. The valley before us is Mitchell's handiwork. He made it like it is – self-taught, with his books, his patience and his attention to detail. For Mitchell, a farmer's life is one that has been particularly well lived. He has spent his time sharpening the clean virtues of work and discipline, and the product of this time is here in front of us – a piece of the midlands that has been shaped by his hands.

There have been other adventures in Mitchell's life, ones that took him away from farming to another relationship with the land.

'In the late 1960s and early '70s I was in the civilian section of the army,' he tells me. 'It was very part-time. I was a farmer, first and foremost. Slowly, I was wooed into the Permanent Force and by the time the border war began I was a full-time soldier. I fought in Operation Savannah in 1975.'

I have brought up the subject of Mitchell's career as a professional soldier, but once it has been mentioned he needs no more coaxing. He is animated now.

'I saw a lot of action,' he says, his voice full of quiet excitement. 'We moved from one town to the next, and there was a skirmish in each place we passed through. I operated a Browning machine-gun mounted on a swivel on top of the vehicle. My job was to scan the bush as we drove north through Angola, and to shoot at any movement in the bush.'

'Dangerous job,' I observe. 'You were a sitting duck.'

'That's right,' he replies, and begins speaking in the present tense. 'You're pumped with adrenaline. If your finger doesn't get to the trigger quick enough, you're dead.'

Operation Savannah is remembered today as a tawdry affair, both politically and militarily. In 1974, a coup in Portugal brought a left-wing party to power, and the new government prepared to relinquish its remaining colonies, including Mozambique and Angola. Both apartheid South Africa and cold war America greeted the news with fear. South Africa faced the prospect of two independent black countries on its borders, both openly hostile, both willing to host the exiled armies of South Africa's and South West Africa's own liberation movements. The US, in turn, saw two Marxist parties, allied to and bankrolled by the Soviet Union, preparing to take power in the heart of the African subcontinent.

In the latter months of 1975, Henry Kissinger, then Gerald Ford's Secretary of State, persuaded apartheid's bosses to send more than 1000 white troops into Angola. At that stage, South Africa's interminable war with its neighbours still lay ahead, and the army was inexperienced and tentative. Kissinger promised that once the South African forces crossed the border they would receive American support – both logistic and human. South Africa was to assist the anti-communist FNLA in its bid to take Luanda, Angola's capital, which was in the hands of the Marxist MPLA. And so Operation Savannah began – apartheid's hesitant induction into the art of invading its neighbours.

By most contemporary accounts, the white army's inexperience and lack of preparation showed badly. The South African Defence Force soon found that its logistical infrastructure was not built to fight a war on the African continent. Trucks designed for smooth asphalt scraped and clattered their way through the wild Angolan bushlands, smashing axles and carburettors, and spewing oil into the Angolan countryside. Battalions of teenage conscripts – stunned by the sudden prospect of real war – were cajoled across the border with lies; it was only on the outskirts of Luanda that many were told they had invaded a foreign country.

The white army lumbered northwards, slowly and hesitantly, and in November a joint South African Defence Force-FNLA assault on Luanda faltered badly. A month later, news came through from Washington that Kissinger had broken his promise. The Democratic majority in America's Congress had hastily passed legislation outlawing military assistance in Angola, and an embarrassed Kissinger had to tell his South African friends that they were alone. Battle-worn and squeamish at the prospect of losing more young white lives, South Africa withdrew its forces from the outskirts of Luanda, and Operation Savannah was over.

Mitchell speaks of none of this. The tactical finesse and political intrigue of the campaign are not on his mind. For him, Savannah is a personal odyssey filled with machinery and courage and the smell of the countryside. He speaks in rapt tones about the weapons at his disposal, about the land off which he lived, and above all, about action and bravery.

I mull over how I might ask my question in a way that does not offend him.

'Arthur,' I ask, 'how did you feel back then about invading a sovereign state?'

'Good grief,' he replies. 'I was a young man, much too young to think about things like that. It was an adventure for me, nothing more.'

At first, I do not believe him. I think that he has sensed the gulf in our politics and feels uncomfortable discussing these things with me. How do you march into another country, your finger on the trigger of a Browning machine-gun, and not ask yourself what you are doing there? How do you engage in mortal combat – kill and face the risk of your own death – without wondering why?

My first reaction is inexperienced and off the mark. Mitchell is telling the truth. I remember doing research a few years ago for a documentary on apartheid South Africa's last major campaign in Angola – the battle of Cuito Cuanavale in 1987. After a brief surf on the internet, I found that hundreds of South African Cuito veterans spend hours of their days shoring up their memories of the battle. There are no fewer than three veterans' chat forums devoted exclusively to the Angolan war. Scrolling through the e-mails and debates of the veterans, I felt I had entered the world of a cult, one that spoke a language I would struggle to comprehend.

Most of the discussion was about G5 cannons, the infamous machines that could hit a target with pinpoint accuracy from many kilometres away. Shooting the cannon itself was an exhilarating feeling, but cheap, short-lived and much scorned. The real work, the work that still commands awe and delight in the cyberworld that Cuito has become, was performed by the ones who sneaked behind enemy lines and whispered a set of co-ordinates back to base so that the cannon had something to aim at. These are the heroes of Cuito's cyberworld, the ones off whom the glory still spills and from whose feats the others nourish. It is as if the battle was fought for the sake of the cannon itself, as if lives lost were lost well if they lubricated the workings of the machine.

Driving back up to the farmhouse with Mitchell, I sense something of the Cuito-cult about him. Half an hour earlier, down at the river bank, he had had trouble starting his jeep. A middle-aged black man dressed in the green overalls of a farm worker spotted our trouble from the top of his tractor and drove over to assist. He and Mitchell conversed sparingly and professionally in simple Zulu. Mitchell fiddled with the ignition, and the black man shook his head disapprovingly, gently pushed Mitchell's wrist aside and began to fiddle himself. Eventually, Mitchell and I climbed into the open carrier attached to the back of the tractor, and the black man drove us up the dirt track on which Peter had been killed, back to the farmhouse.

Mitchell and I are standing on the back of the carrier as the tractor strains up the hill. Shoots and branches from the dense midlands bush spill over onto the road, and we both spend much of the journey ducking an assortment of obstacles. Mitchell is talking about Operation Savannah. His memories have animated his eyes and his mouth, and he is on the point of invoking a heady moment with his Browning machine-gun. He checks himself and puts the story away.

'I shouldn't really talk in too much detail about my personal experiences of the campaign,' he says.

'Why not?'

'It is proper to talk about the campaign in general, but not about my part in it.'

I am battling to understand the ethical code Mitchell has decided to heed, so I repeat myself.

'Why not?'

'It is something that should only be discussed late at night over a whisky,' he replies. 'Over several whiskies. Otherwise it just descends into war stories.'

I imagine myself watching Mitchell as he gets drunk on his memories of soldiering. What will come out? Why must one be drunk to conjure up one's experiences of war? Is it because sobriety must be suspended before one's exhilaration with lethal machines and death can be aired? Is it because sober men know that to use memories of blood-letting as an occasion for boyish excitement is distasteful? This is Mitchell's first and last attempt to draw me closer, to bond over the stuff of male camaraderie. I imagine myself getting drunk with him and listening to his war stories. In my imagination, I am far away from him, alienated by the things that animate him.

Up on the back of the tractor, I see Mitchell as a distilled version of a man – a man created by a second-rate philosopher. He is animated by courage and discipline and revenge – virtues he has brought both to his soldiering and to his farming. Beyond that there is nothing.

A minute or two of silence passes and then Mitchell remembers a story about his Browning that can be spoken of in the whiskyless hours of a working day.

'We were passing through a small town in southern Angola,' he tells me. 'I was up in position behind the swivel. The place was deserted, ominously so, and I thought we would be ambushed at any moment. I heard rustling in the bushes to our right, and then I saw movement. I swivelled the Browning and aimed, but my finger would not squeeze the trigger. I just froze. There was no reason for it. There was every reason to shoot. A moment later, a white man came out of the bush, a Portuguese doctor. If I had squeezed the trigger, he would have been dead.'

We drive on in silence for a few minutes.

'It was an act of God. It was not meant to be. God stopped my finger. We – my family, I mean – we have a lot of faith.'

The thought of God brings Mitchell back to the present – to Normandale and the murder of his son.

'The ground of this province is soaked in blood.' His voice remains steady and soft. But there is anger in it now. 'God will not forgive KwaZulu-Natal easily. There are things this province has not begun to pay for.'

He has never spoken to me of vengeance without invoking God, and he has never spoken to me about God without invoking vengeance. But this time, God and the revenge he will take on Peter's killers are mixed up with memories of the war, and it appears to me that there is a rich relationship in Mitchell's head between soldiering and farming.

Shortly after Savannah, Mitchell left the Permanent Force. The life of a soldier – always uprooted, always settling somewhere new – is not compatible with the life of a family man, he tells me. So he began his 15-year stint as a senior security man in the chemicals industry, where he learned to negotiate with trade unions. It was a long and not unhappy interregnum, but his heart always lay – whether as a soldier or a farmer – with the land. In the early 1990s, he bought Eleanor, the farm that abuts Normandale. Soon after, he left he chemicals industry, and began farming full time.

*

Back at the farmhouse it is lunch time, and Mitchell and I devour a classically English meal of roast chicken and vegetables. The dining room offers no view of the countryside. It is not the dining room of a farmer in particular, but of an English-speaking and bourgeois family in general. It is Linda's domain. He looks for her half-heartedly, but soon returns to the table. He knows and respects that she does not want to talk to me. I have heard from others that things are not good between them. This farm holds nothing for her now, just the prospect of another tragedy.

I wonder what the farm means to Mitchell and why he is prepared to risk another death in the family to avenge what happened there. It occurs to me that I would probably do a better job of understanding Mitchell's wife than of understanding Mitchell himself. Among the things we have in common, we are neither soldiers nor farmers.

I take the liberty of seeing the Zulus through Mitchell's eyes, in full knowledge that I am guessing from afar. He takes in the cultivated river bank and the well-nourished grazing fields, and for him they are the product of a white disposition. The discipline and the patience, the capacity to do everything for the future and nothing for the present, are foreign to Mitchell's Zulus.

'They do not love work,' he tells me. 'They love money. Everything they do is calculated to get as much as possible through as little effort as possible.'

When he praises the Zulus he does so as one praises children.

'They are a humorous people,' he says. 'They laugh at small things. I understand that, and when I work with them I joke about the small things they find funny, and it makes for a good relationship.'

For a second time, I feel estranged from Mitchell, but I hold my tongue; I know that for him the countryside is shaped the way it is by two polar dispositions. Zulus make war and make their women do the work. They see no beauty in the land, or in remoulding it through labour, and so everything, from their souls, to their aesthetic disposition to their understanding of the virtues, is antithetical to the things that nourish Mitchell's soul. They are poor labourers because that is what they are good for.

It dawns on me that there is a special bitterness for Mitchell in the fact that Peter was killed by a Zulu peasant. For a young man to be murdered by the lazy ones as he prepares for an industrious future carries a particular form of revulsion, a double offence against the good and righteous. I remember the worker in the green overalls gently pushing Mitchell's hand from his jeep's ignition, and I comment that his relationship with that particular worker appears to be a special one.

'Yes, it is,' Mitchell replies. 'He is the only one who did not leave when Peter was killed. He stuck it out because it was the right thing to do. And his heart is in his work. He does not cut corners.'

'So different Zulus have different minds.'

A stupid comment, condescending and crudely didactic. Mitchell rightly ignores it.

'He is a Mashabana,' Mitchell says.

'You mean he is a brother of the man you have laid charges against?'

'Not a brother. A cousin, or something. The connections between them are complicated.'

'Yet there is clearly a bond between you.'

Mitchell frowns and stares at the remains of the roast on his plate. 'There are bonds and there are bonds. Blood is thicker than water. I dare not turn my back to him for a moment.'

PART TWO

EIGHT

Drive out of Alanview along the regional artery, and after a short while you have climbed up the back of a steep precipice and are looking into the valley of the Gudla. It is the most powerful and unsettling scene in the southern midlands. A long line of steep hills stretches beyond the horizon, lending the scene a hyperbolic sense of depth. In the middle ground, the first line of hills on the other side of the valley forms the wall of a sharp, deep basin. Despite its depth, the valley is long and wide and disappears into the hills on the left. The Gudla river runs across the centre of the valley, and its amplitude has made the land on either side of it the finest irrigation fields in the area. From the top of the precipice, the vegetables are thickly matted rows of deep green, stretching luxuriously along the length of the valley. An irrigation system tosses streaks of water across the basin, and a black-and-white farmhouse on the far left stamps its authorship on the scene of orderly cultivation.

The pastoral serenity of the valley contrasts sharply with the wild power of the hills. Once you mark this contrast you realise why the scene is so unsettling. The cultivated fields appear fragile and precariously temporary. It is as if nature has lent humankind the use of the valley in a moment of uncharacteristic generosity; as if the wild bush that climbs the slopes of the hills could come down and take the basin back whenever it chooses.

A few kilometres from the valley of the Gudla, you pass a battered old signboard built into the bank on the side of the road. The sign says 'Ndunge', and it points down a poorly built gravel road that appears to go nowhere. Take that road, and the wilderness on either side of you hugs you close. For the first kilometre or two, you drive along the bottom of a steep ravine. The hills on both sides are tall and claustrophobic, their thick vegetation the same as the stuff through which the dirt track on Mitchell's farm is carved.

105

Drive on, and the hills begin to roll back, and the opening vista boasts traces of the power of the Gudla. The old Kriek properties are on the left, the invisible line of dagga plants running alongside you about 700 metres away.

Turn a sharp corner and you are suddenly confronted by a short, steep hill. Once you reach the summit, you are looking down into Langeni. It is beautiful. Through my city eyes, it is too beautiful; there is something banal in its perfect rusticity. Clusters of graceful mud huts, their whitewashed walls crisp and fresh. Gently marked out vegetable patches, rows of healthy mealies growing out of their confines. In the middle distance, a group of women balance clay pots on their heads, making their way up from the bottom of the valley. A dog wags its tail as it trots at their heels. All of this is quietly carved into the grace of the most dramatic landscape I have ever seen.

Call it a cultural village, bus in German and Japanese tourists to talk patronisingly to the Cube and Mashabana women about their maize-grinding implements and their colourful anklets, and the tenants of Langeni could earn a good living.

It is a bad start to my investigation. I need to get this rustic nonsense out of my head. I need to know how these people have negotiated their way through the world for the last three generations. But where do I start? No white person has set foot on that land, except as a landlord, a policeman or a soldier. How does a white stranger stroll in with a notebook and ask all in the vicinity to open their souls? If I were an anthropologist studying the hybrid modes of production that criss-cross breadline households in rural Kwa-Zulu-Natal, I might be tolerated. But I am here to talk about a murder, and it is widely believed in the district that the murderers are here, eat here and sleep here. No stranger in his right mind snoops around in this context.

Indeed, something more profound than race divides me from the Langeni tenants. No matter how sympathetic I am, no matter how deeply I understand their story, it cannot be in the interests of the tenants that the murder of Peter Mitchell becomes a public tale. It is four months since the murder, and the Carton Bay investigators seem no closer to solving their case than they were when it began. If things go on this way, the investigation will lose steam and slowly die. Mitchell and his enemies will be left to battle it out alone. But a book about the Mitchell murder changes things. Then it is back in the public sphere. Then the heat is on the detective service again. And with the pressure to arrest hanging heavily over their heads, the investigators cut corners, get violent, aim for newspaper headlines.

As I look down on Langeni from my car, I have a horrible feeling that this book might shape rather than just record the story, and that if it does, things will not go well for the people in the settlement below me, innocent and guilty alike.

On the other side of the road is the last of the Kriek properties. Beyond it is Izita, a place the police are too afraid to patrol, a place from which a mission priest has just fled in fear of his life. To the best of my knowledge, the only white people who have gone in there as friends are a string of church field workers, laden with school books and food. And even their relationship with Izita has been a fraught and mistrustful one, as you shall soon see.

Cuben, Mike Glossop's predecessor, has offered to introduce me to people he knows on the Izita border. But his relationship with them is that of a private policeman to his informers. I cannot go into Izita on the coat-tails of a man who worked for the dead white man. I will not find out very much.

*

So instead, during the coming months, I hired other people, a string of other people, to go and live in Izita for a few days and to keep their ears to the ground. My first experience with this method was discouraging. I hired an elderly man with a wealth of experience and a wise head on his shoulders. He had spent much of the 1980s building the ANC underground in the townships of the Eastern Cape. A round, bear-like man with a hearty laugh and a hungry gregariousness, he had owned a small shop in the township of Mdantsane, and had used his daily interactions with customers to learn the politics of his neighbourhood inside out. He knew who to trust and who not to. He knew how to build a clandestine organisation in the middle of a densely populated township where few people kept secrets.

Driving past Langeni on his first day on the job, he watched a young woman cross the road between the Kriek farm and Normandale. He stopped his car, got out and greeted her warmly but formally.

'I am looking to buy land somewhere in this area, daughter. What do you know about this land? Is it good? Is it worth exploring any further?'

The woman put down the load of firewood she was carrying and shook her head. 'This is not a good place to buy land, grandfather. There has been trouble here.'

'What sort of trouble?'

'A white farmer who claimed to own this land was killed,' she said, gesturing toward Langeni and the rest of Normandale behind it. 'Since then, the police have been here. They accuse this one and that one of murdering the white man.'

'Why was he killed?'

'He and his father were very cruel men. They made trouble for their tenants.'

'How many tenants are there here?'

The woman thought for a long time and then shrugged. 'Too many for me to count, grandfather. There are nine households. Each one has maybe ten members. There are a lot of people here.'

'What sort of trouble did the dead farmer make for his tenants?'

'You must ask the men. They were in the meeting with the white men. I only know what I am told.'

The sound of a distant vehicle interrupted their conversation. An old white bakkie made its slow way toward Langeni. The woman pointed to the vehicle.

'There is Mr Cube coming with the bread for his shop. He will be able to tell you more.'

The old man hastily thanked the woman for her help, leaped into his car and drove off in the opposite direction.

'I did not want Cube to meet me under those circumstances,' he explained to me later. 'There is a chance that Langeni is harbouring a murderer, and here I am, a stranger, coming unannounced, and asking questions. For all he knows I am a policeman, or a private investigator working for Mitchell. Policemen in uniform have been killed going to investigate crimes in places like that. I am even more vulnerable.'

I understood the old man's predicament, but I was bitterly disappointed. I could not write a book on this murder if the tenants remained elusive. If they were not human beings with histories and motives, they would merely be monsters, Mitchell's monsters, inexplicable beings who cut down his son for a little more land on which to graze their tiny herd of cattle. The tenants could not be a blank screen onto which white farmers projected their darkest thoughts about Africa. And the old man's brief exchange with the young woman was filled with intimation. There was a universe of meaning just beyond my fingertips, and if I failed to get inside it I would have no hope of understanding this murder.

The old man was to be the first of several people whose eyes and ears I employed. When they returned from Izita, I would sit them down for hours and suck every last detail of experience out of them. I would press and press until they were so full of caffeine and nicotine, and the room so full of words and memories and forced inductions, that they would stumble out and hope never to see me again. Where possible, I got them to introduce me to some of the people they had spoken to. Where this could not be done, I got them to describe their time in Izita in the minutest detail; I asked for sounds and smells and the expressions on faces.

In the end, I found out far more than the old man's story had led me to believe I would. I don't know whether it was enough. But I do know that I got to hear everybody's understanding of the events that led up to the murder of Peter Mitchell: farm workers, Izita residents, policemen, schoolteachers, and, most important of all, tenants at Langeni.

Although I planned to understand Izita and Langeni at second-hand, through people whose black skins were the passport to the knowledge I was seeking, I nevertheless got to spend time in an Izita household sooner than I had anticipated. The opportunity came in the form of an unlikely invitation to dinner.

NINE

I was looking for a mission priest who had recently left Izita, but nobody could tell me where he was. Someone suggested that I try asking at a Christian mission a few kilometres outside Alanview. I arrived at the mission at about midday. It was violently hot, and by the time I had made my way from the parking lot to the chapel I was soaked in sweat. An ageing priest with foul breath and a helpful smile told me he did not know the area very well, but that one of the nuns might be able to help me. At the conservatory, an elderly nun with a thick Italian accent called a cleaning woman who lived in Izita. The Izita woman put down her mop and wiped her brow. Somebody had told her what had become of the priest, but she had forgotten. The nun suggested that I try the headmaster of the mission school, so I walked to the other end of the mission grounds to a brown face-brick building, and knocked on the headmaster's door.

His name was Madlala. He had enormous buttocks, a round belly and a double chin. It seems that every petit bourgeois who lives among the destitute is shaped this way; it is his signature. Madlala had known the priest slightly and had a vague recollection that he was now heading a congregation in Mpumalanga, a township of nearly a million people more than 100 kilometres from Izita. Madlala said that two of his students lived in Izita and they were bound to know how to contact the priest. He called his secretary and told her to fetch the two Izita boys from class. While we waited, he spoke about his school.

The Christian mission school was considered something of an elite institution among the blacks in the district. There were schools in places like Izita and the former homeland territories, but perhaps one in ten kids who studied there came out with a matric. Such schools were formally part of the national education system, inasmuch as their students wrote the same matric exams everyone else did. But in reality they had long fallen off the edge of the world. Government gave each school the bare minimum to maintain a rudimentary infrastructure and to pay salaries. The rest came from school fees. Middle-class schools could push fees up quite high and build a decent institution. But in a place like Izita, R500 per year was too high. So the government schools in the area had nothing. They were hollowed out. The buildings were there, people went in and out, but there was little education.

The mission school charged R1 000 per year, double the average in the area, and children came from miles around to attend. Izita is 30 kilometres away, Location A 20 kilometres. Getting to and from school takes half the day, but it does not matter, students come. The high schools in the suburbs of Pietermaritzburg, which had been reserved for white students by law until the early 1990s, are formally open to blacks. But fees at good schools are about R5 000 per year, and the number of people from the traditional lands who can afford to send their children there can be counted on one hand. So in a larger context, the mission school is a fourth- or fifth-rate institution. But in the traditional lands, it is the dream for which one puts money under the mattress.

I asked Madlala how many of his pupils were desperately poor.

'What do you mean? Poverty is relative.'

'I mean desperate. I mean children you worry may not get a square meal in the evening.'

'About a quarter of the kids here.'

'What are they doing here? How can their families afford the fees?'

'You have no idea how resourceful they are. Fees are due at the end of February. In mid-February they will sell two goats. They haven't a clue what they will do the following February, but they will deal with that when it comes. One day at a time.

'Sometimes, a child will not come to school for three or four days. I go to his home and find him sitting there doing nothing. I ask why he is not in school. He'll say that his grandmother died, so there is no pension money anymore and the family cannot afford to pay school fees. Or that all the family's goats were stolen in the night and every cent needs to be saved to replace them. And I reply: "Why on earth did your parents not come to me to talk it over? We can make a plan. You can pay the fees slowly, in instalments."

111

'The child comes back to school but a few months later he disappears again. I go back to the family and ask why he is not attending classes. "This time, there is really no money, Mr Madlala. If we keep sending this child to school, we will starve." They look at me with resentment. They know I am trying to help, but I just remind them that they have been defeated.'

There was a gentle knock on the door, and a schoolboy came into the room. He nodded at Madlala and then came up to me, closer than I was accustomed to, and looked at me enquiringly. He had huge, intense eyes. I was sitting in a chair and he was standing right next to me, so I had to crane my head to look up at him, and he looked back in an unusual manner. His eyes were confidently at work, animated by curiosity; it was as if he was trying to see inside me, not obtrusively, but in a benignly explorative way.

The boy had known the priest, but he did not know what had become of him. He said a friend of his was a preacher in Izita, and he would be happy to introduce me to this man. I thanked him, but said no, I wasn't looking for just any priest, but for this particular one. The boy said his grandfather was waiting for him outside the mission gates, and if we were to carry on talking I must walk with him.

We walked to the gates of the mission, and there was indeed an elderly man waiting there, and although I had not seen him in 12 years, I recognised him immediately. His name was Elias Sithole, and I had last seen him on 15 June 1988 at the Central Methodist Church in downtown Johannesburg.

Back then, I was an undergraduate student and a member of the National Union of South African Students, Nusas, a white anti-apartheid organisation. I sat on Nusas's labour desk, and one of my tasks was to build ties with the trade union movement. Every Tuesday evening a colleague and I would attend a forum called the Congress of South African Trade Unions (Cosatu) Johannesburg Shop Stewards Local. Cosatu was South Africa's largest labour federation, with 13 industrial affiliates and about 1,2 million members. The most taxing question facing the union movement in 1988 was how deeply it should get involved in anti-apartheid politics. The organisations that had led the urban uprisings of the mid-1980s were banned, their leaders in jail. Cosatu, in contrast, remained relatively untouched. It was strong at the grassroots, and a frontal assault on the federation would probably have brought the economy to its knees. So it had to ask itself whether to fill the vacuum left by the banned organisations and become more than a trade union federation, thus risking exposure to severe repression.

The Johannesburg Shop Stewards Local brought together grass-roots leaders from all 13 affiliates once a week to talk about these matters. On 15 June 1988, the evening before the twelfth anniversary of the schoolchildren's uprisings of 1976 – the biggest day on the anti-apartheid movement's political calendar – a group of 30 armed riot policemen burst into the weekly meeting at the Methodist Church. With their visors, their body armour and their assault rifles, they surrounded the meeting while a handful of detectives went around the room searching everyone's bags. A small camera crew followed the detectives, shoving the lens of a video camera in people's faces.

It was a needless exhibition. The people in the meeting were not militant youths, drunk on the exultation of being in a crowd. They were middle-aged workers, tired and sober. The armour, the guns and the men with grim faces were just a reminder that if you protested against the government you were taking risks.

The workers were angered by this gratuitous display of force, and what had been a quiet meeting of labourers slowly but discernibly became a brewing crowd. Somebody began stamping his feet, and others joined him, and within minutes the room was shaking. The riot policemen stiffened, their fingers began twitching on the butts of their rifles.

A short but charismatic man stood up on a desk and put his arms in the air. His name was Duma Nkosi. He was the chairperson of the Local, and one of the most powerful people I had ever met. In conducting the meeting every week, he managed to dart between three languages – Zulu, Sotho and English – all within the breadth of a single sentence, so that everybody understood him at once. Here, with the riot police surrounding the room, he raised his arms in the air and said nothing. The stamping of feet weakened and then stopped. Nkosi let the silence linger a moment before breaking it with a quiet, measured voice. I did not understand a word he said – he spoke no English or Afrikaans, so that the policemen would be deaf to what he said, and I was deaf with them. When he was done, the workers sat down in silence. Nkosi jumped off the desk, walked briskly to the police's commanding officer, shook his hand and asked him cordially if he could be of any assistance. The police conducted their search, Nkosi walking in stride with the commanding officer, watching everything they did with a hawk's eye. Within ten minutes they were gone.

Nkosi opened discussion to the floor. Somebody mentioned the video camera and asked if there would be any repercussions, if workers could expect loud thumping on their doors in the middle of the night. Nkosi said he did not think so. He thought the only people in any real danger were the two Nusas representatives, because the police were very angered when they saw white people at workers' meetings and because the two of us stuck out like sore thumbs.

Nkosi was wrong. Policemen thought twice before laying a finger on a white student. If they did, they would be hammered from all directions: university chancellors, business associations, newspaper editors, advocates. Nkosi knew this. He told a little lie because he thought that student support for the trade union movement was a good thing and he wanted to draw us closer to his forum.

After the meeting, a National Union of Mineworkers shop steward called Elias, a man I knew vaguely and greeted politely each week, approached me. He put a hand on my shoulder, as an older man does with a child.

'Duma said today that you are special because you are white. He is wrong. You must not let his words go to your heart.'

There was no malice in his voice. He simply had something on his mind and felt that I should hear it. He bore no grudge. On the contrary, he smiled at me affectionately.

Were it not for this interaction, I would not have recognised him 12 years later at the mission gate outside Alanview. He did not remember me at first, but after a bit of prodding, his comment after Nkosi's speech came back to him, and he laughed and apologised for having been so blunt. I told him what I was doing in the area, and he whistled through his teeth.

'Dark matters, son, dark matters. It has been coming for some time.'

I told him of the trouble I was having getting into Izita, and he laughed raucously and clutched my wrist in his hand. He insisted that I come for dinner the following night so that I could see for myself how things were in Izita. I asked him how to get to his house and he laughed raucously again. He said his grandson would meet me at the Sarahdale post office at 6 p.m., and the boy with the moon-eyes grinned. He seemed delighted that I knew his grandfather.

*

The evening started uncomfortably. There were seven of us at the table, I understood little Zulu, and the only family members who could speak English were Elias and his grandson. So Elias and I spoke English, the others spoke Zulu, and the youngster, whose name was Sicelo, moved to and fro between us, whispering translations in our ears. Elias insisted on speaking English, even when he was addressing his own family, a gesture of politeness, I would imagine, to his unusual guest. So the boy found himself in the strange role of interpreting a conversation between people who had known each other their entire lives. Despite this awkwardness, it was apparent after a short while that the family enjoyed talking about Izita to a stranger, and the stiltedness of incessant translations soon evaporated.

Elias's family was poor, but not destitute. The house was made of mud and concrete, and consisted of one large room. A small vegetable patch nestled behind the house, and four goats and a cow came to the window periodically and stared at us while we ate our dinner. We ate a rich, yellow, home-made maize meal, boiled chicken and cabbage. I brought a dozen beers and a basket of fruit. I think my offerings were the only items on the menu not grown or raised on the family's small patch of land.

It seemed that under normal circumstances, the house had three bedrooms, their borders demarcated by curtains that hung from the ceiling. That evening the curtains had been removed to make the eating space larger, and everybody's bedroom was on display. An old, greasy copy of James Baldwin's *Go Tell it on the Mountain* lay next to one of the mattresses. I found out later that it was Sicelo's, and that Madlala had lent it to him. Very formal family portraits hung on the walls: stiff men and women, uncomfortable in their Sunday clothes, staring severely into the camera. Everybody in those pictures was either dead or had a job in another part of South Africa and seldom came home. To live in Izita was to be unemployed or retired. To have a livelihood was to live elsewhere, one's presence in Izita registered by a stiff photograph.

115

It emerged during the course of the evening that Elias did not live in Izita. The land on which we ate our dinner was rented by his niece, Sibongile, and her husband, Andile; Elias was here to visit his grandson. He had retired from the mines several years previously, and lived in a township near Pietermaritzburg with the wives of two of his sons, five grandchildren, and two small children who had been orphaned when their mother died in a bus accident. He said he was a regular visitor to Izita and knew something of its politics.

Nobody who lived in the Izita house was employed. Indeed, after all the adults at the table had thought long and hard, between them they counted five people they knew who lived in Izita and had full-time wage jobs. Two were farm workers, one worked in the post office in Sarahdale, and two cleaned the floor at the Sarahdale supermarket. Neither Sibongile nor her husband had worked during the previous decade. They usually generated a small surplus of maize and goat's milk which they sold to a trader. Other than that, the only cash to enter the household came in the form of remittances from family members who lived elsewhere. Sicelo's mother, Elias's daughter, worked as a tea lady in a factory near Pretoria. She had other children who lived in Pietermaritzburg – the Izita house could not accommodate all of her children – and she only came to Izita for ten days a year, at Easter. She did, however, remit some of her monthly wage to the boy's Izita home, and two other family members also sent money home every month. To say that the household was part of an Izita aristocracy would be exaggerating. But its circumstances were unusually good. Most households in the area relied on the meagre state pensions of the elderly. A house run on wage remittances was considered something of a luxury. The boy's school fees were paid in instalments, as well as those of his two cousins, Sibongile's daughters, who also sat round the table. At the mention of their names they looked at me coyly and then bowed their heads and stared at the table.

When Sibongile put food on the men's plates, she did so with the stern deference women show in traditional Zulu households. As she approached the table she got down on her knees, lest she stand above us while serving our food. She did not look me in the eye the entire evening, even when she spoke to me. Once, I caught her staring at me while I sat listening to Elias, and the moment my

116

eyes found hers she swivelled her head away from me and did not cast a glance in my direction again.

Elias and Andile did most of the talking. They said that Izita had changed since the end of apartheid, and that some of the changes were heartening but others were very sad indeed. In the old days, in the 1970s and 80s, Izita was run with an iron fist by Mangosuthu Buthelezi's KwaZulu government. KwaZulu's traditional Zulu aristocracy had for years drawn salaries from the apartheid government, and Buthelezi's relationship with the youths and workers who filled the ranks of the anti-apartheid movement was a hostile one. True, Izita was not formally part of the KwaZulu homeland run by one of Buthelezi's tribal chiefs, like Location B next door; it was mission land and was owned by the Church. But to all intents and purposes it was KwaZulu. The mission school fell under the KwaZulu Department of Education, the headmaster had a portrait of Buthelezi hanging in his office, and every schoolteacher was forced to carry a membership card of Buthelezi's party, Inkatha.

In the mid-1980s, urban townships less than 100 kilometres away were in flames, the youths and the workers rising up against apartheid. But in Izita one did not dare whisper the letters 'ANC'. It was a strange and unnatural sort of silence. It was not as if Izita was sealed off from the rest of the world. All young men left Izita some time in their teens. Some were factory and mine workers by the time the uprisings began, and they joined Cosatu. Others lived among the unemployed youth in the townships of Durban and Johannesburg, and found themselves in the trenches of the war between the youth and the police. And even closer to home, in Richmond, the battle between Buthelezi's Inkatha and the ANC-aligned United Democratic Front raged. One famous Inkatha chief from Richmond took refuge in Izita during the heat of the battle.

So Izita tasted the flavour of the times obliquely, through the travels of people who came home. And much of what they said about apartheid and white minority rule, especially about the land, struck a chord. For people in Izita had always discussed the land. There were many stories about who had ruled this area a hundred years ago, and how their power had been taken away from them.

Why did anti-apartheid politics never come to Izita, I asked. The two men conferred in Zulu for a long time, maybe five minutes. There seemed to be some disagreement between them, an uncertainty about how to reply. I looked to Sicelo for a translation but he put his finger to his lips and shook his head.

Eventually, the men broke off their conversation and Elias turned to me. 'There was terrible faction fighting in Location B in the 1980s,' he said. 'It spilled over into Izita and many, many people were killed.'

'What was the fighting about?'

'If I tell you the specific events that caused anger,' Elias replied, 'you will think them stupid. You will think people here are insane. You will ask why people kill each other over unpaid lobola or an unwanted pregnancy. And maybe you are right. But let us just say that Zulus are a proud people, with lots of memories and lots of dignity, and when poverty takes away your dignity, you fight. It is a question of honour,' he said, chuckling cynically. 'A question of being somebody.

'That is why the IFP/ANC war never really came to Izita, even in the early 1990s, when the fighting was at its most fierce. People were battle-weary. They did not want to stoke the dying embers. So Izita people had a strange, removed relationship to the political war. On the one hand, talk of the injustice of apartheid, and of black rule, struck a chord. But at the same time, the war was just another source of evil.'

'Some time in the early 1990s,' Andile interrupted, 'a very important Inkatha man from a nearby town came to Izita. He wanted to give us guns to fight the ANC. He was chased out of Izita. People said: "Where were you in the late 1980s when we were dying? Why should we kill each other again for your war?"'

But it would be wrong to say that the momentous political changes of the early 1990s meant nothing in Izita, Elias continued. Things changed in subtle but powerful ways. Overnight, things that had been whispered behind closed doors were spoken about on the streets. Nobody planned it, it just happened. Everything was different. Everything suddenly *looked* different. Izita's bottle store was looted two nights after the ANC was unbanned in February 1990. You may think, Elias told me, that the burning of the bottle store meant that politics was already losing its meaning, even though the new era was just two days old. But no. The bottle store symbolised apartheid, you see. For it was owned by a wealthy man, and to be wealthy was to be a member of Inkatha, to be in cahoots with corrupt chiefs and bloodthirsty policemen. So all institutions that smacked of the status quo were suddenly vulnerable. And the people associated with those institutions became nervous.

'But the youth.' Elias shook his head. 'They like war, my friend. Whether it is ANC/IFP, or faction fighting, or crime – they like war. I will tell you why. I have given it much thought. But it is a long story. Be patient with me. I must start with how things were when I was a youth.'

When Elias had first gone to Johannesburg to work on the mines in the late 1950s, he was doing what all young men from Kwa-Zulu-Natal did at that time. They left home and went to the city, and when they got there they worked. There was no question of not finding a job. Everyone worked, and the result was that things in places like Izita got better in the late 1950s and early 1960s, demonstrably better. This was the time of South Africa's industrial revolution, and the factories in the cities needed workers and offered wages that nobody working in the countryside had ever dreamed of. People went away to work, and they brought money back home. Some did not. Some were swallowed up in the towns and the cities and never came back. But many were prepared to bring their money home with them. This money could be used to buy cattle, and cattle gave you a future. Cattle were bridewealth, and bridewealth bought you your own family, your own space in the world, a place in a family lineage. Rural life fed off urban industry, and in the process it became stronger.

That is how Elias recalled his youth, but I suspect his nostalgia has melted the corners of reality. When he spoke of the past he stared into the paraffin lantern, and his eyes lit up with the light of the lantern and the presence of the past, and he appeared to be in a trance. In 1948, a decade before Elias went to the mines, Alan Paton published *Cry, The Beloved Country*. He wrote of a fictional black settlement in the southern midlands, and if he did not have Izita in mind, he was thinking of somewhere just like it. In Paton's book, the past was a beautiful and stable place, just like Elias's past, but by the 1940s, it was gone: the families of the countryside were already being torn apart. The land could no longer sustain cattle for bridewealth, and it had nothing to offer young men, so they went to the city and got lost there, lost to their parents as well as to their own souls. So I suspected that Elias was halfway through a story every generation tells the next, the same story he

119

himself heard as a boy, the same story Alan Paton once told the world.

Things changed in the 1980s, Elias said. Boys would go off to the city, but they would not find work there. They would come home empty-handed, and with neither money nor cattle they could not start families of their own. With no land and no job, how was one to support a wife and children? The 1980s was a time when grown men remained youths; men of 30 or even 40 still living like youths. They could not marry, but they would have children, and this caused a problem. Grandparents and aunts and cousins would be asked to look after children, because the parents had no means to do so themselves. But who wants to look after an illegitimate child, especially when there is not enough money to put legitimate children through school? So a class of children, a whole generation of children, was raised on no-man's land. They found themselves on the margins, not just of the economy, but of their families. And they had to create a future for themselves out of nothing, because they were different, because the futures their forebears had created for themselves were no longer available.

The old man paused and examined his grandson at length. Sicelo stared back at him, his large eyes expressionless.

Then came the unbanning of the ANC and the war with Inkatha, and suddenly the youth had a vocation. They were soldiers. It had happened all over KwaZulu-Natal. Not in Izita. But the fact that it was all around them captured young men's imaginations.

Even back then, at the beginning, Elias had mixed feelings about the new role of the youth in politics. He was as committed as anybody to defeating apartheid, and he knew very well that without the youth, without their wildness and their crazy courage, white rule might have lasted forever. Adults don't overthrow tyrants, he told me. They worry too much.

Yet something was not right. Youths were not meant to rule communities. They should not be calling the shots. But that is what began to happen. Soldiers have power, and it is the kind of power that cannot be contained. You cannot say that the youth must lead when they confront the enemy on the battlefield, but when they come home, they must be obedient children again. It does not work that way. These fully grown beings, who had been excluded from adulthood all their lives, were suddenly men with guns.

When Elias came to visit at Christmas time, the rural villages of KwaZulu were different places. Even on a quiet day, the streets felt fraught. With what? It was difficult to put one's finger on it. With an exaggerated sense of urgency. Even back then, in 1991 and 1992, he was asking himself what would happen to the youth once there was no more war to fight. There was talk of land redistribution when the ANC came to power, of brand-new agricultural training colleges, of large co-operatives of emerging farmers. Some people said that the youth would soon be working the land. Elias didn't believe it for a moment. They were soldiers now, that was their vocation, and even if there was land to be worked, he doubted whether the youth would be prepared to work it.

Elias closed his fist tight, released his index finger from the bundle of digits and slammed it again and again against the table. He had been dead right, he said. What was Izita now that apartheid was dead and Buthelezi had been bought off with a cabinet post? If you had a future, you left. It was an iron law. What idiot with a university degree would choose to live in a slum like this? Which man who had made a name for himself as a thinker in the struggle would choose to work in Izita? He would have to be a fool. The thing is, he said, his voice unsteady and angry now, the thing is, democracy has drained Izita of its good people. Quality leaves here. It does not hang around. And so what is the ANC now, that noble organisation in the name of which people died horrible deaths? The ANC in Izita is run by a bunch of small-time, crooked businessmen who couldn't give a damn about their constituencies. They want to make money, and to keep making it they need power, and that is why they get involved in politics. Politics has become the playground of the corrupt. It is no more than that.

He shook his head in disgust. There was sweat on his forehead and his hands were shaking.

And the youth? Something terrible has happened to the youth. They still think they are soldiers but there is no war to fight. Soldiers without a war are bandits.

Elias pointed a finger at his grandson. That boy must get out of here. There is no hope for a bright boy like him in Izita. He will either get squashed or become an animal. There is no in-between.

Sicelo kept whispering into the ears of his aunt and uncle. He was absorbed in the translation. His eyes said nothing.

Elias took a long slug from his beer, wiped his mouth with his forearm and was silent for a long time. When he started speaking again, he was much calmer. There was a wry, mocking tone in his voice, an unpleasant sort of humour.

The youth are bandits, yes, but what does one mean by the word 'youth'? One is certainly not referring to age. Some of those who behave like bandits are 45 years old and have four children. That is the awful thing about youth today. It is not about how long one has walked the earth; it is about the state of one's soul. Nobody is growing up any longer. Twenty years from now there will be men Elias's age who have not grown up. They will behave as if they have just discovered what they can do. Elias pointed to his crotch, which was invisible, under the table.

What is a bandit? He is somebody who has retained the revolutionary's disrespect for the law. He sees shops and post offices and banks and police stations, and they are nothing but potential targets. The revolutionary was ennobled by the belief that he was going to replace the things he smashed to the ground. He was only sweeping away the old to make way for the new. The bandit just sweeps, just smashes. It is not a means to an end. It is just what he does.

The bandit calls himself an entrepreneur. He says that the world has not given him any opportunities, so he will create his own. Everything he sees, he evaluates. Is it an opportunity, or is it useless? Can I gain from it, or is there nothing for me? The bandit does not respect human lives. That his neighbour has spent a decade building a herd of cattle means nothing to him. He will take it if he gets the chance. You do not feel safe walking around Izita. Not because you could get stabbed for the jacket on your back. It is not as crude as that. You feel unsafe because you feel what is happening in the heads of the people who live around you, and they have ungenerous thoughts. Their way in the world is cruel.

Make no mistake, the small-time businessmen and the youths run places like Izita. They are the only two groups with power: the one has money, the other has physical force. Sometimes they are at war with each other. Sometimes they are in alliance. Always, the relationship between them is tense. And as much as they fight each other, the differences between them keep narrowing. To be a businessman is to be a bandit; to be a bandit, a businessman. Power and respectability do not go together, just as they did not under apartheid. You have either one or the other.

Elias was spinning higher and higher into abstraction, traversing vast stretches of time in single sentences. I wanted him to talk specifics: people, events, detail. But his story had filled him with adrenalin and he was on his own plane. He ignored my questions and continued his monologue until it was done.

I asked him about the white farmers on the border of Izita and why they could no longer farm cattle for fear of them being stolen.

'Is it the bandits and the youth? Is it they who tear down fences and steal cattle?'

'It is difficult to explain to an outsider,' he chuckled, and looked at me warmly. 'Sometimes it is bandits. Sometimes it is that a farmer is cruel, and people want to punish him. But in the main it is because this land once belonged to the Macaba and it was stolen.'

I was stunned by the simplicity of his explanation.

'Ask anyone in Izita who the white farmland rightly belongs to. They will all say Mtini. He was chief of the Amacaba 100 years ago.'

I asked Elias how the land had been stolen. He was vague. Something to do with a census and a tax. He consulted Andile, and the younger man thought for a while and then shrugged. Yes, it was about the census. Some time after the turn of the century, the whites came to take everyone's names. People were suspicious. What were they going to do with our names? But the whites assured the people it was harmless. And then they went away and used people's names to split up Mtini's chieftaincy and take away his land.

The story was incoherent and I did not trust it. But back in Johannesburg I started reading and it soon became apparent what the Izita men were talking about.

The Bambatha rebellion of 1906 has long been canonised by the South African liberation movement. I remember Bambatha's name being chanted at rallies in the 1980s: Viva the spirit of Bambatha, viva! I knew nothing of the details surrounding the rebellion, how big it was, who was involved, how long it lasted. All I knew was what populist pamphlets had told me. Bambatha was ritually mentioned in the cartoonish histories of the struggle that the ANC smuggled into the country during the 1980s. He was, the ANC

123

said, the last independent African chief to sacrifice his life resisting colonial rule. No more than that was ever said.

In fact, the name *Bambatha* rebellion is something of a misnomer. Bambatha was indeed a minor chief in the Greytown area – less than 200 kilometres north of the ground on which Peter Mitchell was killed – and he was killed for his role in the troubles. But the rebellion neither started nor ended with him.

The story begins two years before Bambatha's death. In 1904, the British colonial administration of Natal sent messages to every chief in the colony that it was going to conduct a census of the colony's population. The chiefs were nervous. What was the colonial administration going to do with everybody's names? Local magistrates assured chiefs that it was a mere administrative matter. There would be no consequences.

Black people were not convinced. A state intelligence report filed in April 1904 warned of widespread panic among the black population. 'The Africans say that the Census is for an evil purpose of exterminating or making slaves of the blacks and thus the black races must cohere against a common foe.' This sense of foreboding was not uncommon at the time. Any unusual or unannounced movement of armed white men ignited fears among blacks that something ominous was afoot. In 1902, the administration put troops on the streets in response to the spread of an epidemic in Durban. Rumours soon circulated that all blacks were to be exterminated.

The wariness with which the news of the census was greeted was in fact quite warranted. There was a nefarious agenda behind the collection of names. Like so much in regard to the relationship between black and white since the early 1890s, the agenda had to do with the precariously negotiated balance between land and labour.

For as long as it had existed, organised white agriculture in Natal had complained that Zulus refused to work as farm labourers, a refusal it regarded as little less than criminal. In 1903, a police inspector in the cattle-farming districts around Weenen filed a situation report at the office of the Chief Commissioner of Police: 'With regard to crime,' the inspector wrote, 'the principal complaints made by Dutch farmers to patrols was of the refusal to work on the part of the natives …'

In fact, this 'refusal to work' had a complex set of motives.

Elderly African patriarchs wanted their children and grand-children to work on their own land, and thus sustain their own social and economic domains. Many young African men pulled against the reins of both the African patriarchs and white farmers. They wanted independence of movement and employment. They wanted to be tied neither to their fathers' land nor to that of white employers.

In the last decades of the nineteenth century, the colonial admin-istration and white businessmen alike took a series of measures to curtail the growth of independent African farming and to get blacks to work on white land. In Durban and Pietermaritzburg, white traders refused to buy produce grown on black land. The administration itself passed a host of laws designed to transfer blacks from independent production to wage labour. Most of these involved forcing Africans to acquire cash, and thus to work for wages. Blacks were not allowed into business districts unless they wore European clothing. Additional duties were levied on trade goods for African consumption like picks, hoes and rough blan-kets. A range of taxes was introduced over the years: a tax on each hut in every kraal, a tax on each wife in every polygamous house-hold.

This is precisely what the 1904 census was about. A year after the census was completed, the administration announced the introduction of a poll tax. Every unmarried adult male over the age of 18 would pay a tax of one pound, and the administration would compile a register of adult males based on the 1904 census. The motive behind the tax was clearly to force unmarried black men to work for wages.

The announcement rattled African settlements across the colony. The tax was exorbitant, more than anything that had pre-ceded it, and paying it would require transferring countless men from independent production to labouring on white farms. Rumours of a massive supernatural intervention, tinged with inti-mations of human rebellion, swept across the countryside. Most of the rumours alluded to Dinuzulu, the son of independent Zulu-land's last king, Cetshwayo. Cetshwayo's kingdom had been balkanised after the British victory in the Anglo-Zulu War of 1879, and the memory of a sovereign African state, linked to the flesh-and-blood of a living descendant of its leader, formed a powerful anti-colonial symbol. It was around this time that Africans south of the Tugela, who had fled the emerging Zulu kingdom in the early nineteenth century, began thinking of themselves as Zulus – members of a once proud and independent black state.

Fanciful rumours swept the countryside in the prelude to the rebellion. Some said that Dinizulu had sent hundreds of messengers across the colony, telling blacks to kill white goats, pigs and chickens and to destroy tools of European manufacture. Others spoke less obliquely of the raising of an army to drive whites into the sea.

This is where Mtini and the Macaba come into the picture. The census and the impending poll tax had a particular meaning in the Sarahdale/Alanview area. You will remember that in the 1860s, large tracts of land in the area were bought up by London-based land speculators, in particular the Natal Land and Colonisation Company. The idea was to sell off the land to farmers incrementally. Once the first generation of farmers became successful, the value of the land around them would rise sharply, and the speculator would make a handsome profit. The company got its forecasting wrong. White farming in the Sarahdale/Alanview area remained sporadic until the 1880s, and the value of the Company's land did not rise for decades. In the meantime, the land remained inhabited by black settlements that were rebuilding themselves after two generations of turmoil. Two of the largest tribes on Company land were the Macaba under Mtini, and the Mkize, under a chief named Sigwaza.

The Macaba and the Mkize were well aware that they were sitting on a time bomb. The moment the market value of their land, or the Company's land – that is precisely what was in dispute – rose, they faced removal or submission to aspirant white farmers. This is exactly what was threatening shortly after the turn of the century. Several consortiums of agricultural interests were raising capital to buy land from the Company with a view to establishing wattle plantations. It takes little imagination to see that there are no mutual interests between pastoralists and foresters. Land is used either for one purpose or the other. So Mtini and Sigwaza knew that their land was under threat.

This was the backdrop to the census and the announcement of the poll tax. Black settlements in the Sarahdale area were immediately convinced that the poll tax was tied to a plan to force them off their land. Rumours that black men throughout the district were arming themselves, and that people would refuse en masse to pay the new tax, began to reach the authorities. It is difficult to ascertain how much truth these rumours contained. White intelligence on black politics was as poor then as it is now. 'Part of the difficulty of knowing exactly what was going on among the African population in this period,' the historian Shula Marks writes, 'is that so much of what was reported was little more than unsifted rumour or idle beer-drink gossip. The situation was further complicated by the not unnatural desire of the African informant to give magistrates information which either suited his own particular interests, whether tribal or personal, or which he thought would accord with the magistrate's own views and predilection. As a result, totally incompatible pictures were frequently held by magistrates in neighbouring divisions.'

Whatever the actual case, the authorities took the matter seriously enough to evacuate the white farms of the Sarahdale district and to gather the local white population into a laager. Ultimatums were delivered to Mtini and Sigwaza to hand over all assegais and to bring 'rebellious' subjects into town to be arrested. If the Macaba and the Mkize were not armed yet, the ultimatum and the white evacuation convinced them that they were on the brink of being attacked. Both chiefs hastily assembled armies of young men. There was a tense, 24-hour stand-off during which both sides braced themselves for an assault.

In the end, the two chiefs prudently backed off. The crisis subsided and both tribes began to pay the poll tax.

Concerned that the showdown would create a precedent among black settlements elsewhere in the colony, the authorities decided to punish both chiefs. In March 1906, seven of Mtini's men were sentenced to death for sedition. The sentences were later commuted to long terms of imprisonment.

That was the end of the Sarahdale episode. Three months later, open rebellion erupted less than 200 kilometres north of the stand-off between Mtini's men and the white troops. The rebellion was quelled within a month, its leaders executed. But the Natal administration felt that heavy retributive measures should be taken throughout the colony to deter chiefs from ever again taking up arms. In August 1906, Sigwaza, together with several of his councillors, was deported to the island of St Helena. Mtini was fined 100 head of cattle and his chiefdom – the land of the Macaba – was divided into three sections. By the end of the decade, nearly 40 per cent of the Macaba's land had passed into the hands of white farmers.

This is a long answer to the question of why farmers on the Sarahdale/Izita boundary could not hold onto their cattle in the year 2000. The answer took me by surprise. After all that had happened to Izita during the previous century, the erasure of family lineages, the scattering of kin across South Africa, the emergence of cold bandits and corrupt businessmen – memory was still a formidable organising force. Izita is a place of illiteracy. It has few scribes and keeps few records. And yet an answer to a question about the present evoked an event from almost 100 years ago. To be sure, the 'event' is more a fable than a memory. Nobody remembers precisely what happened or why. But it does not really matter. The 'Census' is simply the symbol of an identity. Nationalism and race are powerful forces here. They animate the hands that surreptitiously harvest tomatoes in the middle of the night.

It dawned on me that Mitchell had run into trouble with his tenants precisely when he announced that he was going to conduct his own census: he wanted the names of everyone who lived on his farm. The connection between that census and the one of 1904 could be no more than symbolic, but I asked Elias about it anyhow.

'Are you saying that Peter Mitchell was killed because Mtini's land was stolen 100 years ago?'

Elias frowned and shook his head. 'No, no. That is impossible. Farmers' cattle are stolen because Mtini's land was taken. Fences are pinched because of the theft of the land. But nobody kills a farmer just so. It is something more immediate, more personal. You don't kill somebody because of a vague sense of history.'

I recounted Mitchell's story of how he had bought a piece of land, laid down a reasonable set of rules – told the tenants that the land they already occupied was theirs, that he would not touch it – and how his son was killed in return.

'No,' Elias replied, 'that is not right.'

I did not understand what he meant: that the murder was not right or that Mitchell's story was not right.

'That is the farmer's story,' I said. 'I have no reason to believe it is untrue.'

'But you do. It cannot be true.'

There was a long, uncomfortable silence.

'I do not know of this Mitchell,' Elias said at last. 'I have never met any of his tenants. But I can tell you that, as I hear it, there is something wrong with the story. People do not spend months planning the assassination of a farmer unless there is big trouble, unless something very serious is at stake. I am the last person to deny that there are many gangsters in this place, but there is something wrong with your story.'

TEN

'Perhaps the easiest way of making a town's acquaintance,' Albert Camus once wrote, 'is to ascertain how the people in it work, how they love, and how they die.' The people with whom I was concerned did not get much opportunity to work and I would never get close enough to know how they loved. So I turned my attention to how they died.

The police mortuary in Alanview is wedged between the charge office and the holding cells. I understand they are building a new mortuary now, right next door to the district surgeon's private practice, which will be extremely convenient for him. The site of the new mortuary is the intersection of Alanview's two busiest streets, and some of the white folk in town think the choice is a little distasteful.

This is not the first time the visible face of death has annoyed them. Two funeral parlours have opened on the High Street in the last two years. Their proprietors behave like anyone who retails to the poor, advertising bargain prices for coffins and individually tailored burials. Their reception rooms are always full. People spill out of the doorway and onto the pavement, talking cheerfully in the afternoon sun. Watching their demeanour, it is difficult to tell whether they are all customers; funeral parlours are places where people congregate.

This public face of death is one of the few outward signs of the AIDS epidemic in KwaZulu-Natal. It is something people don't talk about. 'Long ago, I stopped writing "AIDS" on death certificates,' David Blewitt, the district surgeon, told me. 'Telling people that a family member died of AIDS can be dangerous. They can take out their anger on the messenger. So I state the immediate cause of death, the AIDS-induced disease, and leave it at that.' Writing a book on AIDS in Alanview would no doubt be as sensitive and difficult as writing a book on the murder of a white man. But that is for another time and another writer. I want to tell you about other sorts of deaths – violent deaths – and the soon-to-be-redundant police mortuary that is wedged between the charge office and the holding cells.

Sergeant Ephraim Nadi presides over the police mortuary. I have met him many times before. Like most rural police stations in South Africa, the Alanview station is understaffed, and Sergeant Nadi has many functions. In addition to looking after the mortuary, he is also the police station's public relations officer – he deals with all visitors, the quick and the dead. That is how I met him. I told him shortly after my arrival in Alanview that I wanted to meet as many chiefs in the district as possible. Nadi whistled through his teeth and said it would take a lot of work. I smiled back and said nothing, and during the following weeks we occasionally went chief-hunting together. Nadi would send advance word that a stranger with a notebook was coming, and we would set out a few days later, driving along one of the countless dust roads that link the district's myriad villages.

Throughout our expeditions, Nadi asked nothing about my work. We would drive to a chief's kraal, I would ask the chief questions, Nadi would translate them to the chief, and then translate what the chief said for me, and then we would leave. In the car on the return journey to Alanview, Nadi would not comment on what the chief had said nor on whether my questions had been the right ones. When I probed, he revealed as little as he could. His eyes were always busy. He watched both the chiefs and me closely, and took in much, and thought and judged many things, but he never shared them with me.

Nadi is short, slight, in his late thirties at most. His face is warm, his eyes benignly intelligent. I suspect that silence did not always come naturally to him. It is something he has cultivated over the years. A black man making a career in a white police force learns to hold his tongue. If you have something to say, there must be a good reason for it.

An enormous sign loomed over the doorframe outside Nadi's office: MORTUARY. I asked him whether I could see his mortuary record book. For the first time in the weeks I had known him, he became quite animated. Ceremoniously, he cleared the spare desk in his office of months of accumulated files and papers. He stood

131

on a chair and pulled from a shelf a massive green register book that had been opened and shut many times. He placed it on the desk, offered me the chair and told me to take my time.

I spent seven solid hours thumbing through that extraordinary book. All the while, Nadi sat behind his desk, a never-ending stream of visitors lined up on a bench alongside him. They were all very poor people. Some were barefoot. They had obviously come into town from the countryside to see Nadi. Each held a thin, official-looking piece of paper which he examined for a long time before stamping it and giving it back to them. I forgot to ask him what this paper was and what these people were doing in his office.

Nadi knew as much as anybody about violent death. The police mortuary at Alanview serves an area 100 kilometres long and 50 wide. In the event of any unnatural death in this area, the body has to come to the mortuary to be examined by the district surgeon. Nadi receives each body and prepares it for examination. David Blewitt comes from his private rooms, and he and Nadi conduct the examination, Blewitt talking out loud, Nadi taking notes. I felt it was an eerie vocation, straddling the connection between the forensic and the social, between anatomy and the countless styles of tragedy.

Halfway through my task I looked up at Nadi.

'How did you end up in this job?'

'I volunteered,' he said, setting aside his official-looking paper and his stamp.

'Why?'

He smiled at me and settled back into his work. By the time he replied his head was buried in his papers again.

'It's interesting.'

*

I do not like people who predict our fate by crunching numbers. I do not want to hear that I have a 485 per cent greater chance of contracting cancer than Nadi does, because I ate fast food as a boy while his insides delighted in home-grown maize. But in the Alanview police mortuary, you have to respect the numbers: they tell an extraordinary story. You do not even need to crunch them. Violent death in the Alanview district belongs to young unemployed black people. It happens like clockwork every weekend, and the profile of the victim is always the same.

The mortuary book is marked by the meticulous and caring columns of Nadi's handwriting; there is something studied and ceremonial about the inscriptions. Despite the regularity of the terms that are used, there is little shorthand. M is male, F female. B is black, W white. Other than that, everything is written out in full. I have tampered with one of Nadi's categories: I have omitted the names of the dead ones and of the people who claimed the bodies. Instead, I record their relation to the deceased.

> 7 January 1999 B/M ± 17 years, from Yimba location, Sarahdale, unemployed, found at Izita, assault and head injury. Body collected by mother, of Yimba location.

The body was picked up by his mother but nobody was quite certain of his age. Which suggests he was surrounded on all sides by absolute illiteracy. If he had had a literate cousin or aunt or close acquaintance, his age would have been recorded somewhere in his family's archives.

> 9 January 1999 B/F age unknown, from Wabane Location, Alanview, haemorrhage, stab wound, body collected by acquaintance from Athol.

The woman was murdered 40 kilometres from the home of the person who claimed her body. No family member came to the mortuary, nobody knew her age – and yet somebody buried her. Somebody collected precious money and attended a ceremony to put her in the ground. These are elusive signs. She belonged to a frail and transitory network, rather than a family. Her network knew almost nothing about her history: it could not even guess her age. And yet it cared enough to bury her. A strange burial it must have been. Burials are about families. The personal history of the deceased is borne in the heads of the mourners and inscribed in the nature of the ceremony. This was a burial I struggled to imagine.

I tried to get Nadi to take me to her grave. At first, he was quite excited by the idea. He liked the fact that the signs and records with which he worked mapped things in the physical world. He liked the idea that the codes in his mortuary book could lead him to a grave. But for some reason he lost interest in the project before it was completed, and I never got to the elusive woman's grave.

> 12 January 1999 B/F 30 years, from Nyembe, Alanview, unemployed, found in Raggedhill location, 11h00, gunshot in neck. Body collected by family.

I asked a detective at the police station if I could read the docket in which the investigation of this woman's murder was recorded. The docket revealed little. She had been killed in a shebeen at 11:40 p.m. Witnesses said she was drunk and provocative. She had been fighting all evening with whomever would fight back. There were no affidavits, no formal witness statements. It appeared as if local station detectives had gone through the motions: a drive out to the location, a short interview with the shebeen proprietor, another interview with the next of kin. Maybe they stayed another hour to look for some of the woman's drinking partners. Maybe they didn't.

I interviewed an ancient detective at the Alanview police station who said he remembered the case – an elderly white man who had been in the detective service longer than he could remember. He was wiry, almost skeletal, and his heavy grey moustache looked borrowed. It belonged on a more substantial man. He sat behind his desk in the rigid posture of a bureaucrat. His visitor's chair, in which I sat, was pushed against the wall at the opposite end of the room. Our voices echoed across the emptiness of his office, as if this were a cross-examination in a courtroom. A few minutes into the interview, I picked up my chair and brought it to the edge of his desk. He watched the procedure silently, his face expression-less, then took a pack of cigarettes out of his drawer, lit one and put the pack back. As an afterthought, a small concession to the informality I was trying to create, he took the pack out of the drawer again and offered me a cigarette.

I asked him why so little work had been put into solving this case. If he was offended, he showed no sign of it. Instead, he patiently explained.

Almost all murders in the locations have witnesses, he said. Nine out of ten happen in public. But it is highly unusual for any-body to tell the police what happened.

Why?

The detective thought long and hard. It was clear that he had given the matter considerable attention over the years. Finally, he spoke.

'It's a cultural thing.'

'Most things are cultural things.'

'Ja.'

There was a long pause. I was hoping he would grow uncomfortable and try to fill the silence with an explanation. But this man seemed incapable of feeling discomfort.

'Do you mean it is a political thing? People do not like to deal with the police?'

'No.'

'What then?'

Again, he thought long and hard. 'Well, maybe I am wrong to say it is a cultural thing. Long ago, things probably did not happen this way among the Zulus. But now, in modern times, murder is a private business between two families and they must be left to sort it out.

'If one of the witnesses is a family member of the victim, he will testify, guaranteed. If a witness is not a family member, he will say he has seen nothing. You could threaten him with his life and he will still have seen nothing.'

'So there were no family members among the witnesses to the murder of this woman?'

'No.'

'That is what the investigating officer went to the location to find out? Whether there was family among the witnesses?'

'Yes.'

'And once you found there were none, that was the end of the investigation?'

'Not officially, but in fact, yes.'

I asked him if murder witnesses are ever killed.

'It is expected that they will be killed,' he replied. 'If it is known that somebody will be testifying as an eyewitness in a murder case, it is expected that the allies of the perpetrator will try to kill him. That is how things are done.'

Back to the mortuary book. I have been from 6 January to 12 January 1999 and there have been four murders. A lot of bodies for a mortuary in the quiet backwaters of KwaZulu-Natal. Looking through the rest of the book, it appears that January was an unusually busy time. During quiet months, there are four or five murders. Busy months see 12 or maybe 15. Every month, the victims are the same. They are aged between 17 and 40, they are usually male, they are always unemployed and they are inevitably black.

Other sorts of unnatural deaths are dispersed across Nadi's pages. In 1999, a dozen people were killed by lightning. Of all the death categories, it is the lightning victims who are most likely to be given a pauper's burial. Four out of twelve: 33 per cent. The bodies lie in the mortuary unclaimed for a month. On the thirtieth day, Nadi calls Brickhill and Smith undertakers. They fetch the body and it is never seen again. Nadi writes 'pauper's burial' in his book.

I guess it is not much of a mystery that it is the lightning victims who go unclaimed. It is the wanderers of the midlands who find themselves on the hills or in the valleys when it storms.

Then there are suicides. Generally two or three a month. Most people hang themselves. One or two use guns, but it is unusual. The most interesting thing about the suicide cases is that they share the profiles of those who are murdered. They are young, unemployed and black. Well, almost the same profiles. The suicide band starts and ends younger than the murder band. They start at 15 and end at about 35. I think of Elias's comment about the new generation of youth: a whole generation born into the margins. The signs of their times are etched all over Nadi's book.

My finger goes down Nadi's careful columns and it is all young and black. Suddenly, there is Peter Mitchell.

27 September 1999 Peter Mitchell W/M, 28 years.
Birthplace: Sarahdale. Address: Derbytin Farm
Died at Derbytin 14h00. Brought to mortuary at 14h15 by Sergeant Nxumalo.
Brain damage, 20 G gunshot, head.
Body claimed by A Mitchell, Derbytin Farm.

The first thing that comes into my head is the small error. He was killed at about 14h00, but his body was only discovered at 15h55. It would have been dark by the time he was checked into the morgue.

I picture his body on the slab, Nadi and Blewitt examining its exposed brain. A strong, healthy, white body: it must be among the first to have found its way onto that slab. The district surgeon and his assistant, for all their experience, will never have seen something quite like this before.

And that is the point. Mitchell's name does not belong in this book. It is reserved for the black and the unemployed. The entry above him is B/M, unemployed, 27 years, multiple stab wounds. Below him is B/M, unemployed, 19 years, stab wound.

Seeing his name in that book, one sees something of the shock on the faces of Mitchell's neighbours as they watch his body sliding into the back of the police van. This murder has offended against something visceral and deep. It has never been in the nature of things for a young white man, son of a respectable Natal farming family, to lie dead in the Alanview police mortuary.

I realise that I must meet Paul Mlambo. When something happens for which there is no precedent, something that cannot be explained by the normal tools of recognition, the answers are left to uncharted imagination. The imaginations of those who mourn Peter Mitchell have led them to Paul Mlambo. He has become the key to understanding the new and the unexplained.

ELEVEN

In the first week of March 2000, I left several messages on Mlambo's voice mail. None were answered. I was hoping to hear the sound of his voice at least, but was denied that. The phone was set to the standard greeting supplied by Mlambo's service provider, a white female voice with an impeccable BBC accent. I went to Mlambo's bottle store in Izita. The young man at the cash register was taciturn and wary. Mr Mlambo is not here. Yes, he comes in occasionally, but it is impossible to say when. I left my cellphone number on a piece of paper. The young man looked at it suspiciously and put it in the cash register.

I had time to kill and decided to spend it in the archives at the provincial Diocese of the church that ran the Izita mission. A posse of elderly white women met me at the door to answer my questions. They were all exquisite caricatures of ageing Wasps: heavily starched and mottled skirts, purple hair rinse, gaunt, pale faces. Yes, they beamed, there is plenty of material on the mission in Izita: a biography of Oliver Swift, the priest who founded Izita; several decades of the mission's newsletter; a master's thesis on Christianity and rural development, which uses Izita as its case study.

The archivists steered me to an empty desk, sat me down and began loading the desk with documents. By the time they were done, I was hedged in by three walls of mothballed pages. The archivists had vanished behind the papers, but their voices filtered in relentlessly throughout the afternoon. They broke for tea every 20 minutes, and spoke ill of a woman who had visited the archives that morning. Their gossip kept intruding on the words of the nineteenth-century missionaries in the documents before me, and the heavy KwaZulu-Natal heat pounded my head. In a state of near delirium it suddenly dawned on me what an obtuse researcher I had become. I had scoured the Alanview district for the priest who had fled Izita, the one who had led me to Madlala and Elias and a dinner in Izita. And here I was, at the headquarters of the church that employed him.

I abandoned my trench and strolled up to reception. A black man in a priest's collar sat in the waiting room, his briefcase open in front of him. The receptionist poked her head out from behind her monitor and giggled mischievously at my query.

'The man you are looking for is staring at the back of your head.'

The priest, whose name was Abraham Zuma, looked at me severely and I announced my business.

'You're lucky,' he replied. 'My day finishes at five. After that I'm yours.'

We met in the late afternoon across a conference table at the Diocese. The building was empty, the setting sun squeezed its soft light through a venetian blind, and the stillness lent our meeting a subtle intensity. Zuma was a strikingly beautiful man. His high, sculptured cheekbones gave him an air of aristocracy. He held his body erect. Yet any suggestion of haughtiness was cancelled by the humility of his voice and the absence of malice in his eyes.

I told him I had heard that he left Izita after a series of nasty incidents, and asked if he was prepared to talk about them.

He nodded quietly and began speaking. It was apparent from the measured slowness of his words and his scrupulous attention to detail that he planned to speak for a long time.

'Things began changing in 1996. That is when they started to attack the church. From then on, it became very tough to live in Izita.'

'Who are "they"?'

Zuma ignored my question. The interruption disturbed him. He paused for a long time, staring at his fingers, pushing the cuticles back from his nails.

'I was hijacked twice in Izita in the space of six weeks. The first time was on 27 February 1996. My bakkie was found abandoned 500 metres away.

'The second hijacking was on 16 April 1996. I drove into the mission grounds at 7:20 p.m.'

I would have expected him to say 'some time after seven in the evening' or 'shortly after dark,' as one would in normal conversation. Instead, he used the stiff, precise discourse of a report. As if the records of his trauma were too weighty for casual conversation. As if the heaviness of the event needed to be marked by trivial precision – exact dates, times, movements.

'I pass through two gates on my way home, one at the entrance to the mission grounds, the other at the entrance to my home. A group of men was waiting at the mission gates. They were hoping I would get out of my car to close the gates, but I did not. I drove straight on, through the second gate, into my driveway.

'My dogs were not there to greet me and I knew something was wrong. I jumped out of my car and walked quickly into the house. I walked back out a moment later and there was a man behind my bakkie pointing a gun at me. He said, "Don't move." I thought, whatever this man says, I must do the opposite. In that split second, this seemed to be a good rule of thumb. So I turned and ran back into the house, and as I was running, I heard gunshots.

'They shot for a long time. A number of bullets were found outside my house. Later, I discovered that they had killed my ridgeback. My fox terrier survived. He ran away and hid under the other bakkie that was parked in the driveway.

'While the shooting was going on outside, I phoned the Sarahdale police station. They didn't respond. On the party line, the operator said the police line was engaged. She phoned the Alanview police. They came an hour and 15 minutes later. They went out to look for my vehicle and came back after half an hour. The bakkie was at the side of the road, one-and-a-half kilometres from the mission. They said they had tried to start it but it was dead. The hijackers must have turned off the ignition, not realising that there was an immobiliser. They must have abandoned it when they couldn't start it again.

'I went out with the police to the car. I was not in a good state and was moving slowly. The policemen started getting scared. One of them told me to hurry. These hijackers could come back at any moment.'

The priest emitted a sharp, whistling sound through his teeth, a wordless comment of contempt. It was the only unpleasant gesture he allowed himself during our interview.

'I took my family and left Izita immediately. We went to live in my house in Mpumalanga. I would commute to Izita when it was necessary, for a funeral, a wedding.

'We had sisters living in the mission at that time. I had to leave

140

them there on their own. It was not an easy thing to do. But there was no choice. I was chased out. Over the months, there had been many break-ins. All my possessions had been stolen – radios, televisions, clothes, cushions, the clothes of my wife and daughter.'

The priest cleared his throat and shuffled in his chair. Nearly four years later, telling the story of how he abandoned his mission clearly haunted him still.

'On 17 August that year, the sisters were attacked. A group of young men barged into the mission, took all the sisters' things. They recognised the attackers: they were Izita people, people we see on the streets every day.

'In September, another group of criminals came for a teacher at the mission school. His name was Magubane. They took him from his home – a room he was renting – and demanded money. They were local people, you see, and they knew that Magubane had been collecting money for a school outing, a trip. He said he didn't have the money. Another teacher, a man by the name of Bayi, was keeping it. So they pointed their gun at Magubane, marched him off to Bayi's house, and forced him to knock on the door. Bayi opened up, they marched in and told the two teachers to lie face down on the floor. They found the money, and as they were leaving, one of them shot Magubane through the back of the head. He died instantly.'

'Were they caught?'

'Never. They were never caught.'

As I listened to the priest's melancholy tale, the voice of another priest began to mingle with his in my head. While waiting for our early-evening appointment, I had gone back to the archive and begun reading a biography of Oliver Swift, the British missionary who founded Izita, the black priest's earliest predecessor. It struck me that my afternoon's research had touched the beginning and the end of a history spanning nearly one-and-a-half-centuries: the energetic white proselytiser who founded Izita to spread God's word to the natives, and his defeated black successor, who fled in anguish 134 years later. Separated by a gulf of so many years, I wondered whether the connection between the two men extended any further than a coincidence of name and place.

The biography is a poor one, penned in 1892 by a young English woman by the name of Elizabeth Alfred. She had never set foot in Africa, had little knowledge of the political terrain through which Swift moved, and her lack of confidence expresses itself in incessant reticence. Her commentary is wooden and dull, lacking either suggestion or analysis. The book's only interest lies in the long tracts of Swift's diary entries that Alfred transcribed. In her wiser moments, she stepped out of the book entirely, and allowed the diary to take over.

Refracted through the editorial selections of his biographer, Swift appears to have possessed an awkward mixture of traits: hopeless naivety, rabid cultural hubris, but also an extraordinary prescience in regard to the relationship between black and white unfolding around him. Having settled in Pietermaritzburg in the early 1860s, Swift, a medical doctor as well as a priest, divided his time between a busy medical practice, part-time preaching and a crash course in Zulu. Frustrated by the distractions of his various commitments, and by his growing doctrinal estrangement from his Church, in 1863 Swift persuaded the Church to buy a piece of land from the British Crown in the southern midlands.

The world south of Pietermaritzburg was in a state of great fragility at the time of Swift's arrival. It was not long after the years of turmoil and war which I told you about earlier. And it was less than a decade after the Dutch settlers of 1837 had left in protest against the British annexation of Natal. The African settlements in the area would have been wary of Swift to say the least. An imperialist Zulu army and a hostile Dutch landlord class were the two looming forces that filled their historical memory. A proselytising white Christian, clutching a piece of paper claiming ownership of a chunk of land, talking about establishing a mission, would have been greeted with some wariness.

Astoundingly, Swift was completely oblivious to the fragile political terrain onto which he strolled. For him, the people of the southern midlands were simply 'raw natives in their natural state', a juicy if daunting challenge for a Christian missionary. Indeed, Swift's account of his first meeting with Uzita, the chief of the 400-odd people who lived on the land he had bought, is breathtakingly eccentric and almost certainly untrue. Even Elizabeth Alfred, the most timid of biographers, betrays her scepticism in the words she chooses to report Swift's account of the meeting.

'Swift,' Alfred writes, 'claims to have allayed all of Uzita's fears within a few hours. By the end of the meeting, one of the chief's counsellors had called [Swift] *Yinkosi Yami* – my chief, and Uzita had undertaken to build him two huts.'

The truth of the matter is that the missionaries of mid-nineteenth century Natal were not greeted with the open arms Swift's self-satisfaction suggests. Established African power kept the missionaries at a wary arm's length. Those Africans who did venture onto mission land to make a new life were generally at the margins of established African communities: people with little to lose and everything to gain by joining a strange and foreign sect.

A graduate student named Sipho Cele, who wrote a 12-page essay on Swift in the early 1990s, shows a good deal more insight than his subject does. 'In areas where there was no co-operation between a chief and a missionary,' Cele writes, 'people would hide in the missions to run away from punishment. Indeed,' Cele continues, 'recruitment [to the missions] was in essence a bribe: come and be a Christian and you will get a piece of land.'

If Swift was oblivious to the subtleties of African politics of the southern midlands, or chose to present himself that way, he did have much to say about the moral fibre of African culture. His response was one of unmitigated disgust. Exasperated reports of unbridled misogyny and shameless sloth litter his journal entries.

'There is not a single thing that the Kaffirs do not require to be taught,' he wrote in December 1856, 'from the washing of their bodies to the building of their houses.' Earlier, he commented: 'The Kaffirs are as yet completely ignorant of the very elements of agriculture ... and need constant direction and supervision.' Alfred's account of Swift's relationship to his new converts at Izita is akin to a schoolteacher's relationship with a five-year-old child. 'Every now and again he took the implements out of their hands that he might show them the proper use of them, and how much might by continuous and judicious effort be achieved in a tithe of the time that they usually take ...'

Swift reserves his greatest disgust for the practices of polygamy and bridal payments. 'There is no doubt that they speak of the transaction by which their daughters become wives as an act of sale,' Swift writes. Elsewhere, he caustically suggests that the place of a woman in 'Kaffir life' is that of a plough, an instrument of raw labour.

It is striking how little white discourse on Zulu culture has changed in the intervening years. Reading Swift's diaries, I recall my conversation with Jude Fowler on his farm on the outskirts of Alanview. 'The Zulus are a savage nation,' Fowler said. 'It's the sort of culture where it's not good enough just to kill your enemy. You have to cut his balls out as well. In Zulu culture you can buy a wife. You buy a human being. She has fuck all say in the matter. She's your possession. Like a spade or a hoe.'

Looking across the conference table at Abraham Zuma, I am convinced there is little to connect him to his predecessor. Swift's heirs are not the black clergymen of post-apartheid South Africa. They are the Jude Fowlers of the world, the farmers who work the land on the borders of black South Africa, one-and-a-half centuries of bitter hatred running through their veins.

But reading further, I see that I am wrong. KwaZulu-Natal's white farmers are not Swift's heirs; they are the heirs of his enemies. Swift's mission was to destroy 'the Kaffir way of life' and to teach the black man cleansing labour, monogamy, literacy. Yet as early as the mid-1850s, he knew that to achieve his task he must fight not only traditional African culture, but the mainstay of the white settler project itself.

'There is a feeling among the colonists of Natal,' Swift writes, 'which would very easily pass into a disposition to enslave. They leave their native place where an overstocked labour market makes it difficult for men to live, and come into a country which promises very fair to the enterprise of capital and labour. There is apparently an abundance of *hands*; but to get labour out of them is quite another question ... How are 8 000 widely scattered whites to compel 200 000 coloureds to labour, against their will?'

Elsewhere Swift warns: 'The white man is coming on in increasing numbers and is treading on their [the Kaffirs'] heels in every direction; before they have time to grow into a people another people will have occupation of their places.'

So Izita was founded in the belief that the Christian project could only flourish in the safety of a cloister. Out in the world two evil forces were at work, the barbarism of African tradition and the white desire to enslave Africans and use them as menial labour. Izita was to be a fortress that staved off the world, a place where Africans could become Swift's nineteenth-century Christian version of human beings.

Many mission-educated Africans of the late nineteenth century did indeed play a seminal role in shaping modern South Africa, but not in the way Swift had imagined. The converts may have arrived at the mission gates as outcasts from African society but over the course of a generation many were to become aspiring agriculturalists and fiery intellectuals. Their position as a nascent black bourgeoisie immediately pitted them against white government and agriculture, whose overriding project was to destroy independent black enterprise wherever it arose. With their new-found literary imaginations and their erudition, this incipient African intelligentsia fought back. They scoured African history in search of a foundation for their own dignity. With their pens, they resurrected the Zulu king Shaka and recast him as the founder of an heroic black nation. They lionised Cetshwayo as the last ruler of an independent African state.

Izita was not among the Christian missions that produced African and Zulu nationalism's pioneers. Reading the scant and wooden Izita Mission newsletters from the turn of the century is not enough to discover why. 'Between 1871, when Izita's first black clergy were ordained, and 1900, you do not see the names of black clergy appearing in the Synod register,' Cele notes dryly. 'Where they do appear, they do not voice any opinion.'

Seen in retrospect from the year 2000, Swift's legacy is filled with pathos and irony. During the course of the twentieth century, Izita was slowly but steadily gutted by the very evil of which Swift warned: the white disposition to turn Africans into 'beasts of burden'. Wedged between white farmland and the overpopulated reserves into which Africans were herded in the late nineteenth century, Izita soon became indistinguishable from the neighbouring reserves. Its soil unfit for cultivation, its plots too crowded to sustain its inhabitants, its adult population began to drift to the cities in search of work, just as the architects of the black labour market had planned.

As Izita slid into desperate circumstances, so the relationship between the church and its congregation began to sour. In any sect, the first generation of converts is filled with zeal and passion. But by the time the second generation comes of age, the church is little more than a landlord. In a master's thesis written in the early 1990s, Charles du Toit describes a tuberculosis epidemic that descended on Izita in 1938. Some tenants, Du Toit writes, blamed the epidemic on 'a reduction of available milk due to the rather stringent stock control measures introduced during this period as well as the relative insecurity of tenure. These are seen to have been orchestrated by George Statham – the incumbent of the mission at the time – who was later assaulted and then resigned his charge.'

Mention Statham's name on the streets of Izita today, and you will hear long stories of callousness and cruelty. Statham has found his place in the litany of myths through which Izita residents organise their memory of the last century. 'Statham taught us a lesson,' a retired Izita policeman, who was seven years old at the time of the tuberculosis epidemic, told me. 'The lesson is that in no matter what guise they come, white men are the same. The farmers and the government pushed us into little ghettos, and the Church became the ghetto master, counting head of cattle, extracting rent. In their speeches, the priests spoke out against racism. But in practice, they presided over the ghettos racism created.'

By the time Zuma took up his charge in Izita in 1986, the mission was a hollowed-out place, a place of drifting teenagers and old men and women. In a study commissioned by the Church in the late 1980s, a rural development consultancy reported that 34 per cent of mean household income in Izita came from pension payouts. And yet 58 per cent of Izita was under the age of 16. So Izita had become a place of youth, scores of youth, living off the meagre offerings of the old. Elias's story of eternal children, of boys who grow up but never become men, never become breadwinners, was plastered all over the dry distillations of the consultants' report. I say the 'meagre offerings of the old,' but 'meagre' is something of a euphemism. The consultants reported that mean cash income in an Izita household was R215 per month. Adjust that figure to 2000 prices and the money I spend on petrol to drive from Johannesburg to Izita and back comfortably outstrips the amount an Izita family sees in a month. Thinking back to my dinner with Elias and his family, I realise that by the standards of its neighbours the family is positively wealthy.

The consultants issued a dire prognosis of Izita's future. 'The farm has a low agricultural potential and is more suited to livestock production but even this potential is being reduced by overgrazing, erosion and bush encroachment,' they wrote. 'Despite what potential there is, tenants do not make full use of it, but rely on remittances from relatives working in towns. For most tenants, the farm functions solely as a place of residence, with their subsistence agriculture and livestock augmenting remittances received.'

The consultants saved their sharpest and bleakest comments for the Church. 'The lack of an effective management presence coupled with the general dereliction of the Diocesan-owned buildings showed the Diocese to be unenthusiastic in management and as a rural development agent.' The consultants recommended that the land be subdivided and sold to its tenants.

In 2000, more than a decade later, this is precisely what the Church is doing. Using the post-apartheid government's land reform programme, the Church is selling its land to the state, which, in turn, will distribute it among Izita tenants. In the process of finally pulling out, the Church has found itself locked in battle with some of its oldest tenants.

'When news got out that the Church was giving away its land,' an elderly priest at the Diocese told me, 'old faces, faces we had not seen in decades, suddenly started appearing. People who had long left Izita, and made homes and lives elsewhere, came back to claim their historical right to the land. We told them, no, the land is for people who live in Izita, for people who have nowhere else to go. If we lose this battle, if well-off people from Durban and Johannesburg end up owning the land, then there will be another generation of landlords and exploited tenants. What a terrible legacy for the Church to leave behind.'

*

During the course of our conversation, the priest had lapsed into a monologue of depression and despair. A few months after he left Izita, he was hijacked outside his house in Mpumalanga late one night. This time the hijackers told him to get into the passenger seat and drive with them. Once again, the priest thought to himself, 'Whatever they say, I must do the opposite.' So in a clear and forthright voice he said no, and with his head held high he turned and walked slowly to his front gate. As in Izita a few months earlier, he heard the sound of gunfire behind him, and he scaled his own fence and scampered into his home.

Since then, the priest continued, since his third hijacking in less than a year, he no longer travels at night. By six in the evening, the front gate of his Mpumalanga home is padlocked, and if anyone in his congregation needs something they must wait until morning. The priest complained of the task of keeping the Izita mission alive from so far away. The trip is arduous, he said, and he has back problems. By the time he gets out of his bakkie in the Izita mission grounds, he is in agony, and full of resentment.

There were a host of questions I wanted to ask Zuma, but I felt squeamish about asking them and had spent the last half-hour beating about the bush. I wanted to know to whom, exactly, he had relinquished Izita. It was one thing reading about the encroachment of the bush and the rise of unemployment in the pages of development reports. It was all very well knowing, in the abstract, that Izita had become a place of such overwhelming poverty that Zuma, with his middle-class trappings, had simply become easy pickings for the poor and the desperate. But social degeneration has names and faces. I wanted to know the place the men who terrorised the priest occupied in Izita's political universe.

'Who are the thugs who chased you away? Is it the young and the unemployed? Is it because parents and grandparents have lost control of their children?'

Zuma considered the question and shook his head.

'That is too simplistic. It is not just the young. There are young men with guns who are close to their elders, to their fathers and grandfathers. So one must conclude that there are old men involved.'

'Are you saying you know the people who hijacked your car and shot your dog?'

The priest did not care for the direction in which the conversation was going. He folded his arms tight across his chest and looked at me suspiciously from behind the barricade his body had become.

'My hijackers knew my habits inside out. They were people who had watched me every day for a long time.'

I didn't want to push him any further, but I didn't want to give up either, so I put down my pen and watched him closely. He shifted in his chair, showing me his profile, rather than his face, as if to unlock himself from my stare.

'If you doubt who attacks you,' he said eventually, 'you must greet everyone you meet on the street and look them closely in the eye. Those who do not respond, those who will not make eye contact, they are the ones who know who did it. There is one particular family that comes to church occasionally. Ever since my first hijacking, they have not looked me in the eye.'

'Do you know Paul Mlambo?' I asked.

Zuma winced. It was as if I had slapped him across the face. His head jerked back, involuntarily, and he stared at me with a mixture of accusation and shock.

'Where are these questions leading? What is it you want to know?' His discomfort was palpable. He pointed his face at the far end of the conference table and looked at me warily out of the corner of his eye, like an ancient Egyptian profile painting. 'I think we have spoken enough,' he said. 'It is time for you to go.'

The following day, I phoned the detective who had investigated Zuma's hijacking case, and told him of the priest's alarm when I had mentioned Paul Mlambo.

'Of course you scared the poor man,' the detective laughed. 'Let me tell you why. When the priest's dog was shot, we took the bullet out of him and kept it. A long time later, at the end of 1996, there was the incident on Mr Wells's farm. Two young men broke into his house and held him up. He took out his gun and shot at them. One ran away, the other was killed. The dead one was Paul Mlambo's son. We sent his gun for ballistic tests and found that it matched the bullet we had taken out of the priest's dog. That is why the priest threw you out of his office. He must have thought you had known right from the start about Paul's son. He obviously thought you were making mischief.'

'But it's not as if Paul shot the priest's dog,' I said. 'A parent is not responsible for the deeds of his son.'

'No, of course not,' the detective replied. 'But put yourself in Zuma's shoes. A strange white man comes to ask questions, and just at the wrong moment, he mentions the father of the man who shot your dog. It looks like you are playing games.'

I put the phone down and reeled back in astonishment. The Wells story was legend in the farming communities of Alanview and Sarahdale, and like every legend in the area, it was reinvented by whoever did the telling. I had heard many versions of the tale during the previous months, but none had mentioned Paul Mlambo's son.

Like Arthur Mitchell, Adam Wells farmed on the boundary between Izita and the commercial farmlands of the Sarahdale district. Some time in 1998, Wells and his wife were on holiday in Zimbabwe, and Wells's 22-year-old son, Howard, was alone on the property. On returning from a party late one night, he was shot dead in his driveway. His killers entered the house, ransacked it for guns and, on their way out, took his wallet from his pocket. The killers must have been hopeless amateurs, because they used a credit card from Wells's wallet wherever they went and left a paper trail across the country. A couple of weeks after the killing, the police caught up with them, and they were charged with Howard Wells's murder.

I first heard about the Wells affair from Colin Waugh.

'The theft of the wallet was just an afterthought,' Colin told me. 'It was an assassination, a revenge killing.'

Two years before his son's murder, two armed intruders had confronted Adam Wells in his bedroom. They demanded that he open his safe, and the old man, who had been paralysed in a previous shooting incident on his farm, wheeled his way over to his bedroom cupboard and opened the door. Instead of unlocking his safe, he grabbed a pistol that was buried under a pile of neatly ironed shirts, swivelled round and opened fire on the intruders. He shot one of them dead – Mlambo's son, as it turned out. The other, injured and bleeding, escaped.

'The one Adam killed,' Colin told me, 'was the lover of the Wellses' domestic servant. So she took out a contract on Howard's life as an act of revenge. She had a brother in jail. He was the sort of person who knew where to look for hired assassins. And she paid them, not with money, but with the guns in Wellses' house. Imagine it. She was still working in the Wellses' kitchen while she was planning the assassination of their son.'

'Was she arrested too?' I asked Colin.

'I don't know for certain, but I imagine she must have been. It was clear-cut. She was the one behind the killing.'

A few weeks after Colin told me the story, I interviewed the lawyer who had defended the men charged with Howard Wells's murder. When I told him Colin's tale of conspiracy, he buried his head in his hands and sighed deeply.

'Nonsense,' he said. 'Utter nonsense. The accused were total strangers to the area. They came to Sarahdale to commit an armed robbery. It could have been any of the farms along that border. And no domestic worker was ever arrested. It simply isn't true.'

By the time I interviewed Zuma, I had not got round to investigating Colin's story any further and did not know the truth of the matter. The Wells tragedy struck me as the sort of story that lends itself to myth-making. A white farm on the border of Izita hit three times by armed robbers during the course of a decade, leaving one family member dead, another paralysed; it was a horrific tale, one that lent powerful credence to the idea that the farmers on the Izita border occupied a war zone. Colin had already told a tale with a heavy subtext. The 'opposition' is in your own kitchen; she serves you breakfast every morning. She is the sort of woman whose lover will ransack your house for guns, who knows where to go to hire someone to kill you, who will keep serving breakfast while planning your death.

So why had nobody mentioned Mlambo's son? If every act of violence on the Izita border is splashed onto the canvas of a black onslaught, surely the likes of Colin would have gone to town on the story of Mlambo's son? Surely the moment Howard Wells was killed, every white finger in the area would have pointed at Paul Mlambo?

A few days after I interviewed Zuma, Colin invited me to dinner. I arrived at about seven clutching a bottle of red wine. In defiance of the sexist regime he claimed to enforce in his household, Colin was the family cook. I sat on a kitchen stool drinking wine while Colin, looking camp and overworked, darted between the oven and the chopping board. Occasionally, his wife would wander into the kitchen. He would drop his knife, put his hand on his hip and banish her with a theatrical display of indignation. He was crouched over his oven, peering proudly at his roast, when I told him my news.

'You didn't tell me that the man Adam Wells shot was Paul Mlambo's son.'

Colin froze in that strange pose a moment too long. Eventually, he removed his head from the oven, closed the door, walked over to his chopping board and began peeling an onion.

'I was wondering how long it would take you to discover that.'

He didn't look at me as he spoke. He kept his head down and chopped. And then he abruptly changed the subject. When I brought it up again hours later, he frowned and immediately changed the subject once more.

I could not swear to it, but I was convinced he was lying to me. For a man who prided himself on his prowess as a professional soldier, and especially on his ability to gather intelligence, the thought that so juicy a piece of news had passed him by embarrassed him.

151

And so it should have. The whole episode revealed just how little the white farming community knew about the people it had named as its enemies. The world beyond the Izita boundary was foreign to them. The news they did receive came in hushed tones and was exchanged for a small wad of banknotes. Bought information is impure. It is shaped by the desire to please the buyer, to give him what he wants. It dawned on me that the stories white men gathered about Izita might well depart very little from the stories their own imaginations had invented. The politics of Izita came to men like Colin in disparate fragments. Piecing the bits together was left to them.

Driving away from Colin's house that night, I knew Mlambo was to be an important figure in my tale, but only by the suggestive tales that gathered around him: the man who the whites swore was chasing them off their farms; the man whose name made the priest wince in his chair, as if he had been struck; the man whose son was shot to death as he tried to rob Adam Wells of his guns.

TWELVE

The ANC office in the centre of Alanview resembled an abandoned warehouse. It was a massive, largely empty space, about 30 metres long and about 10 metres wide. A third of the way into the room stood a tiny desk, just big enough for an adult to tuck his legs under. A receptionist sat idly behind it, a middle-aged man in the chair opposite her. The man and woman were framed by a thousand images of South African President Thabo Mbeki, some upside down, some sideways, a few the right way up. At first, I thought the local ANC branch must have employed an interior decorator with an eye for the cynical and the surreal. The image seemed like a strange satire of George Orwell's *1984*. Someone had toyed with Big Brother and made him look silly: he was all turned in on himself and couldn't see the room he was meant to be watching, and there were just too many of him to take seriously. In fact, the image was quite accidental. It was almost a year since South Africa's second democratic election, and the warehouse-like office was crammed with leftover campaign posters – literally thousands of them. They filled about a third of the office space, stacked haphazardly from floor to ceiling.

The receptionist stopped her conversation with the man opposite, and looked up at me enquiringly. I walked through the empty space to her desk and told her I was looking for Paul Mlambo. It was a replay of my meeting with the priest. The receptionist raised her eyebrows and nodded her head at the man in the chair.

'You're Mr Mlambo?'

He neither nodded nor shook his head, just looked at me curiously.

'I've been looking for you for some time. I've left several messages on your voice mail.'

'Yes, yes,' he replied. 'I have a terrible habit of deleting messages

153

before I have had time to write down the phone number. Besides,' he continued, looking at me more closely, a deliberately suspicious look on his face, 'we need to sit you down, ask you a few questions, see who you are.'

Mlambo remained seated. From two feet above his head, he seemed a short, stocky man, with a large belly. He wore a short-sleeved polyester shirt, the buttons undone to the top of his stomach. For an odd moment, he reminded me of a caricature of the Jewish or Indian factory boss: short, squat, bare-chested, presiding over a small kingdom with a brash and leisurely air.

I gave him my business card, told him I was writing a book on rural crime and that I wanted to know something about Izita.

'Who sent you to me?'

'Trevor Sibiya.'

Mlambo nodded. Sibiya was a veteran political activist from the Alanview area, and had been elected to parliament in South Africa's first democratic election. I had met him at his office in the parliamentary precinct in Cape Town two months earlier, and he had in fact mentioned Mlambo's name in passing. Mlambo paged through his diary, a strange gesture, since it was entirely blank, and agreed to meet me at the ANC offices at nine o'clock the following morning.

That night, I glanced through my notebooks, recalling the various things white farmers had said about Mlambo. 'He is heading a devious land distribution campaign,' read one entry. 'The ANC can't buy farms, so they would rather steal them.' And a few pages later: 'Peter's murder is the culmination of a political campaign to undermine Mitchell's farming operation. Mlambo is the brains behind the campaign. He chose Mitchell strategically. Normandale is simply a wedge. Once you get it, you can begin a rolling campaign across the commercial farms.' And still another comment: 'Mitchell is the toughest farmer on that border. He is the kingpin. Whack him and you get a lot of credibility in Izita, especially if you are a leader without much power, looking for a bit more.'

It struck me that none of the comments I read had anything to say about Mlambo as a human being – his character, his conduct, his quirks. The Paul Mlambo in my notebooks was a cipher. He filled in a space – the apex, to be precise – of a cold conspiracy to drive white landowners away and to move onto their farms. There was just one moment in my notebooks where Mlambo threatened, fleetingly, to take on a personality. It was the legendary moment on the eve of the 1994 election when he stood up on a platform and told the assembled crowd that under the ANC everything from the Gudla to the trees would be theirs.

'Are you absolutely sure Mlambo said this?' I would ask.

'Absolutely. In fact, he said more than that. He told people to go to the white farms and take them.'

'How do you know this?'

'Informers.'

'Reliable informers?'

'Extremely reliable. I know how to run informers. I have ways of double-checking.'

*

At nine the following morning, Mlambo ushered me to a desk in the far corner of the hollow office space I had visited the previous day. As we settled into our chairs, I grinned and pointed to the jumbled collection of Thabo Mbeki posters.

'I think the president deserves better than that.'

Mlambo looked up and took in the scene. 'Yes, I see what you mean,' he smiled, chuckling to himself. 'I'm sure we can make an arrangement which is – how shall I say – more appropriate to his status.'

That was the richest, most meaningful exchange that passed between us. For the rest of the morning, Mlambo put on the most astonishing performance. He sized me up and became whatever he imagined I would expect him to be. I am not only talking about the words he chose. It is usually possible to learn something about anyone, no matter how reserved and cautious his discourse. Body language, mannerisms, a fleeting facial expression, the way one's interlocutor looks one in the eye. Mlambo revealed nothing at all. He was entirely blank. He knew that I had come to look for him in his capacity as an ANC man and that I had got his name from an ANC activist. He also knew I was not from the area, and presumed that the minutiae of local politics would be lost on me. So he became a cardboard effigy of a rural ANC leader and a small-time businessman – as viewed from the distant concrete of Johannesburg. He sounded like testimony delivered at a hearing, transcribed and filed in a minor archive. I would indeed have learned no less about him if I had read what he said to me that morning on a piece of paper.

I found out a great deal about Mlambo in the months following our interview. Between then and now, I have asked at least a dozen Izita people what they know of him, and each knows quite a lot. But at the time I knew very little, and much of the wonderful irony of his performance was lost on me.

I started by asking him about the biggest problems he faced in the area. I thought he would respond to the question as a community leader and that he would interpret 'the area' I referred to as Izita. Instead, he responded as an ANC official, and a regional ANC official at that: 'area' he interpreted as the ANC region – a vast stretch of the southern midlands.

'Our most worrying problem is intimidation,' he began. 'At a provincial level, the Inkatha Freedom Party talks toleration and peace; but at the grassroots, they speak a different language. At Santaville, for example, you cannot hold an ANC meeting in safety. Same applies to Location A.'

'And in Izita?'

'Well, Izita is different. It is an ANC stronghold and there is no IFP branch. Mind you, there are a few IFP members there and we work happily with them. We allow them to organise meetings freely.'

'What needs to change? How can you get Inkatha to back off?'

'The problem is the amakhosi, the traditional leaders. Some are understanding, but most intimidate the people.' Mlambo paused, leaned forward and launched into a piece of oratory that I had heard on civic movement platforms around South Africa countless times before. 'You can say this particular chief is good, that one is bad, but if you do that, you are just toying around with the symptoms. What we need are wards of voters, not submissive royal subjects. Chiefs appoint their friends. These people must be replaced by elected officials.'

Some of the irony of Mlambo's words was apparent to me at the time. I knew then – and he clearly did not know that I knew – that in addition to being an ANC activist, he was the induna – Chief Macaba's official representative – in Location B, which merges with Izita. So when Mlambo spoke derisively of the amakhosi's henchmen, he was speaking of himself. This was a man who wore

156

many hats: Mlambo the democrat and Mlambo the aristocrat traded places, depending on the audience. If I had come to see him not in the ANC office but at his bottle store in Izita, and if I had told him I was working for a centre-right research institute, studying the plight of traditional leaders, he would have told a very different story.

That was just the beginning of the exquisite cynicism Mlambo's comments betrayed. The rest was lost on me at the time. A few days after my meeting with him, I found myself in the passenger seat of a car carrying two middle-aged Izita women to Alanview. A large, 72-year-old Zulu man sat behind the wheel. I had employed him a few weeks earlier to snoop around Izita for me, and he had dropped what he was doing and taken up the assignment with relish.

'You don't know a soul in Izita,' I had said to him. 'How are you going to collect information?'

He giggled and grinned at me. 'I'm going to pick up hitch-hikers.'

'Hitch-hikers? I need to see this. I want to come with you.'

The old man brushed my request aside. 'Don't be ridiculous. To get information, you have to let the conversation flow. With you I'll be translating Zulu to English, English to Zulu. It will be like a courtroom. Besides, people don't talk with a white man in the car. They assume he is up to trouble.'

'Just once. I'll come along once, and then I'll leave you alone.'

The old man gave his grudging consent, and at eight that evening we drove out toward a bus stop on the outskirts of Izita. As he had predicted, the bus to Alanview was more than an hour late, and a small group of women sat patiently at the side of the road. He wound down his window and began a garrulous conversation, interrupted occasionally by bouts of hearty laughter. Ten minutes later, we had a cage of four squawking chickens in the boot and two women in the back seat.

For a good 20 minutes, the two women complained volubly about the state of public transport. They shook their heads and clucked their tongues, and in return, the old man told an interminable story about the day he was stranded without a car and was forced to get around Durban by bus. I could only understand snippets of his monologue, but I gathered that he was presenting himself as a sweet, senile old man with too much time on his hands. Gradually, the conversation turned to Izita, and as we

157

reached the outskirts of Alanview the name 'Paul Mlambo' rolled matter-of-factly off the old man's tongue.

The two women began laughing raucously at the mention of Mlambo's name, and the old man raised his eyebrows and asked to be let in on the joke.

'That man is a big problem in this area,' one of the women said. 'He was always Inkatha, from way back. Then, suddenly, after the 1994 election, he changed to ANC.'

The old man's eyes opened wide and he whistled meaningfully. 'Turncoat,' he exclaimed. 'You're saying the man's a turncoat?'

'That is exactly what he is. The ANC cleaned up in Izita in 1994 and suddenly our friend Mr Mlambo found that his bread was buttered on the wrong side. So he switched.'

'Just like that,' the old man replied, keeping up his performance of exaggerated incredulity.

'Well, not just like that. People made trouble for him. The youth marched on his house, demanded that he attend a meeting and explain himself. Now he is too controversial a figure to do very much. He moved out of Izita and bought a house in Alanview. He keeps a low profile.'

When I heard the two women's story, I was convinced it was wrong. This was the man who stood in front of a massive crowd in 1994 and told people that if they voted ANC the white farms would be theirs. This was the ANC kingpin, the man who was about to deliver the world to Izita, by whatever means.

A week after the car journey to Alanview, I was introduced to a woman who had once lived a stone's throw away from Mlambo's house in Izita.

'This Mlambo,' I asked. 'Is he ANC or IFP?'

'That depends which way the wind is blowing,' she replied. 'I'm convinced that he carries two membership cards in his back pocket. You see, Mlambo never held a public meeting to renounce his IFP membership. He just quietly slipped over. And there was no fuss in Inkatha when he joined the ANC. Chief Macaba did not fire him as induna. So that's why I say maybe he is both.'

Finally, I met a high-ranking figure in the provincial structures of the ANC to get some clarity. Yes, he confirmed. Some time after the 1994 election, Mlambo began making overtures to the ANC provincial leadership. The matter was discussed at length.

'One of the biggest problems facing us in the province was the allegiance of traditional leaders to the IFP. To make inroads into rural areas, you must have the amakhosi on your side. So, when the induna of an IFP chief tells you he wants to join the ANC you don't just say no.'

'Was it an easy transition?'

'It was more difficult than we imagined. You see, Izita is not a very politicised place. The war between the ANC and Inkatha in the early 1990s never really got there. So we thought, this will not be a very controversial move. This man does not have blood on his hands.

'We were almost right, but not quite. There was a group of ANC members – youngsters, young men – who had fled Izita before the 1994 election and had taken refuge at the Kwazungu hostel, at the other end of the province. We went to them and said Mlambo is ANC now, he is on our side, it is safe for you to come back. And they replied, what are you talking about? This is the man whose party chased us out of our homes. Now you waltz in and say he is on our side and everything is all right. Bullshit.

'It took a lot of work on the ground to pave the way for Mlambo's transfer into the ANC. Things are okay now, but his name is tainted among ANC people in Izita. He will never be a successful operator there. But that doesn't matter. We didn't bring him in to be a charismatic organiser. We just wanted to make inroads into the amakhosi, to have an ANC man running the area.'

Over the months, a picture of Mlambo started coming together. He was born to a well-off family – well-off in rural KwaZulu terms at any rate – and spent much of the 1980s near Dludla, a tiny coastal town less than 100 kilometres east of Izita. His family occupied a minor position in one of the local aristocracies. The family was wealthy enough to send Mlambo's brother to university to study law, and at some point in the 1980s, he opened a small legal practice in Pietermaritzburg.

Mlambo himself led the typical life of an ambitious Zulu aristocrat during the 1980s. He took up a position as a chiefly representative in his home district near Dludla, and he opened a taxi business, running passengers between Dludla and Durban. By all accounts, his business thrived in the mid and late 1980s, and by the time FW de Klerk ordered Nelson Mandela's release from prison in February 1990, Mlambo presided over a considerable taxi fleet. And, of course, he joined the IFP, as would any low-ranking Zulu aristocrat who sought power and wealth under Mangosuthu Buthelezi's homeland administration.

In the late 1980s, a man in Mlambo's position would have greeted the prospect of democracy in South Africa with reservations, if not with downright hostility. In official liberation movement discourse, the indigenous African aristocracy was a rotten, hollowed-out institution, irredeemably corrupted by its century-long association with white rule. Closer to home, in Natal, civil war raged between IFP chiefs and ANC-aligned workers and youths, and the prospect of an ANC-led South African democracy was bad news for anybody whose livelihood resided in the posterity of royal Zulu power. How close Mlambo got to the front lines of the civil war during his time in Dludla, I do not know. I have spoken to several people who knew the conflict and its protagonists well, and none have heard of him. He appears to have kept his head low, worked on his business and hung back from the trenches.

It is reasonable to assume, though, that a man who ran a successful taxi fleet on the Natal south coast in the late 1980s witnessed a fair amount of violence. The taxi industry was then, and remains now, devoid of regulation, and if a successful proprietor wanted to keep his route, he often had to pay protection money to a national taxi association. In the business world where Mlambo cut his teeth, groups of armed men were put on national taxi association payrolls as a matter of course.

Some time in the early 1990s, Mlambo moved from Dludla to Izita. I have never learned why. Nor have I learned whether he managed to hold on to his Dludla taxi business after his departure from his home town. The KwaZulu-Natal countryside is rife with rumour, and I heard many conflicting stories about Mlambo's Dludla business, but could verify none. On his arrival in Izita he was appointed induna to Location B and given a healthy chunk of land on which his sizeable herd of cattle grazed. He opened a bottle store in Izita and began running a taxi service between Izita and Alanview.

Izita was a docile place in regard to party-political violence, and the move to Izita took Mlambo about as far as he would ever get from the IFP/ANC conflict. His role in the war was marginal and sporadic. In 1992, he gave refuge to an IFP leader from Richmond, a man with a host of vengeful, grieving families on his tail. But that appears to be as close as Mlambo ever got to the province's political violence.

When the ballots of South Africa's first democratic election were finally counted in the first week of May 1994, Izita had voted en bloc for the ANC, and Mlambo found himself living on enemy turf. His move from Dludla had been an ill-timed one. But by then things had changed. Living in a solidly ANC area did not herald the doom and disaster he might have expected it would a few years earlier. Fearing that its election victory would drive both Zulu and Afrikaner nationalists into guerrilla warfare, the ANC played a pragmatic game with its foes. Buthelezi was coaxed into post-apartheid South Africa with the promise of a senior cabinet post, and the country's new constitution guaranteed the amakhosi a place on the government's payroll. So the likes of Mlambo were saved by the carefully bargained compromises that shaped the first years of South African democracy.

Nonetheless, being a member of the IFP in an area that had voted overwhelmingly for the former enemy was not good for business. A few months after the election, a group of ANC youths quietly called for a boycott of Mlambo's bottle store. A few weeks after that, word got round that his taxis were out of bounds. Just before Christmas, his shop was looted. Ever the pragmatist, Mlambo realised that his history had become an albatross around his neck. Well aware that his position in the Zulu aristocracy gave him bargaining power in the strange new politics of democratic South Africa, he began making overtures to the provincial leadership of the ANC. To his pleasant surprise, the ANC was interested, very interested.

So Paul Mlambo reinvented himself. A shrewd and intelligent man, he learned to wear the manner and the discourse of a radical democrat lightly. By the time we met in his office in the centre of Alanview, he was a past master. I asked him about unemployment in the area, and he answered in the manner of a seasoned trade unionist.

'We really feel let down ... no, "let down" is too weak a choice of words: we feel betrayed by Sappi.'

Sappi is a multinational forestry company that bought up vast chunks of the Natal midlands in the 1950s and became the area's largest employer. It is the company Jude Fowler curses every morning for robbing the midlands of its natural water and starving out its indigenous life.

'Sappi used to hire half of Izita for harvesting and trimming,'

Mlambo continued. 'Really, it fed Izita for many years. People used to work there by day, come home at night. They had an un-employment fund, a pension scheme – now all that is gone. A few years ago they retrenched their whole workforce and employed a private labour contractor to recruit workers. With the private con-tractors, you get nothing. You get hired one day at a time, at a measly wage, and the next morning they can tell you they don't need you anymore.'

Why did Sappi do this? Was there trouble in their workforce?

'Money,' he replied, holding out his hand and rubbing his thumb against his index finger. 'They wanted to cut back costs. They have no allegiance to the people of this area.'

'And farmers? Do they employ any people?'

'A handful. But not enough to make a difference.'

He was about to move on, but checked himself and went back to the question. He began to name each farmer on the Sarah-dale/Izita border, one by one.

'Kevin Jakobs, he employs maybe four or five people. Barry Cummings employs very few. He just farms cattle, and cattle is not a big employer. Mrs Draker, more than Cummings and Jakobs, but not much more. Maybe ten workers. Then there is Mr Mitchell. During harvesting, he employs quite a lot of temporary employees. Between 30 and 40 women. But he pays them peanuts. R10, some-times R12 per day. It's a sign of how poor this area is that people are prepared to work for that sort of money.

'In fact, the biggest source of income in Izita is not wages. It is old-age pensions and disability and disease funds. A few people still work in Durban, but most have come back. They sit around doing nothing.'

'Is that why Mitchell's son was killed? Because he is an unfair employer?'

Mlambo answered much too quickly, and for the first and last time, stumbled on his syntax. It was the only moment during our conversation he showed the slightest hint of discomfort. 'I really can't … I don't … I really can't say why the Mitchell son was killed. It came from out of the blue. It is a mystery to me. I really can't comment on it.'

'But it is the talking point of Izita. Everyone has theories about it. Surely you have some ideas.'

'I have some ideas, but I don't know that they get to the truth of the matter. Those people who live next to Mitchell's farm, they kept complaining to the police that he impounded their cattle as soon as they wandered past the Ndunge store. Now, beyond that store, there is a public road. It is not Mitchell's land yet. So he was stepping out of his own property to impound cattle.

'We called in the police to mediate. We wanted a meeting to sort the matter out, but it never materialised.

'So maybe that is why the son was killed,' he said, shrugging expansively. 'But I can't say for certain. It really shook me when it happened.'

It was a carefully considered answer. It acknowledged that Peter Mitchell was killed as a result of a dispute with his neighbours, but it went out of its way not to finger anybody. Dozens of peasant families lived on the Izita border, and Mitchell had impounded cattle from all over the place. In Mlambo's story, Mitchell's tenants were invisible in the crowd.

'Some people say the Mitchells inherited a very bad situation,' I said. 'They say the relationship between Lourie Steyn and his tenants was a very poor one.'

'No, no. That's not true. Steyn got on very well with those people. The Mashabanas, the Cubes, the Mabidas. No problems.'

I could understand why Mlambo was being evasive about Peter's murder. It is not an issue about which one shares confidences with a stranger. But I didn't understand why he was being disingenuous about Steyn's relationship with his tenants. He must have known very well that Steyn tried to evict the Mashabana family in the mid-1990s. I let the issue pass and moved on.

'The unemployment in the area, it brings a lot of crime for the farmers, doesn't it?'

'There are many, many young criminals in the area,' he replied, nodding in earnest agreement. 'They stole more than 100 head of cattle from Cummings. Jakobs has lost a lot of cattle too. And it is not just the farmers who face problems. In the location itself – in Izita and Location B – they steal everything they can get their hands on. Cattle, goats, even furniture. I myself have had terrible problems. During the Christmas period alone, my bottle store was broken into three times. My brother's shop, four times. It is all young boys. They steal my liquor and go and sell it in the shebeens.'

Mlambo reeled off a long list of violent crimes that had hit Izita in the last few years. Mostly, he covered the same ground as Abraham Zuma: the schoolteacher who was shot for his collection money; old man Ntshangase who was gunned down on the day he went to collect his monthly pension payment. Judiciously, Mlambo made no mention of the priest. I prodded him gently.

'Izita is a small place. The criminals are surely not anonymous. You must know who in the location makes a living from crime.'

He responded immediately. 'I have my suspicions about the Sikosana family. After each hit, the young Sikosanas disappear to Pinetown. You do not see them for another six months. Then suddenly they are back, and then there is another hit, and they are gone again. It makes one suspicious. I have no clear evidence, and nor do the police, but it is an odd coincidence, don't you think?'

The Sikosanas were among the oldest and most respected families in Izita, and I am not sure why Mlambo was making mischief for them. Maybe he was privately amusing himself – throwing out wild and scandalous accusations in front of a researcher on whom names would be lost. A few days later, I phoned the patriarch of the Sikosana family, an octogenarian who had left the area and lived in the Pietermaritzburg township of Edendale.

'Talk to *me* about Izita,' the old man chuckled. 'My ideas for that place were thrown out the window long ago. If you are interested in archaeology, you can come and dig me up. If your work concerns the present, I will only waste your time.'

I twisted the old man's arm into meeting me anyhow, but when I arrived at his house in Edendale it was empty. I still have no idea why Mlambo wanted to finger the Sikosanas for a series of murders.

I believe that when Mlambo complained of the anarchic youth of Izita and the persistence of violent crime, he was being entirely sincere. A man who lives in a place of Izita's wildness and destitution, and whose life is everywhere marked by visible signs of relative wealth, does not have an easy time. When I met Trevor Sibiya, the Alanview parliamentarian, I mentioned that I had been told of Mlambo's problems with crime.

'Small businessmen always get robbed in rural areas,' Sibiya replied. 'Mlambo has a lot of cattle. He seldom sells his cows to anyone because he does not need to. That's what causes his subjects to believe he's rich.'

It was an obscure comment for a city boy like me to digest, but it was in fact laden with insight. I recalled a conversation I had had about two years back with Peter Delius, one of South Africa's most gifted historians. He had recently written an extraordinary book which was in part about intergenerational conflict in Sekhukhuneland, an area in the far north of South Africa nominally run by a Pedi aristocracy.

'In the old days,' Delius had told me, 'when wealth was measured in cattle, there were established ways of dealing with economic inequality. It was understood that a rich man would loan cows to a poor man, especially when it came to such crucial events as the payment of bridewealth. There were subtle, often symbolic ways of redistributing assets, and so wealth was tolerated.

'Today we are dealing with new and difficult forms of wealth – the relative wealth of a trader or a general dealer – and how a poverty-stricken community copes with this wealth is not a straightforward matter. A small-time shopkeeper can only let things go on credit so many times. At some point, he must call in his debts if he wants to make his own ends meet. So there you are: in a sea of unemployment and malnutrition, there stands a man who exudes the outward signs of prosperity and there is no way to deal with it, to make it tolerable. So he becomes a target, especially for the youth.'

Mlambo was a man wearing two albatrosses round his neck. He was not just a former Inkatha man who had cynically, transparently, swapped sides when the tide of history turned against him. He also made his money selling taxi rides and liquor to the destitute. And it appears that he was not very adept at making his wealth tolerable to his neighbours or his customers.

There are, of course, many men in the KwaZulu-Natal countryside who are both relatively well-off and hold public office with transparent cynicism, but nonetheless manage to wield a great deal of power. So why was Mlambo not one of them?

Shortly after our meeting, I interviewed John Aitcheson, a stalwart of Natal liberalism and an academic at the university in Pietermaritzburg. Aitcheson had never heard of Mlambo, but he did know a great deal about KwaZulu-Natal's petty aristocrats.

'There are all sorts of indunas – good ones and bad ones – but let me tell you a little about the nasty type,' Aitcheson said. 'He will earn a living getting kickbacks from all kinds of things: weddings, certifying birth and death certificates. He will set up various associations which demand compulsory membership and compulsory fees.'

'But to rob people in that way,' I replied, 'he surely has to wield a great deal of coercive power.'

'Coercive power, yes, but not as much as you might think. A lightly armed group of men can wield immense power in a rural village. But the induna would have to exact resources to pay for them. His young henchmen have no principled allegiance to him. The moment he can't reward them, or the moment they sense he is losing his grip on power and that defending him might not be worth the risk, they abandon him or turn on him. So a fair-sized chunk of the induna's kickback money oils the wheels of his coercive machinery. And it is a precarious piece of machinery. He has to service it constantly.'

There is some evidence that Mlambo once tried to become the sort of induna Aitcheson described – and that he failed. Towards the end of my research, I went to KwaMashu, Durban's largest township, to see an elderly man whose family had rented land in Izita since the late nineteenth century. It was mid-afternoon, and dozens of children in blue school uniforms wandered up and down the dusty township streets. At every third or fourth house, a man or woman stood at the picket fence idly watching the street life outside. I knocked on the front door of a modest house, and a middle-aged woman received me and ushered me into a tiny living room. The old man was having a bath, she told me, but she would tell him I had arrived.

A large colour TV set, mounted on a waist-high pine stand, dominated the small room. American cartoons, their soundtracks booming out dubbed Zulu voices, followed one after the other as the afternoon wore on. While I waited, three generations of the old Izita family drifted in and out of the room. Two little girls, about four years old, sat in front of the set and giggled, soon got bored, and went to play in the back yard. An elderly woman set up an ironing board in the middle of the living room, her attention alternating between the clothes she was pressing and the images on the screen in front of her.

After about 90 minutes, the old man himself walked into the room. He wore shorts and no shirt, and carried in his right hand a white vest, which he only put on about two hours later, as I was leaving. He had a full head of stark white hair, and his face beamed with satisfaction. Settling into a comfortable armchair, he leaned back leisurely and began sipping a milky cup of tea. In some households, the elderly are subtly patronised: they are tolerated and humoured by those with a life to lead. This was not one of those households. The old man was thoroughly in command. The living room quietly cleared while we spoke, and the voices coming from the kitchen were respectfully hushed.

The old man had a precise memory and a sharp, mischievous wit. Events in Izita's history that I had dredged up after interminable hours of archive work rolled off his tongue all afternoon. The past was rich and sharp-edged in his hands. Each event sparkled with the copious pleasure he derived in recalling it.

When the conversation turned to Paul Mlambo, the old man's eyes lit up with insouciance. He didn't utter a bad word about Mlambo, but his careful choice of words, combined with the mischievous expression on his face, was subtly ridiculing.

'In the mid-1990s, Mlambo had a group of boys,' the old man said. 'Not many, maybe four or five. They wore their guns on their hips, where everyone could see them, and they breathed fire. At meetings, they would arrive together, surrounding Mlambo, and they would boast about their strength.' The old man sat upright in his chair, contorted his face into an expression of exaggerated arrogance and began speaking in a self-important tone. '"We can kill anyone we want to," they would say. "You think we are joking? Try and cross us and we will see who is laughing."'

'One of these boys was Mlambo's son. Not the son of his wife, an illegitimate son. Then this boy was killed, by Mr Wells, the farmer in the wheelchair. And that was it. That little gang broke up. We never saw them again.'

'What did that mean for Mlambo?'

'It meant he was very weak. You strut in with all this talk, and then your boys run away – it does not look good. After those boys fled, people broke into Mlambo's store every month. Then he himself left Izita and bought a house in Alanview. It was a bad thing to do. He lost more respect. I have not been to Izita for several months, but I hear there is a move to oust him as induna. People are saying they want somebody who is dedicated to their interests. They are tired of this man.'

A few months after my visit to the KwaMashu family, I learnt that Mlambo had been appointed to a position in government that took him away from Izita for much of his time. Izita had not treated him kindly, and he had left it behind for greater things; he was far more fluent in the discursive world of regional party politics than on Izita's mean and volatile streets. He had moved on into a world where the takings were bigger, the going easier.

*

How did the white men who gave me my first impression of Mlambo get things so utterly wrong? The man who had stood on a platform in 1994 and promised the seizure of white land, the shadowy puppet master who sat quietly backstage, masterminding a campaign to terrorise whites into abandoning their farms – who was this man?

Reading through my interview notes again, something about the language in which Mlambo was described suddenly struck a familiar chord. 'From a strict intelligence point of view,' read one note, 'there must be several layers involved in the Mitchell murder.' And another: 'It can't be a coincidence that the hit happened on the Mitchell farm; it is a springboard into the rest of the district.' The tactical metaphors, the tantalising assumptions of conspiracy, the transformation of every farm, every road into a piece on a chessboard; it dawned on me that too many of the white men who had given thought to the Mitchell murder had been trained to think in intelligence agencies, and that this was at the heart of the problem.

At first, the idea seemed a little silly. It is a running joke – especially among people who need to bring hard evidence to court – that intelligence operatives are outrageous fantasists. Reality comes to them in slivers, disembodied, out of context, and they make the most outlandish deductions to put the slivers together into a coherent story. I remember sitting in a government meeting convened to analyse the countless attacks on white farmers that had accompanied South Africa's transition to democracy. Detectives deduced the motivation for attacks by the type of weapons stolen, their value on the black market, the proximity of the crime to known vehicle-theft syndicates. Uniformed policemen discussed common denominators like time of day, proximity to a regional thoroughfare, the age of the average victim. And then the intelligence agents stood up to speak. They produced patchy biographies of a handful of convicted felons – winding, aimless stories – and finally concluded that there might or might not be, depending on how you interpreted the data, a shady national syndicate behind the majority of armed robberies on South African farms, and that x, y or z might or might not be the syndicate's kingpin.

The story of Paul Mlambo told by white men was a violent parody of intelligence work. They had spent the 1970s and 80s thinking of South Africa as a battlefield. When democracy came and their farms were hit by wave upon wave of violent crime, they assumed that while the site of battle, the tactics, the weapons and the soldiers might have changed, the same old enemy was still out there, fighting the same old war. The information that came to them from the other side of the fence was fragmentary, incoherent. It said nothing in and of itself. So they filled in the gaps, and in so doing they painted a picture that had always been in their heads.

If they doubted for a moment that their thinking was right, their understanding of Zulu culture came to their rescue. Zulus live in rigid hierarchies. Everyone owes loyalty to an all-powerful chief; nobody does anything serious off his own bat. If the civilian world is looking suspiciously like a regiment it is only because Zulus are indeed warriors; they have never known peace.

It is true that back in the mid-1990s, somebody did get up and declare that all the land from the Gudla to the trees was his. But it was not said on an ANC platform and it was not Paul Mlambo who said it. It was a member of the Macaba family, which had given Mlambo his job as Location B induna. When I told you earlier about the state of the Gudla valley when the Voortrekkers arrived there in the 1830s, I said that the Africans in the area had scattered and were living nervous lives in the woodlands and forests. There was one exception. A chief named Hlungwini presided over a fairly stable settlement, with cattle and a permanent infrastructure, along the banks of the Gudla.

For as long as anyone in the area can remember, rival clans have quarrelled over who claims direct descent from Hlungwini, and can thus make a symbolic claim to his land. The Macaba family say that they are direct descendants. The Magijimas – a prominent clan in the area – insist it is they. During apartheid, the quarrel was little more than academic; white farmers held title to the land anyhow. But when the ANC came to power and passed legislation inviting anyone who had been dispossessed of their land after 1913 to go to court to get it back, the issue suddenly became live, at least until the Macabas read the fine print and discovered that they had lost their land long before cut-off date. In the interim, the Macabas and the Magijimas threatened to file land claims. As the dispute between them escalated, both made wild and fanciful declarations about the amount of land they occupied in the mists of the past. So it was not unusual, in the mid-1990s, for a Macaba to stand up and announce that all the land from the Gudla to the trees was his.

The Mlambo myth was probably born when a paid informer crafted an edited version of the Macaba-Magijima feud for the ears of a white farmer. Maybe the informer held allegiance to one of the two clans and decided to mention neither. Maybe he surmised that his information would become more valuable if he slipped the word 'ANC' into his report. Or perhaps the farmer himself threw out Mlambo's name, and the informer read the excitement and expectation in his eyes and nodded his assent. Perhaps the informer spoke no English and the farmer strained to understand his interlocutor's Zulu.

Mlambo is far more comfortable in meetings with government agencies and agricultural unions than he is among his Izita constituents, and white farmers would have seen a lot of him, both in his capacity as an induna and then as an ANC leader. For white farmers, Mlambo was the public face of power in Izita. They had probably heard stories of his less gentlemanly propensities, and his posse of armed young men. So when the story of wild and heady land claims began circulating, they put what they reasoned to be two and two together. Their fences were taken down every night, their cattle stolen in large numbers, their vegetables pilfered by the sackful. Several of them had been shot at, one of them, Howard Wells, had been killed. Surely there was a mastermind at work here. Surely they were the target of a cynical campaign.

And so an intricately imagined universe came to life. The thieves and the arsonists who came in the night were mere foot soldiers. Behind them stood their shadowy commander, a man who had promised everything in 1994 and must now be seen to deliver. And behind him, the murky, complicated machinery of the ANC, provincial, perhaps national as well, that either turned a blind eye or gave quiet encouragement. 'My son's murder was not an isolated incident. This is a terrorist war. Mao said that when you kill one, you terrorise 10 000.'

The truth is that by the year 2000, the world on the other side of the Izita border remained utterly alien to white farmers, as opaque as it had been when Oliver Swift wrote of his enthusiastic reception in the mid-nineteenth century. To interpret the information one receives from the other side, one needs to know something of the texture of its daily life. One needs to have experienced the laughter, the anger, the sense of right and wrong that animates it. This is not something that passes between the border of Sarahdale and Izita. The information that is surreptitiously bought is the proverbial message in a bottle. It comes from nowhere. There is no way to make sense of it.

I was about to write that 'myths die hard', but the word 'myth' is bothersome: it would be imprudent to write off as pure fabrication the story white farmers told about Paul Mlambo. They were certainly wrong, amusingly so, about the past they invented for him. But there is always some truth, even in the liveliest inventions, and this one is no exception.

As you can see from the feud between the Macabas and the Magijimas over who settled first on the Kriek farms, and from the things Elias and Andile said about the Macaba's rightful ownership of the land, there was much talk among black peasants and aristocrats about returning land to its pre-colonial proprietors. With the end of apartheid, scores of people dusted off their ancient memories and plunged back into the days of Shaka, nearly 200 years past, in a crazy and unanswerable quest to prove who was first displaced from this land.

And there had indeed been a handful of clumsy and poorly conceived campaigns to occupy white-owned farms in recent years. Several of the southern midlands' small-time aristocrats, their nominal fiefdoms barren and crumbling, had seen in the end of apartheid an opportunity to shore up their dwindling power. A couple of months after Peter Mitchell's death, I met the chief of the amaZwezwe, Chief Zwanini, who presided over a derelict and overpopulated piece of land about 70 kilometres from Normandale. He had received me in a hut he called his 'interview chamber,' a fake Persian rug on the floor, heavy velvet curtains sparring with the rich afternoon sunlight. A wide-screen television set and video recorder had pride of place in the centre of the room, as if they were a family emblem or a coat of arms.

171

g through Chief Zwanini's forlorn kingdom after the
, Sergeant Nadi, who had arranged the meeting and had
..u as my translator, offered a rare observation.

'Did you notice the television set and video recorder?' he asked.

'How could I miss them?'

'Did you also notice that the room we were in has no electricity?'
Nadi turned and looked at me with bright, amused eyes. He
chuckled to himself and was silent again.

A year before I arrived in the district, Chief Zwanini had
mobilised about 100 of his subjects to occupy two white-owned
farms on the border of their territory. The invaders were to cross
the border at about 3 a.m. By sunrise, they would have erected
20-odd makeshift shacks, and anyone who wanted to remove
them would have the unenviable task of demolishing people's
homes in broad daylight.

Zwanini's plan was in essence the move of a desperate man.
About half of his land was communal property, run under his aus-
pices. The other half was held under individual title deed, and
although the owners were formally his subjects, he had little
power over them. During the decade preceding Zwanini's land
occupation plan, swathes of people had moved from the communal
section of the hapless chief's land, and had rented small plots from
the title deed holders, a subtle but bruising protest against the rule
of his indunas. His subjects disappearing from under his nose,
Zwanini believed he had one remaining bargaining card – space.
If he were to encroach on the neighbouring white farms and
expand his fiefdom, his subjects, he calculated, would abandon
their landlords and come running back to him.

As it turned out, Colin Waugh had had his suspicions about
Chief Zwanini for some time, and had bought the eyes and ears of
a member of the chief's advisory council. By the time Zwanini's
would-be land occupiers crossed the border, the whole of the
southern midlands knew of his plans, and a unit of heavily-armed
public order police greeted them at the fence. After a brief but
tense standoff, the police lobbed a tear-gas canister into the crowd,
and it retreated back into Chief Zwanini's territory.

There were other aristocrats in the area who had had their eyes
on white-owned land, some much closer to Normandale. When
the Kriek family finally sold its farms, to a large southern midlands landowner named Matthew Blair, some of the peasant

families who had lived on that land for several generations told the new proprietor that the farms were theirs, not his. Blair called a meeting with Chief Macaba to negotiate a compromise, and the old man gave Blair a stern lecture on his right to the Kriek farms and stormed out of the meeting. Later that afternoon, Blair received a death threat on his cellphone, and another the following week.

The point of these stories is to tell you that there *had* been talk in the southern midlands about taking back white-owned land. The white farmers' story about Paul Mlambo was horribly wrong. The idea of a coherent, province-wide campaign of land theft, orchestrated by a monolithic ANC government, was sheer fantasy. But the fragments from which the fantasy had been pieced together were real enough. In the scrappy, clumsy signature of parochial midlands politics, a handful of chancers had put their names to white-owned farms. And it is probably true to say that Peter Mitchell would still be alive if talk about taking back land were not in the air. It was part of the new mood of the times; the old paternalistic relationship, the one Mitchell assumed to be alive and well when he went down to Langeni to address his tenants, had vanished with apartheid. The new breed Mitchell addressed at the side of the road was no longer convinced that white proprietorship of the countryside was inevitable. They believed they could do something to end it. In that sense, white farmers were right. Their title deeds no longer carried the weight they did a decade before.

So, looking at their inventions generously, you could say that white farmers caught a whiff of the new fragrance of black life in the countryside. They tried to elaborate on what their instincts told them by talking about specific names and plans and deeds, and that is where they began to wander from reality.

And yet even in regard to Mlambo specifically, one would be too hasty to talk of myths. Farmers invented a crazy history for him, it is true, and attributed to him powers he only possessed in his wildest dreams. But their suspicions about him were not entirely without foundation.

Mlambo was close to some of the Langeni tenants. As you will see, one of those who was briefly to stand accused of orchestrating Peter's murder also sat on a 'council' Mlambo had convened in Izita. While I do not know for sure, it is hardly fanciful to conceive that in the aftermath of Peter's murder Mlambo may well have been in a position to take a very educated guess at who had done it, but chose to say nothing. So the question of Mlambo's culpability is indeed an issue in this story, but not in the way that his nemeses would like to imagine.

In May 2000, a group of white farmers met Mlambo and told him to his face they believed he had encouraged the murder of Peter Mitchell. By the accounts I heard, Mlambo was shaken by the meeting and told several people that he feared for his life. I am told that the day after the meeting, an angry and distraught Mlambo cursed Arthur Mitchell. 'The idiot!' he is reported to have said. 'He buys a piece of land, behaves like a clown and gets his son killed. *I* am expected to come and clean up the mess. And if I don't, I am blamed for the murder. Fuck him. I will not clean up his mess.'

You will see precisely what is meant by this outburst when I tell you about Mitchell's tenants' account of their meetings with him. The outburst betrays a particularly brutal and jaundiced sense of Mitchell's own moral culpability. But that is still to come. For the moment, what is interesting about Mlambo's reported comment is the perspective it contains, a perspective the farmers on the Izita border could never countenance. Perhaps there is no need to think of conspiracy and political intrigue in understanding the murder of Peter Mitchell? Perhaps the story begins and ends with what happened between the tenants, Lourie Steyn and Arthur Mitchell. White farmers were constitutionally incapable of grasping that possibility.

THIRTEEN

On a night in early April 2000, two police cars mounted the hill that overlooks Langeni. Louis Wessels, the investigating officer of the Mitchell murder to whom I introduced you earlier, ordered the drivers of the two cars to turn off their headlights and cut their engines. They coasted silently down the hill and ground to a halt in the darkness outside the Cube kraal. Minutes later, seven of Mitchell's tenants were lined up in front of the two cars. The headlights were turned on and Wessels shouted at the tenants, telling them to fix their eyes on the blinding light beams. This was an old, rural improvisation on the one-way mirror into which the suspects in an urban crime find themselves staring. Behind the safety of the lights, an anonymous witness pointed out and named two men. They were Mduduzi Cube – the eldest of the three Cube brothers – and Vusi Mabida – no relation to Ngwane, the petty thief Wessels once believed shot Peter Mitchell. Mabida was 20 years old and lived with his mother on Mitchell's land. After a thorough search of the Cube kraal, the police confiscated two weapons: a licensed pistol and a home-made .303-calibre rifle.

The two men were driven to a police station and charged with the murder of Peter Mitchell. At their bail application the following morning, they were denied bail and sent back to their cells – a standard procedure for those against whom there is a cursorily credible charge of premeditated murder.

I am not at liberty to tell you who the witness in the car was, nor the precise details of how the police found themselves on the trail of Cube and Mabida. A staggeringly naïve policeman – Will Sullivan, whom you have also already met – handed me a file full of affidavits, even though he did not know me from a bar of soap. The affidavits were signed by men who had betrayed Cube and

Mabida, and whose lives may well be in danger if the things they said to the police become known among the Langeni tenants.

What I can tell you is that the arrests of Cube and Mabida were the culmination of some uncharacteristically adroit police work on the part of Wessels and his colleagues. They had confined their initial enquiries – the ones that led them to believe that Ngwane was their man – to Izita, but they were looking in the wrong place. Clermont, the large urban township outside Durban, is where they finally found their pot of gold.

The investigators would have found their trail thanks to a pretty sound knowledge of contemporary rural sociology. It is true that many black men and women born to peasant families in the second half of the twentieth century live transitory lives, wandering between their rural homes and the shack settlements and townships of the cities. But it is also true that they keep travelling the same well-worn grooves. The members of a rural family will generally find employment in just one or two urban businesses. They will establish themselves as gatekeepers to their tiny segment of the urban labour market, and before long, their urban colleagues will consist largely of people with whom they grew up in the countryside. They will frequent the same shebeens, use the same transport routes, and find homes in the same neighbourhoods.

A detective with enough time and patience to discover this micro-history has done well. He knows which parts of the city to sniff around in, which clan and family names to look out for. Before long, he has stumbled across some careless banter exchanged in a shebeen; offers to sell an expensive .45 pistol like the one Peter was carrying when he was killed; the drunken boasting of an inattentive young man.

Of course, the story is not quite as pretty and seamless as that. Getting a number of people to sign sworn affidavits about the identity of murderers does not come easy. 'Solving a murder where the witnesses are black is a curse,' Sullivan told me. 'You have to treat every witness like a suspect. You have to squeeze them.'

*

Wessels spent three or four interminable sessions with Mduduzi Cube in the interrogation room, and he came out with nothing. The detective walked into the room clutching his file of hard-earned affidavits, and he threw every fragment of evidence he had at his suspect. Cube was silent throughout. He sat there, impervious as a stone.

'This was a hard, hard man,' Sullivan told me. 'Four out of five suspects will slip up at some time. You bombard them with words, hour after hour, and soon they begin talking, and that's when you start to win. Speech is a sign of fear, and once there is fear in the room, things are going your way. Cube was the one-in-five. He never opened his mouth.'

Sullivan's words were double-edged. He admired Cube for his strength, but, between the lines, he also berated Wessels for his weakness. 'Perhaps if I had had a crack at him …' Sullivan said. 'The stuff we had against him was pretty damning.' Later, when I tell you more about Sullivan, you will see that his relationship with Wessels was an interesting one: Sullivan subtly scorned Wessels for his incompetence, but he was also jealously protective of his frail colleague – by the time I met Sullivan, Wessels was in deep trouble.

Listening to this second-hand account of Mduduzi Cube's performance in the interrogation room, my imagination stirred and embellished the scene with the things I knew about him. The Cube family's historical memory reaches back three generations. Beyond that, everything is blank. They do not know why their forebears migrated south during the course of the nineteenth century. As I told you earlier, it must be an interesting tale, for most Cubes never moved as far south as the southern midlands. Something unusual must have happened to this family five or six generations ago. The Cubes do know that their grandparents were the children of tenants on white-owned land on the Sarahdale/Izita border. So by the time Mduduzi – and his brothers, Peter and Prince – came of age, the Cube family had for at least three, probably four generations, taken part in that endless and intricate process of negotiating and renegotiating their relationship with their landlords. The whole history of that awkward relationship was in Mduduzi's blood. The thousand forms of silent encroachment, the countless punishments for a cruel farmer, the whole gamut of wordless games by which peasants tested the limits of the rules governing their lives, all this was woven into the fabric of his upbringing.

The Cubes had not lived on Normandale for long – not by the

measure of a century, at any rate. Mduduzi was born in 1961 on a farm adjacent to Normandale owned by a family called Porter. His father and grandfather were also born on the Porter farm. His grandfather is buried there, his father on Normandale. You will remember the story of Bebetu's son, the young farmer who stopped his black neighbours from using his maize grinder and had the throats of several of his cattle slit in return. That is the Porter farm.

According to the Cubes, some time in the 1960s, when Mduduzi was a young boy, the Porters asked the Cubes to leave their land and move to Normandale. The Porter business was expanding, and they required the land the Cubes had been working since the beginning of the century. In exchange for moving, Porter said, he would give seven bags of maize to the Cube family at the end of every harvest, to compensate them for the land they were losing. The exchange worked well for a few years, until Lourie Steyn bought Normandale in 1969. When Steyn settled at Normandale, he struck a deal with Porter to buy the piece of land on the Porter farm that the Cubes had once occupied – the land that produced their seven bags of maize. In accordance with many generations of tradition, the negotiations between the white men trumped the verbal agreement between landlord and tenants, and in 1969 the Porters delivered the last of the seven bags of maize to the Cubes.

I don't know whether the Cube family suffered terribly when Porter reneged on the deal and the bags of maize stopped coming to Langeni. But I do know that the incident has enormous symbolic import in the family history the Cubes relate to their friends. By their lights, their very presence on the Mitchell farm is a product of trickery. That Mduduzi's father is buried on Normandale is the result of an act of deceit – one of the countless deceptions they say shaped the family's trajectory during the course of the twentieth century. By the Cubes' telling of it, the last time they had the freedom to bury their forebears on ground of their choosing was somewhere in the forgotten past, before they were labour tenants.

Several people promised to introduce me to Mduduzi Cube. I told them that I would only meet him if he knew that I was writing a book about the murder of Peter Mitchell, and that it was not my aim to defend him against the charges and accusations that had been levelled at him. After this, each offer of an introduction was withdrawn. Nobody knew for certain what I would say in my book, and nobody wanted to be associated with something that might earn his wrath.

One of the people who offered and then rescinded the offer to take me to Mduduzi told me an interesting story. He and Mduduzi were talking of the Cube family history, and when Mduduzi told the tale of the move to Normandale and the betrayal around the bags of maize, my informant shook his head in sympathy. Mduduzi smiled impishly. 'You know the older generation,' he said. 'They were cowards. Every time I visit my father's grave, I shout at him for agreeing to that crazy deal.'

It was one of the most suggestive and illuminating comments I had heard during the course of my research. Mduduzi and his brothers may have constituted the third or fourth generation of a tenant family, but they were unlike any of their forebears. They were no longer men of the old paternalistic relationship between white and black, not in any meaningful sense. In their late teens, they had drifted to Clermont, and that is the experience that formed them. The burgeoning trade union movement of the 1970s, the heady days of urban insurrection in the mid-1980s, the violent war with Inkatha, the growing power of organised crime in South African cities – these things had moulded the identities of the men Mitchell addressed at the side of the road after he bought Normandale.

Between Mduduzi and his father lay a gulf wider than any that had divided previous generations. It is true that the old man would have honed an impressive arsenal of weapons in his quest to use as much of the countryside as he could. But even on the furthest horizon his imagination could conjure, the land would still be owned by the whites. And so he would never have gone for his master's jugular. He would have accepted the white man's encroachments with a respectful nod, retreated into his hard shell and negotiated things from there.

Mduduzi's generation, in contrast, imagined the whole countryside torn apart and put together again. And when democracy came and they were still the tenants of white landlords, they began to fight a scrappy and opportunistic campaign. They learned the country's new laws quickly, and they used them as hardened and brutal men do. When the landlord tried to change the rules, they would apply for a pro bono lawyer and haul the white man in front of a judge. When two white policemen came looking for them in the night, they would be at the local police station first thing the next morning, laying charges against the landlord, as one equal citizen does with a complaint against another. And when they found themselves in an interrogation room, a charge of murdering the landlord's son before them, they would use the most powerful weapon constitutional democracy handed them: silence.

*

Mduduzi did break his silence to tell Wessels one thing: he sat on a committee that discussed Izita matters, and the committee was chaired by Paul Mlambo. I spent a long time trying to get to the bottom of this committee and where it came from. White farmers, when they heard what Cube had said, called it an ANC committee; the police said it was a 'traditional' committee. I eventually discovered that Paul Mlambo had convened this structure in his capacity as induna. Formally, it was the mechanism by which a petty aristocrat consults his subjects. Informally, it appears to have been a forum through which a remote and increasingly powerless leader keeps his ear to the ground.

For white farmers, it was confirmation that Peter Mitchell's murder was the work of a political conspiracy. Mduduzi's face was not known by white farmers in the area. They knew his brothers Peter and Prince, but many of them only noted his existence after he was charged with Mitchell's murder. 'He was a political plant,' I was told. 'He came in under orders.'

For me, Mduduzi's position on Mlambo's committee only confirmed that Mlambo probably knew a great deal more about the circumstances surrounding Mitchell's death than he would care to admit. There is another reason, which I will share with you soon, why Mduduzi would suddenly have taken an active role in Langeni's affairs after Mitchell bought Normandale, and I find it far more compelling than the conjectures of the white farmers.

*

Wessels claimed to have had a lot more luck with the younger, more impressionable man, Vusi Mabida. By the end of their second interview, Wessels and his investigating team said, the youngster

180

had signed a damning affidavit. I read it at a tacky restaurant table at Durban International Airport, Will Sullivan opposite me, looking nervous, fidgety and very young. In the affidavit, Mabida said he watched Peter Mitchell as he died. He said Mduduzi's 20-year-old son, Bheki Cube, pulled the trigger, that the shotgun used to kill Peter had once belonged to the Mitchells, and that it was stolen from their jeep one day down at the river. He said that Mduduzi was not there when Peter was killed, but that he gave the two boys the weapon, and told them where to go and what to do.

A few months after Mabida signed his confession, I had breakfast with a seasoned old detective. 'How common is it for a police detective to hit a suspect across the face?' I asked.

The detective swiped at an imagined face with the back of his open hand, hard and snappy like an elastic band. 'Like that?'

'Yes,' I replied.

'The trick is to use it only when it will work. Never hit an older man. He will consider it an insult and will lose respect for you. But a youngster – late teens, early twenties – that is a different story. Hit him at the right moment and his memories of childhood will come flooding back to him. He will soon become a small, humiliated boy, standing before a figure of authority. If you have stripped him naked, it is even more effective. He will talk to you. He will need to confess, like you are his father.'

I was in Johannesburg when news of the arrests and of Mabida's confession broke. Whenever I stayed away from Sarahdale for a long period, I would phone Arthur Mitchell from my office in downtown Johannesburg every once in a while. I usually phoned late, after the end of the working day. It was early winter then, and by six in the evening the thick and intimate ambience of the Highveld's twilight would permeate my office. Everyone else had gone home, and there was absolute silence. In those early evenings, I felt as if I had been sucked into a vacuum; there was just Mitchell's voice, nothing else, and I was close enough to feel the subtlety in its tones and the messages they encoded.

At first, the words Mitchell chose were as thin and prudent as ever. He said he was delighted that the two men were behind bars, and was confident that Bheki Cube – named on the affidavit as the one who pulled the trigger – would soon join them. A huge burden had been lifted from his shoulders, he said, and the morning Cube and Mabida woke up in jail, the world seemed different to him.

181

Yes, Peter was still dead and nothing would bring him back, but there was something sweet in justice nonetheless.

The words were predictable enough, but the manner of the delivery was like nothing I had heard from Mitchell before. There was an unexpected lightness in his voice. Soon he was babbling a little, the words flowing with a freedom to which I was unaccustomed.

'I employed them both when they were schoolboys, you know', Mitchell told me. 'The young ones. Bheki Cube and Vusi Mabida. It was about five years ago. I lived in Durban then and farmed on the weekends. I would come over on a Saturday to dip cattle. The youngsters would come and help until lunch time.'

'What were they like?'

'They were nice.' Mitchell chuckled cynically as he spoke. He saw irony and humour now in things that had once only pained him. 'I had no aggro from them. No problems.

'But I have another memory of the young Cube boy. It's amazing how things get stored up in your brain and then something triggers them and they come back to you. The day after Peter was killed, I went to Langeni to tell the women there that I would no longer employ them. As I once told you, the place was deserted that morning. The men who hang out in the Tearoom had vanished. The door of the Tearoom was standing slightly ajar. As I was driving by, this face peered out at me. It was the young Cube and he was smiling at me. A nasty smile. A smirk. I forgot all about it until I was told that he killed my son.'

The lightness stayed in Mitchell's voice when he told this story, and I was surprised by this because it was truly one of the darkest stories I had heard in a long time. It reminded me of an essay by the American philosopher George Kateb I had recently read. Kateb asked why it is that politicians commit evil, ordering the deaths of men and women they have never met from the comfort of their war rooms and their offices. The idea that there is a dark side to their natures, he said, that the underbellies of their souls take pleasure in death, is facile and silly. Nor does it make sense to argue that they know what they are doing and do it anyway. One cannot erect a scale and measure the value of winning against the tragedy of killing the innocent. Such things are incommensurable; they do not fit on the same scale.

Is it not more plausible and more interesting to wonder whether they have simply made an error? Kateb asked. They sit there with their maps and their advisors, and their heads are filled with the rules of a tactical game. The logic of the game abstracts from the value of individual human lives and the tragedy of human deaths. Killing here is registered simply as an instrument in the game, a tool. A president who orders death is drunk on the game. In that moment, there are no human beings, just pieces on a chessboard.

As Mitchell told his story, I thought of the young Cube's smirk and of Kateb's essay, and I wondered whether the young man was not like the president in Kateb's imagination. Twenty years is old enough to absorb what it means for a father to lose his son. To look the father in the eye and smirk is to have forgotten that knowledge. It was an eerie thought, a thought about madness: the tactical manoeuvres in the tussle between landlord and tenants had become the only reality, and killing just another way of winning.

I asked Mitchell what he planned to do now, and the question drained the conversation of its lightness. Something of the tone with which I had become familiar returned.

'I am going to write to the Department of Land Affairs and inform them that I plan to evict the families of the men charged with killing my son. I will also tell them that all negotiations to sell Langeni to Land Affairs, so that they can give it to the tenants, are off.'

'Why? Why punish them all?'

'Because they all had common cause,' Mitchell replied, his voice now as dark as it had ever been. 'They killed my son by omission. They all wanted him dead. That is why not a single soul warned us beforehand. If just one of them had thought that what was about to happen was wrong, we would have been told.'

You will recall that when Mitchell first met with his tenants, he suggested that they might apply to the Department of Land Affairs to take ownership of Langeni. He was speaking of one of the clauses in South Africa's new land reform legislation – the willing-buyer-willing-seller clause. A group of landless families earmarks a piece of land they would like to own. The Department of Land Affairs offers the owner a market-related price for it. The farmer agrees, and Land Affairs buys the land and hands it over to the claimants. At that first meeting, Mitchell's tenants rejected the offer. What difference would it make if they owned their pathetic little ghetto, they said. After Peter was killed, Land Affairs sent a team to Langeni to conduct a rights inquiry. They told the tenants they had no right to Mitchell's land, but that they could invoke the willing-buyer-willing-seller clause and see if he was prepared to sell.

Now Mitchell was telling me he had retracted his previous offer and negotiations were off. I struggled with what he was telling me. On the one hand, I did not like the tone in his voice. It was too menacing, too vindictive. And yet I also strained to put myself in his shoes. To sell to the ones he thought had connived to kill his son – that would not come easily.

Later in the conversation, Mitchell began to talk about farming – for the first time in a long time; buying cattle to replenish the herd that had been stolen over the years; mending the fences that had been torn down. I realised then that what was going on between Mitchell and his tenants was quite simple, really. They had tried to push him off his farm and rob him of his vocation, and now the idea of farming that land the way he had done before his son died contained the most meaning he was ever going to squeeze out of his life. I also realised that his tenants would never leave him in peace. Whenever he dipped a cow, mended a fence or planted a seed, he would be getting his revenge. They would haunt him in the taking of his every pleasure.

Thinking now of that telephone conversation with Mitchell, of his lightness and the future he had begun to imagine, I feel a great deal of pity for him. Neither of us knew then that Louis Wessels had made an awful hash of things. Vusi Mabida's self-incriminating affidavit, the one Sullivan showed me, is called a section 204 statement. A 204 is a nasty piece of work; it dangles the prospect of freedom in front of the accused, but he can only grab it by betraying his accomplices. In the witness box, he repeats the things he wrote in the 204, and if the magistrate is convinced he has told the full story, and if his evidence convicts his co-accused, he walks free.

Naturally, the decision to sign a 204 is a fraught one; the confessor is haunted by guilt and regret. In the empty and interminable days before his trial, there are times he wishes he could undo his deed. It is thus common practice in the South African detective service to get the betrayer to sign his dark pact in front of a magistrate. That way, the law has witnessed the deed; there is no ambiguity, no backtracking.

There was no magistrate present when Mabida signed his 204

with a thumbprint; only Wessels and his assistant were there. A few days later, Mduduzi Cube found Mabida a defence lawyer, who had his client sign another affidavit. I have confessed to nothing, it read. The detectives beat me and forced me to put my thumb to a blank piece of paper. They must have filled in the rest, long after I was back in my cell.

So, a week after the arrests, Wessels found himself back at square one. He had no weapon, no witnesses and no confession. The other affidavits – the ones picked up in Clermont – were enough to arrest a suspect, enough to use against him in the interrogation room, but they were insufficient to bring anyone to trial.

I will probably never know what really happened in the interrogation room between Louis Wessels and Vusi Mabida. I have spoken to several people who know the South African detective service well – defence lawyers, judges, detectives – and they all agree that it is a close one to call. Perhaps Mabida did confess. Perhaps Wessels was afraid that by the time he had arranged for a magistrate, his suspect would have changed his mind, and so he got him to sign his thumbprint there and then. Or perhaps Mabida's subsequent affidavit tells the truth. I don't know.

*

They came for Bheki Cube shortly after nightfall on a Tuesday in May. They brought with them a few rolls of boerewors, a selection of beefsteaks and a crate of beer. There is an abandoned hall on the Sarahdale/Izita border, about seven or eight kilometres from Langeni along the district road. The skeletal frame still stands, but the flesh of the building has long been eroded by neglect. They settled in there at about seven in the evening, cooked their meat and drank their beer. It was close to midwinter and very cold, and they could not light a big fire for fear of making themselves conspicuous. It was an uncomfortable and unpleasant evening.

The white South African braaivleis is a portable ritual. Its customary place is a family's Sunday lunch, but it has other uses too. Read the volumes of the Truth Commission report, or the journals of white soldiers in Angola, or the memories of riot police on township duty, and you will find that it has often strayed from the suburbs and taken its place on the front line of South Africa's racial conflict; a pre-battle affirmation of one's pedigree and one's purpose.

There were five men around the braaivleis. Louis Wessels was there, and his junior partner, David Uys. So was Will Sullivan and another white detective by the name of Justin van Gas. The fifth was Wessels's black informer, Vuyo. He was to act as translator in the crucial interrogation of Bheki Cube.

The stakes were high. The two men in jail were due for their second bail hearing, and if all Wessels could show for the three weeks of his suspects' detention was a dubious statement, there was little doubt that the presiding magistrate would let them go. So if the detectives got nothing from Bheki, they would lose Vusi and Mduduzi as well. Yet, on the face of it, their task was not inordinately difficult. The young suspect need not know the niceties of the admissibility of Vusi's statement. Wessels could take it out of his bag, this very official-looking document, and Vuyo could translate it back into Zulu with much ceremony. By the time he was done, Bheki would believe that the case was wrapped up. The weapon, they would tell him. That is your saving grace. Show us where it is, and things might go easier for you.

The men packed up their braaivleis at around midnight, and drove to the summit of the hill that overlooks Langeni. Like the time before, they cut the engine and the lights and rolled silently down the hill. They had been told that Bheki would be there that night, and they knew that Langeni had no electricity. The tenants go to bed early, and by 12:30, most of the valley's inhabitants would be sleeping deeply.

The men summonsed Bheki from his bed and guided him outdoors. Wessels and Vuyo each grabbed an arm and escorted him into the night, to a secluded place behind the Cube kraal. It was almost an hour before they returned.

Everyone in Izita and Sarahdale has a version of what happened next. I will begin with Bheki's mother's version, which I heard second-hand. The two policemen who had taken Bheki away – the black man and one of the four whites – returned to the kraal with the youngster. Bheki stayed in the shadows, behind the policemen, and she could not see her son's face. The white one began speaking in Afrikaans to his colleagues. One of them went away and returned with a spade, and Bheki led them to a patch of ground on the Cube kraal and nodded. The policeman with the spade handed it to Bheki and he began digging, the policemen surrounding him in a circle, smoking cigarettes and talking among themselves in Afrikaans.

'What is he doing?' Mrs Cube asked the black man.

'That is where the shotgun is buried,' he replied. 'The murder weapon.'

The boy dug three or four holes around the kraal, and the policemen's voices grew more and more agitated, and they began to shout at Bheki and to curse him. They took the spade away, and the two who had disappeared with him earlier disappeared with him again, and when they returned half an hour later, the five policemen stood in a huddle and talked quietly. The huddle dispersed and three of the white policemen took Bheki and the spade and left the Cube kraal, crossed the district road, and began walking into the darkness of the old Kriek property. Again, Mrs Cube asked the black man what was happening, and he said that Bheki had told them there was another gun, one that had also been fired at the scene of the murder, buried on the Kriek land across the road.

A few minutes later, Mrs Cube heard shots, a short volley, too close together to count how many. She waited a long time, listening for activity on the other side of the road, pleading over and over to see her son. After a long, excruciating wait, the black man sat down beside her and said that her son was dead.

*

According to the report Louis Wessels filed the following day, Bheki had told him that he had taken a nine-mill. pistol to the scene of Peter's murder and that Vusi had shot one round from it when Peter's jeep came to a standstill. Bheki, Wessels continued, had said the gun was buried in a plastic bag in an abandoned hut, and he had taken three of the detectives to the hut and begun digging through the floor. After a short time the detectives heard the rustling of plastic, and then Bheki stood up, tore away the plastic bag and cocked the gun. The three detectives drew their weapons and opened fire. Bheki died instantly.

By law, whenever somebody dies at the hands of the police, the case is investigated, not by the police themselves but by the Independent Complaints Directorate. Several hundred people die in police custody and through police action every year, and the ICD is a scrawny organisation with meagre resources and a tiny staff. In reality, it investigates a small fraction of the cases itself.

The rest are handled by police detectives under ICD 'supervision', a polite and legally acceptable way of saying that the directorate is incapable of investigating the case, that a bit of formal paperwork will be done and then the case will be filed and forgotten.

The Bheki Cube killing was one of those the ICD did investigate. The directorate is staffed by a crew of human rights activists, the sort of people who fought the police tooth-and-nail under apartheid. A case like this one, where the detectives are white and old school, the suspect is a young black tenant, and the scene smacks of assassination – it is precisely the sort of case that excites the overworked investigators at the ICD. The directorate's investigators made a lot of noise around Langeni. They asked many questions, and when they were done they handed each tenant their business cards and told them that when the police came round again they should answer no questions, but phone the ICD instead. For this, they earned the wrath of Will Sullivan and Arthur Mitchell, and confirmed the latter's belief that constitutional democracy is designed to ensure that murderers go free. But beyond annoying a couple of white men, the investigators did little else.

Since every eyewitness was telling the same story, the investigators had little of evidentiary value to work with. They commented that the hole they found in the abandoned hut on the Krieks' old farm was suspiciously shallow, consistent with a hole dug in great haste. They said that Bheki's dead body was bruised, consistent with a recent beating. They were surprisingly brief on the countless guidelines the detectives broke when their suspect led them to the weapon.

The guidelines do not carry the force of legal stipulations. They are there to help the prosecutor win his case in court, to show the magistrate that the manner in which the police found their evidence was clean and above board. One of these guidelines suggests that the suspect remain cuffed. He may point out the place the weapon is buried, but the detectives themselves must do the digging. Another stipulates that the scene be videotaped, not by one of the detectives investigating the case, but by a police cameraman with no knowledge of it. There are certain things in particular that must be recorded on video: the questioning of the suspect, the suspect's response, key landmarks on the journey to the scene, the suspect's directions to the precise location of the evidence, and the discovery of the evidence itself. Aside from the cameraman, another officer who is not involved in the investigation should also be present at the scene. Both he and the cameraman must sign affidavits confirming that the evidence on video is indeed what it seems.

Every one of these guidelines was disregarded on the night Bheki Cube was killed. But in a police force like South Africa's, that could mean any number of things.

There is little doubt that many South African suspects are executed by police officers. There are established codes of silence and omission, a collective knowledge of the rules and how best to conceal the moment when they are broken. Several policemen have said as much to my face. A few months before Bheki Cube was killed, I found myself in the station commissioner's office in a farflung district of the Free State. I was reading a pile of case dockets, all of them armed robberies committed on white-owned farms. Time and again, when the suspects were apprehended at the scene of the crime – by police reservists, or soldiers, or simply by white neighbours – a shoot-out ensued and the suspects were killed.

Reading one particular case, I looked up at the station commissioner, who was buried in paperwork behind his desk, and asked him some questions. 'The docket says the suspects opened fire on the police reservists and neighbours who rushed to the scene. It says the apprehenders returned fire in self-defence. Is there any evidence of this?' I asked. 'Were cartridges from the suspects' weapons found on the scene?'

The station commissioner, an enormous man with countless braais and beers under his belt, kept writing, the subtle trace of a smile about his mouth. He put down his pen carefully, held the paper on which he had been writing up to the light, as if to check for a watermark or a hidden sign, put the paper down and smiled at me, a patronising and scornful smile.

'Mr Steinberg,' he said. 'If the Constitutional Court had not abolished the death penalty, I suspect that those suspects would be down here in the holding cells, waiting for their trial.' His office was a parody of government-issue décor: wooden school furniture and heavily waxed vinyl floors. His boots squeaked noisily against the vinyl as he rearranged his bulk. 'But you know what?' He leaned forward and looked at me aggressively. 'I never bothered to find out.'

He shuffled the papers in front of him, picked up his pen and resumed work. But my questions still niggled at him, and a minute or two later he lifted his head from his work and stared at me menacingly.

'What?'

'If, Mr Steinberg, if the courts were functioning properly, and if the law assisted the prosecutor rather than the defence, then I would go down on my hands and knees looking for spent cartridges. But as things stand, I have other work to do.'

At the most abstract and cursory level, the killing of Bheki Cube fits the station commissioner's bill. As the night wears on, and each hole the youngster digs turns out empty, the investigating officer feels the case slipping from his hands. He thinks he has his man, but the rules of evidence and confession have wrapped him in their web and he is no longer in control. And yet the guilty one is here, right in front of him; it is night and the place is quiet and deserted.

I have my own ideas about what happened in the abandoned hut on the old Kriek farm. I must wait until Will Sullivan returns to these pages before I can tell you in full, because I gleaned much of the story from the expression on his face and the tone of his voice. For the moment, let me say that what happened was complicated and emotionally fraught. I very much doubt that the policemen in that hut had a premeditated a plan to kill their suspect.

I never shared these doubts with Izita people, because if I had, I would probably have been ejected from their homes and sent on my way. Bheki Cube was killed in the early hours of a Wednesday morning. By Saturday, everybody knew about it. And they were all saying the same thing: 'The Cube son was killed by the white man whose son was killed.' I say 'everybody', rather than 'all of Izita', because the routes that such news travels are complicated. There are old Izita families now living in KwaMashu, in Edendale and in Clermont, and by Saturday morning, one or another version of the story was at all of their breakfast tables.

One of the people I had employed to get information for me lived in KwaMashu, more than 150 kilometres from Izita. On the Friday after the killing, I phoned him, and asked him to visit every one of the Izita homes in KwaMashu we had found during the course of our research. He visited three homes the following day, and in each one the conversation revolved around the homeboy who had been shot dead by the white man. Some said the farmer himself pulled the trigger. Others said that he paid two white policemen from Durban to assassinate the youngster. Still others said that the policemen had a braai on Mitchell's front porch after they killed the Cube boy.

An idea came to me which at first struck me as too trite to write down. In Izita, the Cube killing had already begun to play the precise role the Mitchell killing had played among white farmers in Sarahdale. It took its place in the annals of myth before the body was cold. It fanned out and absorbed everything and became an icon of all that was wrong in South Africa's young democracy. A strange thought came to me. If I had been black and had begun my research in June 2000, the narrative you are reading would have been reversed. I would have started with a racist white farmer and his old-school policemen who roamed the countryside with their guns blazing as if apartheid had never died. Perhaps I would have befriended some whites to speak to the white farmer for me, and as the narrative progressed through the layers of my discovery, the story would have grown more complicated, more troublesome.

As it happened, Mitchell himself did more than anyone to shape Izita's myths about the death of Bheki Cube.

*

I met Mitchell on the Saturday after Bheki was killed, at about the same time my colleague was driving around KwaMashu visiting the homes of Izita families. By now, my meetings with Mitchell had become tightly ritualised. We met in Colin Waugh's lounge on a Saturday morning, Colin's Eton-thin sandwiches before us, our backdrop the slightly hysterical tempo of disobedient dogs and a grumpy teenage step-daughter.

Mitchell was in the bathroom when I arrived, and I began chatting to Colin about Bheki's death. Always a perceptive and well-armed man, Colin quickly reversed the journalist-subject relationship, and he watched me studiously as I answered his questions.

'Well, Colin,' I said, 'they broke every procedure in the book and that in itself is cause for much suspicion.'

'Yes, indeed,' he replied. 'Which broken procedures bother you in particular?'

'No cameraman, for instance. And why was Cube not cuffed?

That is very odd. One of them could have dug for the weapon.'

'What the hell do you expect? A film crew in the middle of the bush?' The voice was Mitchell's, not Waugh's, and it came from the passageway that leads off from the lounge. There was viciousness in it, and accusation. I had never heard Mitchell speak that way before.

He entered the room and instantly calmed himself, recovering the soft-spoken manner to which I was accustomed. He greeted me warmly, asked how I was, and settled into the chair he had sat in the day I met him, when he had told his story from beginning to end.

Colin and I were silent, and Mitchell took the cue that the floor was his.

'The detectives had tea at my place on Tuesday,' he said. 'They are hard-working boys. It's not easy. So why not make their lives a little more comfortable?'

It was a strange and awkward opening, a clearing of the throat, and Colin and I sat impassively and waited for more.

'On Wednesday morning, I went down to my irrigation fields,' Mitchell continued. 'I said to my labourers on Wednesday morning, I said: "The Cubes took my son, now the good Lord has taken one of theirs."' His upper lip was taut with tension as he spoke. If he took any pleasure in what he said, it was lost among more haunting and difficult emotions. 'There was general delight among my labourers. But that was irrelevant. I was sending a message to the Cubes.'

*

Not long after the Cube killing, Louis Wessels and his junior David Uys were suspended from the Carton Bay Murder and Robbery Squad and criminal charges were laid against them. Believe it or not, the detectives' trouble had nothing to do with Cube's death. They stood accused of fraud. The fund from which the squad paid its informers was suddenly empty, and the charge was that Wessels and Uys had spent months dipping their fingers into it. Wessels booked himself into the police psychiatric hospital in Pretoria and was diagnosed with chronic stress. Whether he willed his illness or whether the prospect of sitting in the dock genuinely made him ill, I do not know. But Wessels was exempt from attending his own trial – which drags on as I write – on the grounds that he was too sick and unstable to be there.

The Mitchell case was handed to a Carton Bay Murder and Robbery detective by the name of Ben Steenkamp. Steenkamp was due for some hard-earned leave when Wessels was suspended and, a few days after the case became his, he left town. I never found out whether anyone had bothered to tell Steenkamp of his new case. In any event, on the day Mduduzi Cube and Vusi Mabida were scheduled to attend their second bail hearing, neither the accused nor their docket arrived at court. An outraged magistrate telephoned the Murder and Robbery Squad and cursed its hapless receptionist. At 3:55 that afternoon, five minutes before the court was scheduled to close for the day, Cube and Mabida were delivered to the holding cells beneath the court. The magistrate struck their case off the roll, and told them they were free to go. He then turned to the constable who had driven the accused to court and ordered him to drive the free men to their homes.

Of all the strange things that happened in the investigation of the Mitchell case, this, if not the strangest, is certainly the most emblematic. The Mitchell murder was probably the most important – the one subject to the most pressure – of the many hundreds that the Carton Bay Murder and Robbery squad were investigating. Yet the squad had strayed so far from its business that it had forgotten about the case's existence. The killing of Bheki Cube and the subsequent amnesia about his case are surely symptoms of the same malaise. A detective unit that has fallen to pieces is a violent and unpredictable one, and yet its violence has no apparent purpose. Its members can kill a suspect one day and forget about his co-suspects the next.

There can be little doubt that if Cube and Mabida had been delivered to court on time, they would have been set free anyway. They had been in detention five or six weeks and there was not a shred of admissible evidence against them. Arthur Mitchell was either never told this or decided to forget it. For him, the murderers of his son were free because they and their docket never arrived at court.

When I dialled Mitchell's number a few days after Cube and Mabida were released, I thought I would be received by a man on fire. I was ready for the maniacal voice of someone who had given the criminal justice system its chance and was now going to do what his guts had always told him, to behave like a man who inhabits a lawless frontier. I was in for a surprise. The voice at the other end of the telephone was sickeningly dead. I don't think I have ever spoken to a more deflated person in my life. Every word was delivered with great effort and pain. It was like listening to a voice that came from the bottom of a well – ghostly, disembodied and excruciatingly lonely. I gave my condolences as if speaking to a man whose son had been killed all over again. I think it was indeed Mitchell's darkest time.

*

I met Will Sullivan seven months after the death of Bheki Cube, on a November morning in 2000. It was one of those awkward situations where two people who have no idea what the other looks like, and who have sensitive business to discuss, agree to meet in a busy public place. I caught an early-morning flight from Johannesburg and arrived at Durban International Airport at about 8:30. We had agreed to meet outside the domestic arrivals terminal. I scanned the hundreds of faces that passed by, and one in four or five looked like it might belong to a police detective. A tentative voice called my name from somewhere behind me, and I turned round to find myself looking at the most detective-looking among them: blond and aryan with a chubby baby face, mid-twenties, late twenties maybe, blue jeans and short-sleeved checked shirt, no gun. Sullivan examined me closely; the fashionable Danish spectacle frames, the upmarket Samsonite laptop bag. He registered the cultural distance between us, and his body language was nervous and shy.

We went into the terminal building and upstairs to the airport restaurant. Usually, it offered a close and unobstructed view of the powerful jets as they lifted themselves into the air. But the windows had been boarded up for renovations for the last six months, and the planes outside were noisy but invisible, the restaurant dark and gloomy, its tackiness accentuated by the absence of a view. Sullivan had that irritatingly deferential habit of ordering only what I ordered, no more and no less. I felt exhausted already, the interview barely begun.

I asked him detailed questions about the events preceding the arrests of Vusi Mabida and Mduduzi Cube. I wanted to know who had signed the damning affidavits and how Louis Wessels had got them. My questions were too detailed, too nosy, and I was still a total stranger, so I expected him to respond with professional reserve. Instead, the detail overwhelmed him and he stumbled over the Zulu names and got lost in the sequence of events.

'Maybe you should just read the docket,' he said. 'That way you will have just the facts.'

He went to his car to get the docket, and took a long time to return. I was convinced he had grown suspicious and fled, and I cursed myself for my sloppy forthrightness. But he returned, sure enough, clutching a police-issue file as thick as a dictionary, and to my astonishment, he put it in front of me and told me to take my time. It was all there; the names of the witnesses, their statements, the investigating officer's notes. As I read, I marvelled at how the colour of my skin had shaped the trajectory of my entire investigation. These were secret affidavits; the prosecutor would only give them to the accused on pain of being thrown in jail. Those who signed their names had taken their lives in their hands by doing so. And here I was, a stranger pawing through pages of other people's fates. That I was white was enough for Sullivan to trust me implicitly with the lives of black witnesses. I was tempted to remind him that I was a journalist, and that we were only meeting at all because I was publishing a book. But I held my tongue. The journalist in me was tearing like a hyena at the flesh of this unexpected feast, and I would not have stopped myself for the world.

The affidavits provided Sullivan with a useful structure, and he turned out to be a very good storyteller indeed. Each witness and suspect his tongue crafted came out rich and alive, in the very specific way that a detective's characters are alive; how they resist and how they break, how they outsmart and are outsmarted.

I waited until Sullivan was deeply buried in his detective world and then asked him a question in his capacity as a white man; I wanted to know what it would mean for him to pull the trigger and end one of their lives.

'Did they tell you why they did it?'

'The youngster said the land belonged to them,' he replied. 'He said it was theirs because they were born there.' He shook his head and gave me a disgusted look, searching for my complicity in his disgust. I gave it to him; I shook my head. 'They are brain-damaged,' he added. 'Simple is not the word for it.'

Formally, Sullivan had no connection to the Carton Bay Murder and Robbery Squad. He was based at the Durban regional detective office. In 1998, the Carton Bay Murder and Robbery Squad landed a difficult, high-profile case. The daughter of a well-known local businessman had been kidnapped, and the abductors were asking for ransom. The overworked and overwhelmed Murder and Robbery Squad sought help from the Durban office, and Sullivan was dispatched to Carton Bay to head the investigation. He solved the case quickly; the businessman's daughter was returned unharmed, and three men were sentenced to long terms in prison.

'How did you crack it?' I asked.

'Cellphone,' he smiled. 'The idiots communicated their demands on a cellphone. It took one call to MTN to get the kidnapper's name and address.'

While working on the kidnapping case, Sullivan got to know Wessels well, and when, a year later, the Mitchell docket arrived on Wessels's desk, he phoned Sullivan and asked for help. So Sullivan joined the Mitchell case in an auxiliary role. He did very little of the delicate coalface work – interviewing suspects, collecting affidavits. That was left to Wessels. Early in our conversation, Sullivan was very protective of his colleague. When I hinted that the investigation had been a disaster, he shrugged and ignored me. But he didn't keep up the collegial solidarity for long. Talking about the case, his irritation got the better of him.

'Right at the beginning of the investigation,' he said, 'all the Cubes were interviewed. The Carton Bay detectives wanted to hear their alibis. Peter and Bheki Cube submitted contradictory statements. Peter said he had gone into town and asked Bheki to mind the Tearoom. Bheki said he was not at home that day. The detectives missed that. Can you believe it? Days after the murder, there was a gap, and they missed it.'

Months later, when Mduduzi Cube and Vusi Mabida failed to arrive at court and their case was struck off the roll, Sullivan drove down to Carton Bay to find out what was going on. It took him three hours to locate the Mitchell docket; it was buried in a storeroom in a heap of forgotten files and papers.

'I picked up the docket, walked out and drove back to Durban,' Sullivan told me. 'So I shouldn't really be holding this docket. It's not my case. But I couldn't leave it there to be eaten by moths. That's not right.'

'Why? Your caseload must be enormous already. Why take an after-hours case?'

'I met Arthur Mitchell years ago, when he was a security man at a chemicals company. I worked a case at one of his plants.' He paused and smiled at me as if this explained everything. 'There's a connection, you see. I was meant to solve this case.'

I marvelled at his reasoning. His identification with the dead white man, the enthusiasm of a young detective whose heart is in his work, all mixed together and made coherent by some home-spun superstition.

'But your task is such a frustrating one,' I said. 'Going over old ground to clean up someone else's mess.'

Sullivan nodded. 'I need to find Vusi Mabida and take his statement all over again. He's disappeared. Mduduzi Cube has told him that if I find him, I will kill him. But I have discovered where he is hiding.'

Again, Sullivan told me the name of the place where Mabida had taken refuge. It rolled casually off his tongue like the name of a B & B or a scenic spot worth visiting.

'Problem is that where he is hiding, you can hear a vehicle coming from miles away. I'll have to go in with a helicopter. And I will. I'll do that. It's just a question of timing.'

'Given what happened to Bheki Cube,' I said cautiously, 'Vusi probably believes it when people say the police will kill him.'

It was all Sullivan needed to talk about that night.

'There were three of us with him in the hut,' Sullivan said, and he watched me very closely as he spoke. 'He stood up with the packet in his hand, threw his spade at Louis and cocked the gun. Louis and I opened fire. Louis missed. His bullets sprayed all over the place. Mine hit. All of them. The bullets came from my gun.' Sullivan stuck his chin out at me, a vulnerable gesture, like he was taking the idiom – to take it on the chin – quite literally.

His choice of words, and the sequence in which he arranged them, were odd. Louis missed. That came first. That was the most important. And then the vulnerable chin and the taking of responsibility. My bullets. Why not just 'We shot him,' or 'He cocked his gun and we killed him'? Why the detail, unsolicited, unnecessary?

I believe that what happened that night is betrayed by Sullivan's strange description of Bheki's death. It takes a lot for a policeman to sink his colleague. That is the oldest and truest cliché about cops on the streets. A colleague slips up and you take it on your chin. It is noble. You feel good. Your bonds to your colleagues grow richer and deeper. I would be surprised if the bullets that killed Bheki Cube came from the barrel of Will Sullivan's gun.

FOURTEEN

It is late June 2000, four-and-a-half months before my meeting with Will Sullivan.

'Is that Mr Steinberg?'

'Yes, it is.'

'Good morning, Mr Steinberg. Mike Glossop here from Alanview Farm Watch. I'm not sure whether you remember me.'

It was a puzzling way to resume contact. Earlier in the year, I had clocked up many hours with Mike Glossop. We had driven along every forgotten district road in the Alanview area, Glossop chewing my ear off on subjects ranging from the virtues of Margaret Thatcher to the difficulties of shedding weight in middle age. Calling me 'Mr' and nervously asking whether I remembered him made me wonder whether there was another Mike Glossop in Alanview.

'Mr Steinberg, I read about your report to the government in the newspapers. You are right. The security forces lack proper intelligence and sufficient personnel. I want to tell you that I have a little operation going here that has solved the problem. We are doing terrific work. If you have a minute, I want to tell you about it. If you like it, I want to ask you to hand it on to the top brass, to the sort of people who make real decisions.'

I smiled to myself as Glossop revealed the source of his awkwardness. He had an authority problem, like a boarding-school boy who craves recognition and is convinced from the outset he has already been robbed of it. Despite the fact that he was a good 15 years older than me, the stuff Glossop had read in the papers that morning had turned me into one of those cruel dispensers of reward and esteem who had littered his past, or one of the dispensers' emissaries, at any rate.

'A couple of minutes, Mr Steinberg. I won't take up too much of your valuable time.'

A few months before Glossop's phone call, the Ministry of Safety and Security had commissioned a colleague and me to tour the country and assess government's capacity to combat violent crime on commercial farms. We had had a ball stampeding through the hinterland's racial frontier. We interviewed a white vigilante hired by farmers to mete out punishment to those who stole their potatoes. Sitting in his own living room, he wore an assault rifle over his shoulder and large bags of depression under his eyes. He spoke of himself as 'The Executioner', the man who holds the social fabric together with the threat of death, and he quoted from the work of Joseph de Maistre, the dark nineteenth-century thinker who wrote that humanity's abiding feature was its taste for violence. We met a black chief who called white men 'baas' to their faces and organised a vehicle-theft ring behind their backs, and a labourer who swore that God would smite white farmers by replacing the semen in their scrotums with insecticide.

We wrote our report, which noted with formality and academic understatement some of the madness we saw, and when Glossop read of our work, he assumed I was on first-name terms with the men who run South Africa's criminal justice system.

'I have hooked up with the Gudla army commando,' Glossop continued, launching himself into that rapid frenzy of words I knew so well. 'They have seconded five of their part-timers to me. I have manpower now. And with manpower, I have the trust of the locals. The information is pouring in. I have people travelling 80 kilometres on a bicycle to tell me that their neighbours are stashing weapons.'

The commandos are the part-time civilian component of the South African army. In their earliest form, they were units of farmers and traders who left home with their rifles on their backs to defend their remote farms from the blacks in the early nineteenth century. In the 1970s and '80s, the commandos were shored up by the Afrikaner nationalist government and became training grounds in the fight against Afrikanerdom's new enemies, the communists and the ANC. They were the means by which the apartheid government kept the minds and the trigger fingers of white men trained on the invisible enemy in the bush. Back then, farmers joined the commandos in their thousands. They dressed up in camouflage every night and bonded like men at war.

When democracy came to South Africa, white men left the commandos in droves. The enemy in the bush was now running the national army, and many whites would be damned before taking orders from their erstwhile foes. Those who remained trained their energy on the growing wave of violent attacks on white farmers. Some became useless boys' clubs, humoured and ignored by police and army alike. Others have been remarkably effective, policing the countryside with an efficiency the police force will never match. Still others became violent bands of vigilantes, combing the countryside for faces they did not trust, tying men to trees and leaving them to starve, burning homesteads to the ground in the middle of the night.

Bands of armed and uniformed white men in South Africa's new democracy are not good for public relations, and the commandos had to find black faces to fill their ranks. White and black were never going to work side by side, as equals, to fight crime in the hinterland. They do not trust each other enough. So, as a second best, commandos around the country picked unemployed black men off the streets of rural towns, put them in uniforms and gave them a tiny stipend for their trouble. The black men were mute and submissive, and they obeyed orders.

These are the sort of men the Gudla commando put in Glossop's charge; drifters picked off the streets of small coastal towns, hungry enough to wear the white man's uniform and to obey his orders for a handful of coins.

I remembered the tale Glossop had spun about 'accommodation' in the countryside. The blacks who live and work on white farms are an aristocracy, Glossop had said. They have jobs and they have found a way out of the ravaged rural ghettos. Protect them and they will protect you from the hungry and the unemployed.

'You say the information is pouring in,' I said to Glossop. 'You mean from workers on the farms? You are solving their cases and so they are helping you?'

'No, no. Oh, no. It is much more impressive than that. We are going deep into the locations, into places the police have always regarded as no-go zones, like Izita. When the people there see that we are serious, they realise that we are their saving grace. Nobody wants a neighbour who hoards weapons. Everyone wants the neighbourhood bully off the streets. So they come and whisper in our ear, and we go in. I'm telling you, they're pouring in to talk to us, from miles away.'

'Mike, that sounds ...'

'You see, in essence, our interests are the same. People talk crap about no trust between races. But we are all after the same thing. A troublemaker is a troublemaker. Hated by black and white. Show them you are serious, and we are all in it together.'

'Mike, I'll ...'

'Look, we stay within the law, as far as we can. You go to some-body and ask him nicely for the AK 47 he's hiding, he'll tell you to get lost. You've got to slap him around a bit. Otherwise you'll get nowhere. No real violence. Just a bit of pressure. A bit of urgency.'

'Mike, write this all up, and I promise to give it to a divisional commissioner in Pretoria. But I can't promise that he'll read it. In fact, I'll be surprised if he does. I have much less influence than you seem to think.'

A few days later, a 15-page document arrived in the post: Glossop writes like he speaks: a neurotic torrent of wild prose, so excited it doesn't know where to begin or end. I put it in an enve-lope, wrote a cursory covering letter, and addressed it to a man who I knew would throw it in his wastepaper basket. I thought of Glossop and his new stream of informants, and felt a cold shiver go down my spine. A man is irritated by his neighbour and tells the overenthusiastic white man of a hidden stash of weapons. He sits in his hut chuckling to himself as he hears the commotion next door.

*

A week after Glossop's call, I went away for three weeks, to New York to report to one of the organisations that funded this book and to Berlin to visit friends. I thought very little about Mitchell and Glossop and the people I had met in Alanview, and I did not read a single South African newspaper. In Berlin, I sat every morning at a sidewalk café in the inner-city district of Kreuzberg and read the *International Herald Tribune*, the *Financial Times* and the *New Yorker*, slowly and at leisure. The mid-morning streets were shared by homeless men and women who scavenged in the litter bins, and Turkish housewives who popped in and out of the Turkish delis, their veils plastered to their faces, their arms filled with their shopping. The housewives and the homeless were invisible to each other; they walked through separate worlds. By noon, the streets were filled with young children returning from school. They taunted the bag ladies with Turkish curses and German verbs, and the bag ladies gathered the shreds of their dignity and shouted back.

As I watched these daily skirmishes, the rest of the globe washed over me, dream-like and illusory; the distilled and formulaic prose of global newspapers makes everything look the same. South Africa was mentioned twice in the newspapers on my table. In mid-July, South Africa lost its bid to host the 2006 soccer World Cup to Germany, and the *Tribune* carried a picture of Sports Minister Ngconde Balfour, giant tears rolling down his swollen cheeks. A few days later, South African soccer star Benni McCarthy scored a goal and then allegedly lifted his index finger to thousands of Zimbabwean fans in the Harare National Stadium; 13 people died in the riot that ensued. The self-righteous *Frankfurter Algemeine Zeitung* said in its editorial the following day it was just as well the World Cup had steered clear of Africa.

*

I returned to Johannesburg in late July to find an urgent message on my voice mail, left by a colleague in Durban whom I had asked to keep an eye on things in Alanview.

'Jonny, Mike Glossop has been charged with murder. Phone me.'

At work, there was a fax waiting for me in my letterbox. It was a copy of an article in KwaZulu-Natal's *Morning Post*:

> An Alanview magistrate yesterday expressed shock at the way investigations were being conducted in the case of six South African National Defence Force members and a police reservist charged with the brutal murder of a Grayton Farm resident, Mr Ronnie Zizini on July 1.
>
> Appearing before magistrate Mr N Rheeder were SANDF members Mr Nkululeko Mdlalosi, Mr Bradley David Jones, Mr Elliot Soni, Mr Matthews Ncongo, Mr Siphiwe Jackson Nzuzu, Mr Phineas Xaba and police reservist Mr Michael James Glossop.
>
> The seven face a charge of murder and two counts of assault with intent, after the death of Zizini.

Zizini (34) died after an R4 rifle was allegedly repeatedly thrust in and out of his anus by the accused in full view of his family. The repeated assaults resulted in severe injuries to his internal organs, which resulted in his death.

The accused claim they were on a search for illegal firearms when the alleged murder and assaults took place. Residents, however, claim Zizini's death was as a result of continued brutality by soldiers who had been sent to Alanview to protect them.

The second charge of assault with intent stems from the severe assault on a neighbour, Mr Boeti Mbantshe, who, according to state evidence, was beaten and also displayed scars on his buttocks indicating an assault similar to the one suffered by Zizini.

Rheeder expressed shock at the investigating team's not opposing the bail application, when five of the accused had no physical addresses appearing in their dockets. The State also did not oppose bail.

Furthermore, two of the accused had been granted bail in an after-hours bail application last Thursday.

Rheeder questioned the regularity of the two accused, Jones and Glossop, having been granted bail after hours while facing a Schedule 5 offence, which by law could be done only during normal office hours.

There were other faxes in my letter box. One was a copy of a letter, dated 2 June, a few weeks before Zizini's death, signed by a University of Natal violence monitor, Maude Henderson, addressed to the police area commissioner and the commanding officer of the SANDF in KwaZulu-Natal:

On the night of Tuesday 30 May 2000 the homestead of the Mgabi family at eFuze, Athol, was searched – without a warrant – by men claiming to be police and army members. The men allegedly had no identification insignia ... Two men, believed (from uniforms) to be army members, were wearing balaclavas. During their search these men were responsible for maliciously damaging property ... It is alleged that other houses were searched that night, and some people were beaten by these men and have opened cases at the local police station. It is further alleged that these security force members have a list of people they are targeting, and that these people just happen to be deemed ANC ... Is it usual for members of the security forces to wear balaclavas whilst engaging in such activities ...?'

Henderson wrote to the SANDF commanding officer again on 28 June 2000:

Copy of letter dated 2 June 2000, which I had tried to fax to yourself (and subsequently discovered that it had not gone through) follows for your attention.

I understand from Commissioner Randall that this matter has been discussed with SANDF representatives, and he has undertaken to provide me with a written response to my letter.

In the meantime, raids by members of the SANDF have continued in this area, with serious allegations being made about damage to property and a variety of human rights abuses ... There seems little doubt that amongst those participating in these illegal activities are members of commando/Farm Watch units.

And finally, on 12 July, 10 days after Zizini's death, an exasperated Henderson wrote to the police area commissioner:

Despite my drawing this disgraceful matter to your attention on 2 June, following which you informed me that you had brought the matter up at a meeting with army officials, the pattern of abuse continued, not only in Athol, but also in Alanview. Members of what *appear* (since I have had no confirmation from yourself exactly which army members are involved; however, my local sources maintain they are commando/Farm Watch units) to be the very same unit that allegedly inflicted horrific torture on Mr Ronnie Zizini of Grayton Farm in the Alanview area, which led to his death.

Two of the facts reported in the *Morning Post* article were wrong. Glossop and the other white man were not in the room when Zizini was tortured. They were waiting outside. A few days after Zizini's death, a worried and astute Colin Waugh set out to find just how far outside the room the white men had waited. Two eye-witnesses told him Glossop was a good 300 metres away. 'That's out of earshot,' Waugh thought to himself, and he got his witnesses to sign affidavits.

The other mistake in the newspaper report was that Zizini had been tortured in full view of his family. When Zizini's wife stood in front of a police line-up, she could not identify the men who had killed her husband. In fact, the soldiers had cleared the hut and dealt with Zizini alone. A murder without an eyewitness is difficult enough, and on the forensic side of the investigation, things were not going that well either. When the police arrested the seven men, they confiscated a plastic packet, which they said was placed over Zizini's head while he was being sodomised, a rifle, which had traces of human faeces on its barrel, and a jacket, which was said to have been used to wipe the barrel of the rifle when the soldiers were done. I phoned a technician I knew at the police forensic laboratory in Pretoria and asked how the examination of the evidence was going.

'Take a guess,' he laughed. 'It's the usual story when organic evidence is transported across the country. By the time it gets here it is tarnished and useless. If they do get a conviction, it won't be because they found shit on a rifle barrel.'

So right from the beginning, it seemed unlikely that Glossop and the other six would be convicted of murder. And indeed, I learned much later, shortly before the publication of this book, that the state abandoned its case against Glossop before it reached trial.

When I was told of the scenes outside the Alanview courthouse on the day of the five black soldiers' bail hearing, I cursed myself for having been at the other end of the world. Two groups of protesters converged on the court that morning. The first, about 150 strong, was led by Alanview's mayor, a young ANC activist named Joseph Majola. The crowd carried home-made banners saying 'Farm Watch Out', and 'Stop Killing Us'. A delegation of protesters handed police representatives a memorandum. Among other things, it said that 'the actions of the SANDF in this area are typical of those of a foreign army invading enemy land. The

SANDF must be investigated and those who are not here to protect us must be removed ... We insist that the police reservist, Mike Glossop, be removed from the reserve.'

The second group of protesters consisted of the colleagues of the five black soldiers charged with murder. Newspaper reporters tried all morning to understand precisely what they were protesting against. By mid-morning they produced a spokesman who said the group demanded that all charges against their colleagues be dropped. A senior army official attending the bail hearing, clearly embarrassed, told his troops that if they did not return to barracks they would be court-martialled.

By the time the bail hearing began, it looked as if things might turn nasty. Majola's protesters danced and chanted at the gates of the courthouse, waiting for the five soldiers to walk free. The nervous Alanview police station commissioner phoned the nearest public order policing unit, nearly 100 kilometres away, to request a crowd control unit. Fortunately, the outrage of the presiding magistrate saved the day. He railed against the detectives investigating the case, as well as against the prosecutor, neither of whom had opposed the accused's bail application. The magistrate himself denied bail, set a date for a further bail application, and instructed the army to vouch that, were the five part-time soldiers let free, they would be confined to barracks. The soldiers were led back into the holding cells and the crowd outside, victorious, at least for a day, drifted home.

Glossop was not at the courthouse that day. He was at home, behind locked doors, his pistol loaded and ready for trouble. There is a part-time secretary at Alanview Farm Watch whose husband is a senior prosecutor in the district court. It seems that strings were gently pulled, and that the two white men were whisked into an after-hours bail hearing on the day they were arrested.

If the colour of the black soldiers' skins denied them the luxury of an early release from prison, their uniforms earned them fine treatment on the inside. On the Sunday after the bail application, a man I had employed as a researcher drove past Athol police station, where the five were being held. There was a braaivleis in progress on the little lawn behind the police station, he told me. Lots of meat and crates of beer. Some of the men around the fire he recognised as patrol policemen. Others looked vaguely familiar. They looked just like the ones in the dock at the Alanview bail hearing.

By the time I arrived back in South Africa, Alanview's white farming community had spun its own story about what had happened on Grayton Farm. It was an extraordinary education in the workings of small towns. During the course of my research, I had found that the white community was as fractious, the tactics of its internecine wars as dirty and mischievous, as anything a novelist might have invented. There are many stories I have chosen not to tell for fear of losing myself in gratuitous gossip: criminal charges laid against a teenage boy for sleeping with his 15-year-old neighbour; an openly gay man whose business was boycotted by half the district. And yet, within a few days of Glossop's arrest, every white man and woman – enemies and allies alike – had precisely the same story on their lips. It goes like this.

The morning after Ronnie Zizini was interrogated in his home, he walked the five kilometres from Grayton Farm to the district surgeon's rooms in Alanview. The white doctor examined Zizini thoroughly, gave him some painkillers, and told him to fill out an assault form at the police station. Zizini walked back to his home, and by the following morning he was dead.

'How does a dying man walk ten kilometres in a day?' I was asked. 'How does a man bleeding to death from the inside stroll into town and back? And how does an experienced and competent doctor not notice that his patient is dying? We have our sources, you know, *good* black people. We are told that Zizini's family was very unhappy with him. They wanted to know why he was bringing trouble home, why seven soldiers came knocking at the family's door. We are told that on the night he came back from the doctor, the women were removed from the hut and Zizini was beaten, badly beaten. We believe that is why he died.'

On my first night back in Alanview after Glossop's arrest, I had dinner with a couple who own a farm a few kilometres from town. Throughout my research, I made a point of spending time with people who were not close to Mitchell or Waugh. I worried that by homing in too narrowly, I would get a distorted picture of the farming community, and these peripheral contacts acted as a check on my perceptions. We ate a hearty farmer's dinner of roast beef, creamed vegetables and boxed wine. Anthony was among the most taciturn human beings I had ever met. On the several occasions I had dined with them, he had sat there all evening, gloomy and silent, listening closely to the conversation. Occasionally, he would snigger meaningfully at something that was said and I would look up at him enquiringly. He would offer a few words of explanation and resume his silence. His wife, Nicola, made up for his lack of words. They streamed out of her all evening, sometimes bitchy, sometimes kind, always curious.

They asked what I was doing in town, and I told them that Glossop's arrest had brought me.

Anthony frowned and looked up suspiciously. 'But that is unrelated to the subject matter of your book.'

'Well, it is somewhere on the border of my subject matter,' I replied. 'I have spent a lot of time with Glossop. There is a chapter about him in my book.'

He frowned again, looked at his plate carefully, and chose a vegetable to put on his fork. He chewed slowly, swallowed, and spoke into his plate. 'But it has nothing to do with Peter Mitchell's murder.'

'Yes and no. Every murder in this district is connected, in a way.'

There was a long, awkward silence, and Nicola took the cue.

'Very disturbing, this Mike Glossop business. Very disturbing.'

'Yes, it is,' I replied.

She stared at me, absorbing the expression on my face, trying to work out if we were disturbed by the same thing.

'Suspicious,' she continued. 'Very suspicious. When Peter is killed, nobody is arrested for months. But a white man fighting criminals … he is arrested the very same day. Something very odd is going on.'

'Maybe,' I replied, 'maybe he was arrested because he was seen there, and because when an army operation ends in murder, the stakes are very high.'

'No, I don't buy it,' she replied, reading my face closely again. 'Something is going on.'

'Are you suggesting that Glossop has been framed?'

She shrugged, expansively, meaningfully. 'Who knows? All I know is that he was the one person doing something about crime in this area. And they locked him in jail.'

Her husband kept staring at his plate, then chose a floret of creamed cauliflower to impale with his fork.

*

Colin Waugh was probably the unhappiest white man in Alanview. Right from the beginning, two or three months before Zizini's death, Waugh had pitted himself against Glossop's commando project. He had been overruled by the more excitable and enthusiastic of the Farm Watch's directors, who insinuated that he was jealous of the project because he had not thought of it first. They were wrong. The truth is that Waugh was far wiser than they were.

'I can't have Glossop running around the countryside unsupervised,' Waugh told me a few weeks before Zizini's murder. 'They're looking for illegal firearms, for heaven's sake. Operations like that draw accusations. Where will the security forces be when something explodes?'

Since the murder, Colin had been having a torrid time. He had tried to defend himself and his organisation, and then Mike Glossop, in that order, and the two tasks did not always sit well together. He had told reporters that Glossop had been acting in his capacity as a police reservist, not a Farm Watch employee, and that those who claimed Farm Watch was running a campaign of terror were malicious and dishonest. Asked why Glossop had not been suspended from his job at Farm Watch, he replied that suspects are innocent until proven guilty and that suspension would be unjust. In fact, he could neither have suspended Glossop nor expressed remorse, if he had wanted to. Many of the farmers who sat on Farm Watch's board thought of Glossop as a righteous crusader and a martyr. He had been cut down in action, fighting a just war. Waugh was their employee.

I met Colin at his house the morning after my dinner with Anthony and Nicola. He was waiting for me at his front gate, his body language urgent, his facial expression gloomy.

'How are you?' I smiled.

'Pretty under the weather, thank you. I am not a popular man at the moment.'

'I can imagine. What's been going on?'

'I am under personal attack. Severe personal attack. After Glossop's arrest, Paul Mlambo and Trevor Sibiya went to see Randall, the police area commissioner. They told him that I am running the police and army in this area, and that I must be stopped. Randall told them to their faces they were talking nonsense.'

'Well, Colin, that is to be expected.'

'That's not all. Inkatha has jumped on the bandwagon, and so have the provincial minister of safety and security's nasty little henchmen. There is a campaign against me.'

'Perhaps if you were less indignant and expressed some shock at the killing you would look a little better.'

'Gentle, Jonny, gentle. I am in a fragile state. Very much under the weather.'

'What do you think happened out there?'

He began to tell the standard story of the healthy walk to the district surgeon and the irate family members. For once, I discarded my reserve and cut him off.

'Come on, Colin, that's a load of nonsense and you know it.'

He looked back at me forlornly. 'Jonny, I honestly don't know what happened out there, and I cannot turn on my man. I cannot tell the world he is guilty, when I really don't know myself.'

*

Later that week, I arranged a lunch-time meeting with Joseph Majola, the Alanview mayor who had led the protest at the soldiers' bail hearing. It turned out that Majola had a job at the Alanview fire station, and that's where we met. The entire place was deserted when I arrived; it was just me, Majola and two beautiful red fire engines.

I had been a little lazy in setting up the meeting with Majola. By rights, I should have approached him via a provincial network of ANC activists. That way, I would have been solidly kosher by the time I met him face to face, and he would have spoken to me without reserve. As it was, a part of me had begun to grow resentful of the laborious and ritual-laden paths to my interviewees, and I had phoned him directly. So a white stranger wandered into his fire station, and my business card and a brief summary of my credentials evoked a sympathetic and generous smile, but little candour. Majola was young and affable and clearly had much to talk about, and the persistent reserve he displayed throughout our interview seemed to go against the grain. After 45 minutes, I had filled barely a page of my notebook, and as I got up to leave Majola apologised to me.

'You probably don't work for the Colonel,' he said. As you may recall, 'The colonel' was Colin Waugh's designation in the district. 'But maybe you do, and I can't take the chance.'

I smiled back at him. 'I know. If I were you, I would probably do the same.' He returned my smile with genuine warmth and I imagined, erroneously perhaps, that if this interaction had happened half an hour before, the interview would have been far more productive.

*

I had learned by now that at least half the time I spent in Alanview was down time. One meeting would end at ten in the morning, the next would begin at midday, and the two hours in between were empty. Sometimes, I would sit in my car or in the town's solitary bar, reading my interview notes and jotting down my impressions, or I would get absorbed in archival work. Other times, I would drive around town and watch – openly, aimlessly.

I had more than an hour to kill before my meeting with Majola at the fire station, and I parked my car outside the gates of a high school in downtown Alanview. The kids streaming out of the school grounds were all black, and I wondered whether I could tell from their manner and the way they wore their uniforms which were the children of Alanview's tiny black bourgeoisie and which were embarking on the long journey back to the shantytowns and locations. In my rear-view mirror, Glossop's unmistakable profile – crooked nose, thick black moustache, sagging triple chin – shot past.

I followed Glossop's car down Alanview's main street, until it turned off into a leafy lane. He parked outside an ancient double-storey house, got out and began walking toward the front gate.

I rolled down my window and called his name. He turned, looked at me unsmilingly, and came up to my open window. It was an exaggeratedly unequal uncounter, Glossop staring down at me from a few centimetres away, while I squinted up at his face.

'Did you ever give my document to the big brass?' he asked.

For the first time in the many months of my research, I had to summon all my resources to suppress laughter. 'Yes, Mike. I gave it to the divisional commissioner, as I promised.'

'Any response?'

'Like I said at the time, he probably threw it away.'

Glossop wiped his moustache, irritation and disappointment on his face. 'Well, I've been oiling some other channels as well, in the army. If I knock on enough doors, one of them will open. There's been a hiccup in the operation, as you must know. But it's no more than a hiccup. It's a good idea and it must go on.'

'Mike, I'm going to come down to Alanview for your murder trial. It's on 22 August, right?' I deliberately said 'murder trial' rather than 'trial', but I failed in the execution. As I said 'murder', my voice and my face betrayed a hint of queasiness, and Glossop responded with silent and subtle scorn. He knew, not only that I felt he was guilty, but that the idea of his guilt made me recoil from him, partly out of distaste, partly from a primitive and instinctive sense of fear.

'We slap people around a bit, as I told you on the phone the other day. Because that's the name of the game. But this ...' He made a shovelling motion with his hands, a rifle barrel digging into the flesh of human bowels. He raised his eyebrows and let his eyes linger on me as his hands shovelled. 'None of that.'

'You were framed?'

He nodded severely. 'Local elections coming up at the end of the year. Palms to be greased, votes to be counted.'

I remembered that Majola was defending his local government seat and hoped to be re-elected as mayor. 'I'm on my way to see Joseph Majola now,' I smiled. 'Should I ask him how he framed you?'

'Majola's small fry,' Glossop replied. 'He's on the periphery. It goes much deeper than that.'

'How deep?'

'Maude Henderson has some field workers in the area. She's enthusiastic and naïve. They whisper nonsense in her ear.'

'Who's paying them?'

'Let's not talk names just yet. One day, I'll sit you down and we can talk names. For the moment, let's just say this: politics and crime go hand in hand in this province. The one lubricates the other. So if you are competent at fighting crime, as we had become, you ruffle some feathers. Put some noses out of joint.'

'You stepped on the toes of a classical politico-criminal mafia?'

Glossop saw that I was humouring him, and his lips tensed with irritation. 'I'm glad for this trial. I'm glad for the publicity. They have framed me, but it will expose them. People will be asking a lot of questions by the end of this trial.'

It dawned on me that I was not listening to an eccentric or lonely voice. I pictured Glossop in huddled conversation with his allies on the Farm Watch board. I am convinced they believed this story from the bottom of their hearts.

I told him to phone when he was ready to tell me of the conspirators behind his arrest. He said he definitely would, but I never heard from him again.

Driving from Glossop's house to the fire station, I recalled writing something about him much earlier in my research. 'Glossop blusters a lot,' I wrote. 'But he also has the perceptive irony of one who is not from these parts. I think he senses something of the logic of these unspoken rules, and I think this knowledge is the cause of some loneliness. I stare at Glossop as he stares out over his client's fields, and I sense that he is watching himself from far away, wondering what on earth he is doing at this ungodly hour, stalking the destitute as they fill their sacks.'

I had to laugh at myself as I recalled these lines, one of the many moments in my life when my judgement of character had been hopelessly poor. And then I thought about it for a while and began to wonder whether I not been right after all. Glossop did indeed feel like an idiot guarding tomato fields in the early hours of the morning. It reminded him of all those dispensers of prestige who had looked through him, as if he was invisible, during the course of his life. He had abandoned the tomato fields for the locations, his flashlight and night-vision glasses for his fists, to draw himself closer to his image of himself. He was bored and humiliated, and the locations' gun smugglers, real and imagined, gave him the opportunity to reinvent himself.

PART THREE

FIFTEEN

It is time to talk about the tenants' side of the story. I have agonised a long time about how to tell it, drawing dozens of mind maps on crisp white paper with a box of felt-tipped pens, throwing each in the dustbin and starting again. The problem is not that the story lacks colour or depth. On the contrary. I would love to tell you about some of the people who attended the two meetings between Mitchell and his tenants, the things that made them smile and laugh, the things that contorted their faces into expressions of hatred. Failing that, I want to tell you about the people I hired as investigators, how their capacity to seduce and to charm led me to the story I am about to tell you.

The problem is that nobody who features in this story allowed me to write about them. Nobody named the killers. Nobody said anything that the police do not already have in their bulging file of affidavits on the Mitchell murder. But that was not good enough to reassure anyone. Who knows what events the publication of this book may precipitate? The nine families who live on Normandale are largely illiterate. Most will not read the book themselves, but they may well be told what is in it. This information will pass through many hands before it reaches Langeni, and each narrator will make countless adjustments as his own imagination helps him spin the tale. Broken telephones create rumours, and rumours themselves are often vicious tales, laden with villains and betrayers. So it is hardly fanciful to imagine that at some time in the future, in the common fund of wisdom that small communities gather, somebody in this book, somebody whose identity is revealed by a phrase or a gesture, will be named as the person who fingered the convicted ones, the person who took a breadwinner from his family.

I have at times felt bitterly disappointed – at other times angry, I admit – that pivotal characters have refused their place in this

217

book. I am disappointed in part because I was robbed of some pleasurable ways of writing a story. But something more important than that is also at stake. It is the question of credibility. There is something amusing about my adventure, is there not? I smugly tell you of the white men who have gone to Izita to get information and chased their own tails. And yet I am surely one of those white men. I too am forced by the colour of my skin to employ others as my eyes and ears, and I am therefore prone to all the failures of my predecessors. I announce up front that I will not tell you how the material was gathered. You will not see, and you will therefore be unable to evaluate, the people who spun the tale, their motives, their character, the veracity of what they say and do.

I should tell you I am certain that nobody I spoke to told me a clean or transparent story. Everything in my notebooks ranges between propaganda and untruth. And the fact that I am white only partially explains why people chose to say the things they did. Before his body was cold, Peter Mitchell's death became the sort of story about which people embellish and fantasise. It was never just about the death of a single white man; it was always an emblem. When black peasants cursed the Mitchells and told me that they and their rules were evil, they were not really talking of a particular white family, but of a stylised and abstract family, one that condensed, and smudged the distinctions between, three generations of white families in general. Just as Peter Mitchell would not have died if his father had bought Normandale some time in the past, so the stories black people told about his father's rules and conduct would have been very different in times past.

Aside from the circumstances surrounding Lourie Steyn's departure from Normandale, few of the hard facts I will relate are contested. Most of what I tell you about the two meetings between Mitchell and the tenants was confirmed, as you will soon see, by Mitchell himself. Indeed, there is very little controversy about the veracity of facts; it is in the interpretation of those facts, in the subtexts, in the meaning of the unspoken, that things become difficult. For me, that is one of the most remarkable features of this story. The rules Mitchell laid down for his tenants were orthodox; countless white proprietors had established the same strictures over their tenants' lives during the course of the twentieth century. And yet, while most of them lived to a ripe old age, Mitchell's son died as a result of the anger these rules evoked. So, on the one hand, this chapter unfolds around the announcement of each of Mitchell's rules. And yet it is not so much the rules themselves, as the things that had changed in the heads of those who heard them, that is the key to our story.

*

There is another reason why talking about the tenants' side of the story is a difficult task. An explanation of a murder is often read as a justification. And to justify this particular murder is essentially to say that Arthur Mitchell brought death upon his son, perhaps the cruelest thing one can say of any parent.

Nobody who writes a murder story has the last word on why the event he describes took place. Each reader will draw his own conclusions. All I can say is that the idea that Mitchell's murder was a just one fills me with horror. And the fact that many of the people I spoke to did, as you will soon see, express satisfaction at the news of Mitchell's death, is probably the most disturbing thing I encountered during the course of researching this book. But enough said; there is a limit to how much the writer can protest.

*

As you may well expect, precisely what happened at the beginning is contested. The tenants have one version, white farmers another. I will begin with what I was told by some of Mitchell's tenants.

When Lourie Steyn finally threw in the towel and left his farm for good, he called a meeting with two of his older tenants. As with Mitchell's meetings in the months to come, the precise words the white man chose would shape many of the events that followed. They were slippery, ambiguous words. When the landlord was finished speaking, the two old men were uncertain of his exact meaning.

Steyn announced, I was told, that he was leaving, but he said nothing of his increasingly desperate phone calls to Arthur Mitchell, nothing of his desire to find a buyer. What he did say was: 'I am leaving now, and I will not be back. I want you to look after my farm. If there is anything you need from me, here is my cellphone number.'

219

Look after is a curious choice of words. What does it mean? I remember attending a black-tie dinner in the early 1990s hosted by a large South African mining house. The master of ceremonies, a senior executive at the company who carried himself with the air of a feudal baron, began his speech by describing his position in the company.

'I look after our gold mining interests,' he said, his modesty so transparently false that the room instantly filled up with the fragrance of his self-importance.

Look after, here, is a leisurely description of proprietorship. And this is precisely how the tenants understood Steyn when he told them to look after his farm. 'It is yours,' they read between the lines. 'Take it and enjoy it.'

It would be silly to deny that this is a strangely eccentric interpretation of what Steyn said. After more than a century of proprietorship, white farmers were not going to abandon their farms with an awkward euphemism and a weak smile. The tenants' powerful desires of wish-fulfilment had clearly robbed them of their sobriety. But look at the background to the relationship between Steyn and his tenants, at the things that had passed between them in the preceding years, and the thoughts that crossed the tenants' minds are not quite as eccentric as you might think.

If the tenants' version is indeed correct, why didn't Steyn tell them that he was selling the farm, that there would soon be a new landlord? After months of speaking to black peasants in the midlands, it became apparent that it was a common practice of white farmers to tell their tenants of their commercial plans in riddles and snippets. When the Kriek family sold their farm at about the same time Steyn sold his, they also failed to inform their tenants that there would be a new landlord. The farm's new proprietor, a large southern midlands landowner by the name of Matthew Blair, was greeted by a group of enraged families when he came to claim his new land.

Perhaps this practice is an age-old expression of paternalism – they simply don't need to know, it is not their business. Perhaps the paternalism is mixed, as it must be, with a subtle assertion of ownership and power – the land is ours, not theirs, why should they know the finer details?

But there is something else about Steyn's alleged choice of

words, something more immediate to his relationship with his tenants. Steyn went to his tenants to announce a decision, one of many that a landlord will take in the course of his life. He had *decided* to leave his farm. Yet both landlord and tenants knew that he was putting a face-saving spin on the truth. Steyn had in fact been pushed off his farm. The steady stream of cattle thefts, the fields that burned in the night, the death threats, the shooting of his foreman, Lottering, the shots fired at his son – Steyn had not *decided* to leave, he had been defeated by a long, brutal campaign of psychological warfare.

So Steyn's words – *look after* – were laden with irony. He was trying on the discourse of the assured paternalist, but he was not wearing it very lightly. The cook looks after our culinary needs. The gardener looks after the flowerbeds. This *look after* clutches in vain at the legacy of paternalistic confidence. Steyn pretends that he is still in control, that even after his banishment, the servants are still just minding his estate. The irony was not lost on Steyn's audience. They humoured him and allowed him his pathetic display of dignity, but in truth they understood *look after* the way the mining magnate used it; the farm was theirs.

*

There are times when I struggle to believe it, but people swear that when Arthur Mitchell called a meeting of his new tenants in February 1999, they were convinced he was an interloper. Who is this man to claim the farm? Steyn said nothing about a new landlord. When the meeting was over, Prince Cube rummaged through his papers to find Steyn's cellphone number. The familiar voice at the other end was nervous and embarrassed. 'Yes, it is true. I sold the farm to Arthur Mitchell. He makes the rules now.' Long after that telephone conversation, after Peter was dead and officials from the Department of Land Affairs came to Normandale to talk to its inhabitants, the tenants still did not believe that Mitchell was the rightful owner of the farm. Maybe there was a conspiracy between Mitchell and Steyn? Maybe the whites make up their own laws when it suits them? They told the Department's official that Mitchell had stolen their land, and when the official smiled back at them politely, they ordered him to go to the title-deeds office to find the truth. To this day, the residents of Langeni still refer to

Normandale as 'the Steyn farm', as if everything that has happened since February 1999 can be erased by the words one chooses to name things.

*

When I was told this story, I phoned Lourie Steyn and asked him whether any of his tenants had called him on his cellphone early in 1999 to ask whether Arthur Mitchell had bought Normandale.

'They might have phoned my son,' Steyn replied. 'Must have been my son actually, because I don't remember anyone phoning. I never even gave them my cellphone number.'

'That's odd,' I replied. 'They insist it was you they called.'

'Ja, very odd. Because it wasn't me. And if it had been my son, he would have told me.'

'They say the first they knew of Mitchell owning the farm was when he called a meeting with them.'

'No, no,' Steyn laughed. It was exactly a year since I had met him in the Adristad hotel, and he appeared to have forgotten how uncomfortable he had felt that day. His voice was light; he was amused by the story. 'I told my two indunas, two old men, that Mitchell was taking over. There was no question of them not knowing.'

'What were the indunas' names?'

'Now you're asking a difficult one,' Steyn replied, and he strained to remember. 'It will probably come to me as soon as I put down the phone.'

'They say you did not mention Mitchell,' I continued. 'They say you asked them to look after the farm.'

'I may well have said that,' Steyn replied, laughing heartily. 'You know, it's just something you say when you are leaving. But I also told them that Arthur had bought the farm. They knew what was going on.'

*

I will never know which story is true. What I am pretty certain of is that by the time I arrived on the scene, the story of Steyn's last words had become a truth that everyone at Langeni believed. The insistence that Land Affairs produce Mitchell's title deed, the out-

222

rage that greeted me when I told people Steyn's side of the story – if the tenants' account of Steyn's final exchange with his 'indunas' is a myth, it is an extraordinarily powerful one.

There is a sense in which our story becomes more interesting if Mitchell was indeed cast as an interloper in retrospect. For even if his formal ownership of the land was not in itself a crime for his tenants, there is little doubt that the things he did when he took over robbed him, in their understanding, of any right to ownership. In the weeks preceding Mitchell's February meeting with his tenants, he made his proprietorship known in no uncertain terms. If the tenants had pushed back the frontier between themselves and Steyn, and had begun to use more and more of his land for their own purposes, Mitchell's first move was to force them back into the confines of Langeni. He began by hiring people to guard the borders of his farmland closely. Cattle that drifted over the border were impounded, and, in some cases, their owners charged a R50 fine to get them back. People who wandered onto Normandale to collect firewood were escorted back to the boundary of Mitchell's land. His employees watched closely for the hunters who came onto Normandale and Eleanor in pursuit of zebra, buck and warthog. The tenants found that they had become trespassers on land they believed they had won from Steyn.

So even before Mitchell met his tenants in February, they knew that their victory over Steyn had in fact turned against them. The new proprietor was out to roll back each and every one of the small victories they had won over the preceding years. Time was running backwards; the status quo from a decade past appeared to have returned.

Thus far, I have been telling you a somewhat formalistic and empty story. There is a battle over turf; as the battle proceeds, the boundary demarcating what is his and what is theirs shifts this way and that. But I have said little about the content of the battle, about what was at stake, about why the question of where the boundary lay was so important. I must ask you to be patient; the remainder of this chapter is precisely about these things. For the moment, bear in mind that Mitchell was not unknown when he addressed his tenants at that first meeting. He had said nothing, but the meaning of his proprietorship had already been established by his actions. Late in my research, when I was quibbling with Mitchell about the exact details of his first speech to his tenants, he interrupted me. 'It does not really matter what I said,' he told me. 'My fate was sealed before that, by what I had done. I was preventing the blacks from using my farm for poaching and grazing. That was the real issue.'

Mitchell is right, but only in part. Had he addressed his tenants the day he bought Normandale, before they knew how he would run his farm, they would have interpreted every one of his rules very differently. Everything Mitchell said can only be understood against the backdrop of the preceding battle between Steyn and his tenants, a battle the tenants erroneously believed they had won.

*

I have often discussed with Mitchell his demeanour and his tone at the two meetings he held with his tenants. He considers himself particularly adroit at labour relations. 'I was there in the front lines when I worked for a large chemicals company,' Mitchell told me on several occasions. 'I was there on the eve of a strike when the stakes were high and temperatures were flying. I am trained to deal with these situations. I am firm and confident, but I never lose my temper.'

I can imagine Mitchell with his firmness and his civility, the head of each tenant family standing before him next to the district road, his son at his side. He brings to the proceedings what he takes to be a businesslike and formal air. He speaks with the authority of a landlord, with the voice of a man who means what he says when he issues rules and regulations. He wants no ambiguity. He wants everything crystal clear.

On the other side, from the audience's vantage point, things do not quite look that way. The short man with the thick red neck and the bulging belly, the man the blacks call 'Kahle' – Softly, or Gently – gathers the tenants together and addresses them in clipped tones. ('Why do you call him Kahle?' I ask. 'Because when workers handle his expensive equipment, he is worried they will break it. "Kahle!" he shouts. "Gently!"') He is clutching a piece of paper and he reads from it. Few people understand his rapid English. They listen to his tone, they observe the way his mouth and cheeks move. The upper parts of his face remain immobile and expressionless. His eyes are cold. Then the Zulu policeman translates what Kahle has said, and people gasp in anger.

I am reading through the minutes Mitchell took after the first meeting with his tenants, the one on 20 February 1999. One of his rules reads: 'Cattle and goats must be controlled, as strays going onto the rest of Normandale will not be allowed. Normandale has now been declared a conservation area within the Ndunge game reserve.' The next rule reads: 'No trespassing or firewood collection will be permitted on Normandale farm. Persons found on Normandale without authority will be in breach of these rules and may be evicted from Normandale. It is the responsibility of the family head to ensure that all family members comply.' And a further rule: 'The keeping of hunting dogs is not allowed. No hunting or snaring of game will be allowed on any of my properties.'

The tenants would have pricked up their ears at the words 'conservation area'. For as long as anyone can remember, the land around Izita and Sarahdale has teemed with zebra, warthog and an assortment of buck. In pre-colonial times, each kraal kept a pack of hunting dogs and at least one member of every family would learn the craft of making traps. A warthog would provide a meal for an entire kraal; a large buck would provide two or three. By the time white farmers settled in the area in the late nineteenth century, hunting was long established as an integral part of local subsistence.

White farmers have always loathed hunting dogs. Read through farmers' diaries, the minutes of agricultural association meetings, court records in the far-flung districts of Natal – for the last century farmers have shot hunting dogs, tried to outlaw them, evicted tenants for keeping them. Part of this loathing is born from an aesthetic sensibility. The white middle class has a romantic relationship with the countryside. It is okay to clear the fertile valleys, to till the soil and sow vegetables in the rich earth of the river banks. But the animals that roam the countryside must be left alone. They are graceful and innocent, and the idea of savaging them is repugnant. Hunting them for sport is another matter entirely. For that is a battle of wits. It is about the guile of the animal, its capacity to evade death. The hunter and the hunted are as intimate as lovers; man and animal are joined by a mystical bond. But tearing them down and chopping them up for those fire-blackened pots is vile. Hunting dogs make whites wonder about the souls of their black neighbours.

There is another, more pressing reason why white farmers hate hunting dogs. The problem, of course, is that a hunting dog seldom distinguishes between a warthog and a prize dairy calf, and there is no doubt a long and proud history of dog handlers who have encouraged their animals' indiscretions. When a white farmer finds a calf lying in a pool of blood, its throat ravaged by canine teeth, he wonders whether the violence has not been subtly displaced, whether his neighbour is not sending him a message packed with anger and hatred.

Over the decades, as black and white honed a vast array of tactics in their quiet, internecine battles, the owning of hunting dogs became loaded with many meanings. It is about subsistence, to be sure, about putting a good meal on a poor family's table. But it is much more than that. It fires a message across the racial frontier. You use the countryside in your way, we will use it in ours. And if the two should become incompatible, we shall see who wins. You may have taken the land, but you will not dictate how we live our lives. That is our call, not yours.

So when the tenants heard the rule about hunting dogs, they were not surprised. Their parents and their grandparents had heard the same rule, and they had flouted it when they could, obeyed it when prudence demanded. But the words 'conservation area' lent a new twist to the old game, and left a bitter taste in the mouth.

Successive generations of white farmers on the Sarahdale/Izita border have waxed lyrical about the awesome beauty on their doorstep. The living-room walls of some farmhouses boast amateur landscapes that are dreamy, pretty, hyperbolically pastoral. But it took until the early 1990s for farmers to realise that beauty meant money – lots of it. The zebra and the buck are already there. The unspeakable beauty needs no maintenance. Erect a tall fence around the wild, uncultivated land you have never used, sprinkle the valley with simple wooden cabins, lay down some dirt roads, and you have a game lodge. There is an American niche market for this sort of tourism; seduce it and you can charge in dollars.

There are no tourists yet. The idea is still in its infancy. But there are many plans and lots of talk, and for the peasants in the area, it is war talk. The whites have never used all their land. They fence off fields for their cattle, they plant vegetables in the narrow, fertile strips on the river bank. But the wild bush land has always been used by the blacks, to hunt, for its firewood and its water. It is one of the corners of the countryside the peasants have refused to give up. So for the whites to fence in the whole countryside, to claim the zebra and buck that have always roamed there – that is no small thing. Across the district, blacks speak of the coming game farms as a betrayal.

For Mitchell's tenants, the advent of game farms finds its place in a long and sensitive history of the bushland. 'It is like when the forestry companies bought up the land in the 1950s,' one of Mitchell's tenants told me, 'taking huge stretches of it, tearing it to the ground, as if nobody had ever lived there, as if the way we lived our lives did not matter. Forty years later, it is happening all over again. We are being boxed into our little ghettos. Kahle is telling us we will not be allowed out. We will waste away on our little strips of land.'

There is little doubt that white farmers' decision to farm game had a great deal to do with their increasingly acrimonious relationship with black tenants. 'The blacks stole our cattle in such numbers that beef farming has become impossible here,' one of Mitchell's neighbours told me. 'We need to find new ways of earning a living. And if that means taking sections of our land which the blacks have used, it is too bad. They have brought it on themselves.'

*

There is a fourth rule recorded in Mitchell's minutes, this time from the second meeting, held on 28 August 1999, shortly before Peter's death: 'Each tenant family on Normandale is restricted to five head of cattle. Cattle are not to graze other than in the designated area. From Tuesday 30 August cattle outside the designated area will be impounded. After one warning, if this continues the owner of the cattle will be given notice to move off the property.'

Mitchell gave me a copy of his minutes only after I had spoken to his tenants, right at the end of my research. It was from them, not him, that I heard of the cattle rule. When I was told about it, I asked Mitchell how he had arrived at his numbers. Why five head of cattle per family?

'What must I do?' he replied irritably. 'The informal rule of the district is five head per family. If I make an allowance for my tenants, word gets out and others demand more from their landlords. I can't do that to my neighbours. Each has his own situation. Besides,' he continued, 'I never enforced that rule, not once. I told them about it, yes, as would any farmer in the district. But I never once counted each family's herd.'

A week or so after I was told of Mitchell's cattle rule, I met a tenant who worked and lived on a farm close to Normandale. I was introduced to him in the haphazard, incidental way so many of the people in this story came to me. A black colleague in Johannesburg overheard me talking about my research and told me that, many years ago, a distant cousin of his, a policeman, had been posted to Sarahdale for a six-month period. The policeman had a friend who was still in touch with a man who knew the district well, and he, in turn, still kept in contact with a tenant who lived two or three farms away from Normandale. Fast tiring of wild goose chases, I came close to abandoning the search for the elusive friend of a friend of a relative before it even began. But I went through the motions, contacted the policeman, then the policeman's Sarahdale friend. Perhaps it was the allure of nostalgia that egged them on, but both men were more enthusiastic about the project than I was, and a couple of weeks after starting my enquiry I found myself driving to Izita with both of them in the back seat.

The policeman was an elderly man by the name of Msane. He was dressed in off-duty blue jeans and a heavy checked shirt. Overdressed for a hot midlands afternoon, the sweat poured off his obese face in my rear-view mirror. I never learned his first name. He was introduced to me as Captain Msane, and he clearly enjoyed the sound of his title, so I never suggested calling him anything else. The old policeman was loud and voluble, and spent most of the trip railing against South Africa's new constitution.

'When you want to arrest someone, you have to haul this little constitution out of your pocket,' he shouted from the back seat, shaking my shoulder for effect. 'The print is so small you have to take your reading glasses out of your breast pocket. By the time you are ready to commence business, the criminal has shot you in the head and has moved on to his next robbery.'

The policeman's friend, a middle-aged man called Mzi who owned a small clothes shop in KwaMashu, smiled privately as Msane rambled on. At one point during Msane's tirade, my eyes met with Mzi's in the rear-view mirror. He winked at me and chuckled silently.

Arranging to meet the tenant was marked by all the delicacy and awkwardness to which I had become accustomed. A white man clutching a notebook does not just pitch up at the home of a black tenant asking questions about a murder, especially not in view of the tenant's neighbours. If anyone were to be arrested for Peter's murder in the weeks following my visit, my subject would be in serious trouble. So the two black men left me on the side of a district road about 15 kilometres from Sarahdale and made off in my car in the direction of Normandale. I spent the next 90 minutes throwing stones at a fence pole, tallying the proportion of hits to misses.

The tenant who climbed out of the car later that afternoon was in his late thirties and was dressed in the green overalls of a farm worker. He refused to tell me his name or which farmer he worked for. When I asked him questions about his personal history, he stared silently at the gathering sunset. Mzi, who acted as my translator, was a study of unobtrusiveness. He translated my questions with an earnest expression on his face, and when the tenant failed to reply, he sat there, as silent as the tenant, his face inscrutable. So I turned the discussion to more abstract questions, and recounted to the tenant a favourable interpretation of Mitchell's five-head-of-cattle-per-family rule. I said that Mitchell was only following the district's informal rules, that he had had many problems of cattle trespassing on his land and that he had a business to run. Mzi frowned for the first time and shook his head.

'Let me phrase that differently,' he said to me. 'We don't want to lose this man so early.'

'No,' I replied. 'Phrase it my way. If he gets offended, I will learn something from that.'

Mzi bowed his head and looked at the ground. He began with a preface dissociating himself from my views, apologising for them, and when he was done the tenant looked at me violently, cursed me under his breath and walked away. Mzi gave me an irascible glare and chased after the tenant, and the two men held a long conference in the middle of the district road. At length, they headed back to my car. The tenant motioned for me to sit and he joined me on the gravel at the side of the road, close up, his breath in my nostrils. From that close distance, he began to shout at me.

'Five head of cattle! Five head!' He stretched his hand out in front of my face, showing me five digits. 'Do you know what happens to your family name when you are restricted to five cattle? It disappears. Never mind that your family has been carrying its name for 200 years. Never mind that the spirits of your ancestors are shouting and cursing you. No cattle, no family name. It disappears for ever, and nobody can ever get it back.'

'You're talking about bridewealth, lobola.'

'Ah, but the white man is a quick one,' the tenant replied. He was a transformed man. His taciturn silence had given way to loud disdain and the barking of his voice against the quiet countryside buttressed his confidence. He turned his face from me scornfully and addressed Mzi. 'He has learned something already. Let me teach him a bit more.'

He touched me for the first time, slamming his hand down on my thigh and holding it there, pressing it for effect every time he wanted to emphasise his words.

'I don't know what the word "poverty" means to you. But let me tell you something about what it means here.

'There are two ways of dying from poverty. The first is when you have no food and you slowly waste away. The second is when you have no cattle and your sons cannot marry. They will have children, but the little ones will not be your grandchildren. They are vagrants, human beings with no ancestry. And then you have died because your family has died. You have disgraced everyone who came before you.'

I knew too little of the tenant's personal history to evaluate the meaning of his testimony. I wondered whether he himself had been born out of wedlock and had spent his life roaming the boundaries of a family history he had no right to claim. Or perhaps his own children were born 'vagrants'; perhaps the death of his own lineage was the albatross he wore around his neck.

Guessing at the source of his anger, I listened to what the tenant said about Arthur Mitchell. Long before Peter was killed, the tenant told me, the rules Mitchell laid down in February 1999 became infamous across the Sarahdale/Izita border. Their perniciousness lay in their subtlety. It is not as if Mitchell's cattle rule chased people off their land. He did not send in policemen and bulldozers. Things were far more delicate than that. There are quieter and more intelligent ways to destroy people. Take the mechanism by which a family survives through time, slowly, quietly choke it, until the family gradually melts into thin air. This is more devastating than a physical assault, the tenant told me. The white man assaults your dignity, your very being. He spits on you like you are a beast with no name and no history.

I told the tenant I did not believe him when he said that in February Mitchell already had the reputation of an evil man. Mitchell was only following the ways of the three generations that preceded him. What was different here? What was so distinctively evil about Mitchell? Listening to the translation of my questions, the robust, remonstrating tenant who had burst into existence at the mention of the cattle rule vanished as quickly as he had come. Once again, he put on his taciturn face and stared mutely at the twilight. He refused to answer any more questions.

Driving away from the meeting, I felt more strongly than ever that in the wake of his son's death, Mitchell had become an emblem among the blacks in the district for generations of unexpressed anger. On the journey from his home to my post on the side of the district road, Mzi and Captain Msane would have briefed the tenant about my business. By the time he met me, he would have known what talking about Peter's murder to a white journalist meant, that the murder was a beacon representing the district and its politics. A white man has died after a scuffle with black tenants. There is a story to tell, and much hinges on who was right and who wrong, who was victim and who villain. Had I met him before Peter's death, I wonder what the tenant would have told me about Mitchell's rules.

The story of lobola and the death of family lineages resonated powerfully. There were many people living in Izita on their own land, rather than white land, whose cattle had slowly dwindled such that they too could never pay bridewealth. But it is one thing when the root of your indignity can be related directly to your own poverty, and the political forces that have caused your destitution are abstract and invisible. It is quite another when the humiliation relates directly to the rules of a rich white landlord, and the instrument of your suffering has a name and face. Then the betrayal of which Charles van Onselen spoke is particularly bitter; the relationship with one white man in particular eats into the most tender and sacred places in people's souls.

I wanted to discuss these things with Msane and Mzi, but they were of little help. As we drove into the darkness I prodded them on their interpretation of the tenant's words. Both responded reluctantly in lean, unfinished sentences. Msane's freewheeling excursions into homespun philosophy had been put aside for another time. Mzi was as private as before. A delicate estrangement had crept into our encounters since the meeting with the tenant, and much of the return journey went by in silence.

*

I called Lourie Steyn again, this time to talk about cattle.

'Ja, all my tenants kept cattle,' he said. 'It was one of their perks.'

An interesting choice of words. They grated against the things the tenant had told me at the side of the road. For Steyn, cattle were a 'perk', a little extra the paternalist allows out of the goodness of his heart. For his tenants, they were the symbol and guarantee of their identities. It is impossible that Steyn never absorbed this during his 30 years in the district. He knew about bridewealth and about the measure of a family's weight and pride. I marvelled at how thin his empathy must have been during the course of those decades.

I asked him to tell me roughly how many head of cattle each family kept, and whether there were large discrepancies between the families.

'We used to keep books on who had what,' he told me. 'But that fell away about ten years before I left. You know how it is with blacks and cattle when a son or a daughter gets married; cattle kept coming in and out. It was too difficult to keep track.'

'So there were no restrictions on cattle numbers.'

'Ja, of course there were restrictions. Otherwise there is too much grazing. Langeni can only take 60 or 70 head. More than that and you have a disaster.'

'There were times when you told people to get rid of cattle?'

'Not really, no. They balanced each other out, you see. One family would have 12 head, another only two head. So it didn't get to the point where people had to sell or cull.'

'What about the district rule?' I asked.

'What rule?'

'That each family can only keep five head of cattle.'

'Oh, ja. There was that. Average of five or six head per family. But it wasn't a strict rule. It was more a rule of thumb.'

It is here that the relationship between Mitchell's rules and the things he did before he uttered them becomes crucial. A new proprietor on the Sarahdale/Izita border who announced that each family was restricted to five head of cattle could have been saying a number of things. He might have been giving a merely formal nod to a half-forgotten stipulation. Or he might have been indicating a rule of thumb, a rough limit that was to be negotiated in the give-and-take of a daily relationship. Yet, given the fastidiousness with which Mitchell had been policing his farms, it is unlikely that his tenants understood him thus. He told them that he wanted their names, that he would be keeping a check on what they built, on who came and went. All these things together constituted the meaning of Mitchell's cattle rule, a sign of how he would enforce it. He appeared to be saying that those with 15 head of cattle must get rid of ten. True, he never implemented the rule, but that hardly mattered. By his tenants' lights, if he had not yet counted their cattle it was because they had not allowed him to. They had shown him they would fight back.

The things Steyn said about cattle began to shed light on something that had been bothering me. It had occurred to me some time before that the families who had been most vocal in their resistance to Mitchell appeared to be the ones with the least to lose by his new rules. Among the Cube and the Mashabana brothers, several had full-time jobs and homes in Clermont. They also had vehicles and licensed guns, a sure sign that they were far from destitute. They seemed to be less dependent on the countryside than most. The line dividing peasant from proletarian is a blurred one, but the Cubes and the Mashabanas had had far more success in the cities than their typical neighbours. I would have thought, at first blush, that the front line in the fight against Mitchell would be occupied by those with everything to lose, people whose entire incomes, homes and identities lay in the future of Normandale. I wondered what it was about the Cubes and Mashabanas that raised the stakes so high. Why did they invest so much passion in the countryside, when much of their well-being was located elsewhere?

The answer should really have been obvious from the beginning, for the more success people like the Normandale tenants have in the city, the more valuable their control of their countryside assets becomes. A home and a job in Clermont do not erode the importance of cattle in the countryside. On the contrary, cattle are the store of one's success, an emblem of one's escape from destitution, a guarantee that one's children will marry well and that one's lineage is secured. It occurred to me after speaking to Steyn that the Normandale tenants who had fared best over the last generation were precisely the ones who would fall furthest if Mitchell were to implement his cattle rule. As with the question of hunting, the import of Mitchell's new regime was far more than symbolic.

*

Another rule in Mitchell's August minutes: 'No additional huts or buildings will be permitted without the authority of Mr Mitchell.' The February minutes are more ominous: 'No further building without the authority of Mr Mitchell. Breach of 6(3) and 10(3)b [Mitchell is referring here to clauses in the Extension of Security of Tenure Act, which governs his relationship with his tenants.] Failure to comply may lead to eviction.'

There is a difference between the way this rule is worded in Mitchell's minutes and the way it actually came out when he addressed his tenants. The difference is crucial, and when I heard the tenants' version I went back to Mitchell and quoted them quoting him, word for word.

'Yes,' he said. 'They are right. That is how I worded it.'

'No additional huts or buildings permitted without my authority,' Mitchell told his tenants. And then he added: 'When you want to extend your accommodation, you come and speak to me. I will come down to Langeni and I will personally assess whether the extra accommodation is necessary. If it is for a daughter, or her husband, if it is about family, then it is fine. But if it is about bringing new families onto my property, I will not permit it.'

I recounted Mitchell's building rule, and the way in which he intended to implement it, to all sorts of South Africans – white conservatives, white lefties, middle-class black urbanites, and black people who grew up in rural KwaZulu-Natal. The response to the building rule from those in the last category – those who had tasted something of peasant life in the midlands – was in most cases the same. Their faces would grimace in a strange hybrid of disgust and pain, as if an invisible bond joined them to Mitchell's tenants, causing them to share in their humiliation. Then they would compose themselves and nod sagely. 'Ah, so that is what happened. You see now that it is no great mystery that the son was killed.'

I was astounded by this response. When it came once, I did not take it that seriously. But then it came again and again. Throughout my research, I did not for a moment think that the rural black people I met would express unambivalent satisfaction with the murder of the white man. The pervasive rage, the powerful identification with the killers, was awesome and shocking.

When I heard about the building rule and was confronted by these unexpected responses to it, I immediately went looking for Elias. He was a wise and judicious man, with an instinctive distaste for the biblical morality of murder and revenge, and I wanted his response in particular. The old man proved difficult to find. I had only visited his niece's house in Izita once, after dark, and when I went looking for it in daylight I soon got lost. I stopped several people on the roadside and asked for directions, but it seems that nobody in Izita co-operates with a white stranger. Everyone shrugged and walked away. Elias had also given me an address in Edendale, but when I went looking for him there, nobody had heard of the street name he had given me. Long after I had abandoned hope of ever finding him, I got an unexpected call on my cellphone. Strangely, he did not announce himself or even say hello. He just said: 'I hear you have been looking for me.' I recognised his voice immediately and smiled at his awkward telephone manners.

We met in a pub in downtown Pietermaritzburg in the middle of a weekday afternoon, a place where white men in suits and ties go to drink together after work. We arrived a couple of hours before the after-work rush, and the place was empty, its staff listlessly wandering the dark, thick carpets. Elias was probably the pub's first and last black working-class patron, and the alien surroundings unnerved him. In his unmistakably working-class attire – fake snakeskin shoes, smart polyester trousers, supermarket-shelf baseball jacket – he resembled an off-duty waiter, mooching about at the end of his shift, his uniform squeezed into a plastic supermarket bag. He hunched over our table, making his body small, and spoke in a conspiratorial whisper. Ironically, his behaviour made him conspicuous, and the white bartender eyed us with ungenerous curiosity during the course of the afternoon. I wished that I had met him in his own home, where he commands the authority of a patriarch and speaks with the weight that is his due.

Elias listened intently for the six or seven minutes it took me to tell the story. He betrayed no emotion, just sat there in his awkward posture. When I was done, he took my pen and began doodling on a serviette – he drew gyre-like cords that started in a tight ring and spiralled outwards, like a vortex or a tornado.

'The rule itself is no surprise,' he told me, still doodling, his eyes switching between mine and the serviette. 'It is one of the oldest rules set down by whites for blacks, and very few people have died because of it. What Mitchell got wrong was the question of style, of approach. He should have gone down to Langeni with a crate of beer, black people's beer. He should have invited the heads of the families to drink with him, asked them something about their lives, how they supported themselves, where they got their firewood, how many family members had good jobs. And then he should have said, "Listen, the nine families that are here I can live with, side by side, in peace. But nobody else is welcome. I have a farming operation to run here and I can't have hundreds of families living on my land. So, do me a favour. Build by all means, when your daughter gets married, when kids are born. But don't build in order to bring strangers onto the land."'

I silently scorned Elias's idyllic fantasy of what was possible between white farmers and black tenants on the Sarahdale/Izita border, but I did not challenge him on it until much later.

'This business of coming onto the land to make a personal inspection,' Elias continued, 'it was a very big mistake. When I first listened to you telling me the story, what went through my mind was, "This man wants these people off his land. He has decided to destroy them." First you have the five-head-of-cattle rule, which, as you rightly say, touches on raw and painful questions of lineage. Now the man is saying that you cannot give birth without him examining the size of your wife's stomach. You cannot bring a man or a woman into your household without the white baas coming down to examine the marriage papers. If the white man says no, where must the newborn baby sleep – on the roof? Where must the newly-weds conceive their first child – in their parents' bed? The white man decides these things.'

'That is a jaundiced interpretation. It expects the worst.'

'No, you are wrong. The worst is in the rule itself. The rule itself says the white man comes down to your home and counts your wives and your children. He walks into your bedroom and measures it, sees how many people it can hold. He decides whether you make love to your wife in private or in front of your children. You are no longer the head of your family. The white man is.'

'So what should Mitchell have done?'

'Respected human dignity. You do not march into people's homes and count them like goats.'

Later that afternoon, Elias and I fought a complicated, disturbing fight, all in hushed tones, the barman watching us from ten feet away. But there are some things I must tell you before we get to that.

*

There are two more rules I should mention. The first you have already heard about from Mitchell himself: 'Mr Mitchell must be provided with a list of family heads and family members living on the property.' The second is more an announcement than a rule: 'Photos of all kraals will be taken in due course for control purposes.' Mitchell did not in fact take these photographs until December 1999, after Peter was killed.

In Mitchell's version of events, you will remember, it was the taking of names that caused all the trouble. Mhila Mashabana stood up and chastised the white man. 'We do not give our names to *umlungu*. He will use them against us.' When Mitchell told the story, Mashabana's anger was not easy to fathom. There was something abstract, almost mystical about it. But against the backdrop of the cattle rule and the building rule, and Mitchell's determination to push the tenants back into the confines of Langeni, they interpreted the taking of names and photographs in a very specific way.

For the taking of names and photographs was now clearly understood as a mechanism of surveillance and policing. Mitchell was going to police the boundaries of his land, as well as the occupancy of Langeni itself, very closely. Names and photographs were to be used in the exercise of enforcement and control. And yet there is more than that. All of Mitchell's rules were ominous for any of his tenants who planned to defend their victory over Steyn. Why did Mhila Mashabana lose his temper over this one in particular? Perhaps because it was so personal. Perhaps the idea that his name and a photograph of his home would sit in a filing cabinet up at the white man's farmhouse, to be taken out and used against him, perhaps that is the image that lit Mashabana's fuse.

There are a few other things I should tell you. In Mitchell's account of the two meetings, he is a paragon of grace. In the face of much provocation, he keeps his cool, talks in quiet tones, never takes the bait. 'You don't want me to take your names. Okay, there is clearly a problem. We will leave it for now.' At the time, I found his account of the meetings a little puzzling. By the time the second meeting was convened, some of his tenants had told him to his face they would flout his rules. Others had threatened violence against him. Why should he remain serene and gentle under the circumstances? Surely he would be asserting his authority.

And indeed, Mitchell's first account does not quite tally with the way things actually happened. Mashabana was the vocal one at the February meeting, and in the months between the two meetings, Mitchell prepared a plan for him. When the question of names was raised at the August meeting, Mashabana again stood up and railed against the white race. This time, Mitchell took a carefully worded eviction notice from his bag, handed it to Mashabana in front of the assembly, and told the translator to tell the troublesome man to pack his bags.

I tell this story, not to catch Mitchell out for being dishonest with me; his account of the meetings was not dishonest, it was just unperceptive. And that is the point. Mitchell believed that he was behaving like a company representative at a wage negotiation. He could not have been more wrong. The relationship between a company and a trade union rides on its formal equality. It is, after all, a *negotiation*. Each reminds the other of the weapons he has not yet brought into the room – the right to strike, to go-slow, the haunting spectre of retrenchment. A compromise is struck, shaped by the balance of forces, and by the skill with which each side brings the image of its power to the other.

All Mitchell has taken from this arena is its colourless formality. He was not negotiating, as one does in wage talks; he was laying down a set of rules. His interaction with his tenants could not have been more foreign to the relationship between a company and a trade union. It is an unfortunate combination: the mindset of an ancient paternalist and the manner of a modern negotiator. They don't go together. For Mitchell's audience, the businesslike formality of the negotiator speaks of coldness, while his paternalism is a sign that nothing has changed.

*

I am reading over the notes I took at my first meeting with Mitchell in Colin Waugh's lounge. Each page is greasy and well-thumbed and covered in the fluorescent colours of an assortment of highlighters – I have read them countless times. This time, I am looking for two things in particular. The five-head-of-cattle rule, and the part of the building rule that says Mitchell will make personal inspections. I have begun to think I must have forgotten about these things somehow. But there is no reference to either rule. Mitchell never mentioned them.

He did not deliberately hide these rules from me. I am convinced of that. He just did not think they were important enough to mention. Everyone who tells a story cuts and edits, instinctively, unconsciously. The things that are inconsequential are trimmed or erased. That Mitchell edited out the very two rules that angered his tenants so, that he did not see the rage and humiliation they fostered, brings into relief his terrible ignorance of the people on his doorstep. The silences, the things he did not say, lie close to the source of his tragedy – for a moment, at any rate.

The truth is that nothing that passed between Mitchell and his tenants was new. The white farmers and black tenants of the midlands have always jockeyed over cattle numbers, over the right to bring extended family onto the property, over the integrity of fences and grazing land. It was there in the 1840s, when the Voortrekker Raad passed a law capping the number of black families residing on a white farm. It was there in the tale William Beinart told about the politics of cattle and fences in nineteenth-century Umzimkulu. There has always been a quiet struggle over who owns the countryside, and it has always boiled down to the smallest of details – the number of this family's cattle, the building of that hut. Mitchell and his tenants were tracing the lines of an old battle, one whose contours had been shaped and reshaped over a century and a half of history.

So what went wrong? One version is that Mitchell was locked in a time warp. He played the old game as it was played in the 1940s and 50s. Back then, in the heartland of white baasskap, it was understood that the landlord laid down the rules unilaterally. He told his tenants where they could shit and where they could sleep, and in return he built schools for their children, paid medical bills for the ill, and bought coffins for the dead. It was also understood that the limits of each rule would be quietly tested, that the precise meaning of words would take shape in the course of a silent and tacit negotiation.

But the Normandale tenants of the late 1990s were a different kettle of fish. While they kept their rural homes, they were of the generation that had migrated in a great wave to the cities and in spirit they were urban men. Their formative experience was not the baasskap of the fields but the wild and crazy years of urban insurrection. They cursed their fathers for their shameless submissiveness. I remember Mduduzi Cube's reported words when he told the story of his family's move from Porter to Steyn. 'You know the old folk. They made too many compromises.'

Mitchell laid down his rules for the ears of a generation that was long dead. The old Cube who agreed to move to Normandale when Mduduzi was a boy would have sat listening to Mitchell impassively, his dignity sheltered behind an impregnable shell. He would have behaved like the archetypal stoic, whittling down his needs until they fitted into a space the white man could not penetrate. His children's generation was anything but stoical. They were acquisitive and hardened men, and they were opportunistic to a T. They had taken what they could grab from the countryside, and they were never going to give it back. And some among them were brutal enough to kill in defence of their gains.

This last thought surely complicates the matter considerably. While it is true that Mitchell was an old paternalist, the question is whether any commercial farmer could have dealt with Normandale in the aftermath of Steyn. Would a subtle liberal of the twenty-first century have been spared his son? Or has the battle for the countryside been honed down to a lean, zero-sum affair, where every commercial farmer risks his life to keep his farm? As much as it would comfort me to think otherwise, I am not sure that a genuine negotiator would have succeeded. I am not sure the tenants were ever going to allow somebody to regain Normandale as a commercial farm.

I am driving from Durban to Alanview in the crisp light of an early Saturday morning, a nine o'clock meeting with Arthur Mitchell ahead of me. In the solitude of my car, I begin to imagine my conversation with him, and it makes me feel anxious. I want to tell him everything I have learned from his tenants, but I want to take care about how I say it. For a man who has recently lost his son, the line between explaining a murder and condoning it is a thin one. I am not sure he will understand what it is that *I* have come to understand. I want to tell him I find it remarkable that he forgot to inform me of the two rules that caused so much anger, that these things reveal an extraordinary ignorance on his part. And yet I do not want to tell him he is responsible for his son's death – things are infinitely more complex than that.

It is Saturday morning in the quiet, middle-class landscape of Alanview. Colin Waugh and I are sitting in his lounge, the obligatory plate of wafer-thin sandwiches on the coffee table, a pot of tea, Colin's black-and-white dogs asleep under the table. Mitchell arrives holding a transparent plastic packet brimming with large tomatoes, just picked from his farm. He is the consummate gentleman, and he tells us so.

'For the woman of the house,' he smiles. 'A good visitor never arrives empty-handed.'

It is 12 days after the killing of Bheki Cube, and beneath the soft-spoken tones and the studied manners, Mitchell is bursting with testosterone. The death has not quenched his thirst for revenge. It has egged him on. He speaks of divine vengeance, and the gap between the gentleness of his voice and the ferocity of his thoughts is chilling. It is a bad morning to talk to Mitchell about his tenants' souls. In his mind, they are only treacherous bastards.

'The five-head-of-cattle rule, Arthur. They interpreted that as a wilful assault on their very identities. They feared that the rule would obliterate their names from the planet.'

Mitchell tilts his head back, looks at the ceiling and grits his teeth. 'What utter nonsense. What monstrous nonsense. It is not I who obliterates people. It is they. Of course, they will give you sob stories. They will tell you they are the victims. They will manipulate you and play on your ignorance.' He stops, shakes his head. Then a new thought comes to him. 'What you are saying helps me. I can begin to picture what happened. The Cubes are the bosses down at Langeni. They control things. After the February meeting, they would have gone round Langeni poisoning people's minds. The white man wants to destroy your lineage. It is either us or him. It is life and death. The Cubes would have stirred that whole place into a frenzy. By the time they were finished, I had become the devil.'

I look to Colin for help. His eyes are busy as he returns my gaze. But he says nothing.

'And the building rule, Arthur. The idea that the white man walks through your house to see how many people live there, to see whether an extra building is warranted. The idea that it is he who decides whether a marriage is legitimate enough to warrant an extra room.'

'All I am hearing here is the dishonesty of the Zulus,' Mitchell replies, waving his arm dismissively. 'You see, they are the ones who abuse power when they get it. They are the ones who destroy another man's life on a whim. So they assume that I will do the same. They think my rules are out to get them, because that's precisely how they would use the rules. They think I think like a Zulu.'

The discussion lasts ten minutes. There is nothing left to say. One of us changes the subject, and we begin talking about the Cube funeral that is to take place at Langeni that afternoon. Mitchell points out that the body is to be buried on his land, that nobody asked him for permission to bury it there, and that if he were a ruthless man he would have it disinterred. He says he must get back to his farm as soon as possible. The funeral will bring a crowd to Langeni, an angry crowd, and he does not want to leave his wife alone.

So he leaves, and as I watch him go, I think of him as one of the old patriarchs who litter the pages of the Old Testament, egging on his God to destroy his enemies. I imagine that he has already forgotten our conversation by the time he gets back to Sarahdale. There are other things on his mind.

When Mitchell is gone, Colin drags me off to the kitchen to watch him make another round of sandwiches. He is peering into his fridge, and I cannot see his face as he speaks.

'Your story is fascinating, fascinating.'

'Why?'

'Because these cultural questions are so delicate, so explosive.

Innocent words and gestures can lead to such terrible misunder-standings.'

'You see why they believed they were being invaded, why they were being humiliated?'

'That is what is so fascinating, yes.'

*

In retrospect, it was indeed an unfortunate day to talk to Mitchell about these matters, the burial day for a 20-year-old man whom every black soul in the district believes was killed at Mitchell's instigation. But the things Mitchell said then, while cast in the words and the tone of the moment, were deeply held convictions. Many months later, when the book was almost written and Mitchell was becoming increasingly wary of the things I might say, he spoke, unsolicited, about the question of his culpability.

'When something awful happens,' he told me in quiet and measured tones, 'you cast your mind back and you wonder whether you did something wrong. We all make mistakes. There are areas in my life I regret, things I did and said that I should not have. But this is not one of them. I wanted to farm. To do that, I had to stop poaching and illegal grazing on my land. That is why my son was killed. It really is that simple.'

SIXTEEN

I am sitting with Elias in the downtown Pietermaritzburg pub. He has put down my pen and has spread out the serviette on which he doodled in front of him. He admires his artwork, rubs his fingers over it until the blue tornadoes smudge and traces of ink accumulate along his fingerprint lines. He drinks his beer leisurely, one modest sip at a time. I have just ordered my second; he is halfway through his first.

I watch him from the other side of the table, and I realise that despite the large, warm place he has occupied in my head for the last few months, we are to all intents and purposes strangers. On the two occasions we have met during the last year, I have treated him with the exaggerated deference one shows to an old man. There are things he has just said with which I want to take issue, and I am not sure that the boundaries of our relationship will allow for it.

'Elias,' I say, uttering his name so as to signal the heaviness of what I want to tell him. 'You talk as if Mitchell should have behaved like a new neighbour in the suburbs. Cracked open a few beers, laughed, told jokes. Do you really think that is possible on the border of Sarahdale and Izita?'

'Why not?' he replies, crumpling up his serviette and pushing it to the corner of the table.

'Because it is not simply a question of finding out about the families, where they collect firewood and draw water. The relationship between these people is antagonistic. He wanted to farm the land they had taken from Steyn. Drinking beer together is not going to make that go away.'

'Yes, their relationship is a delicate one.' He takes another sip of his beer and nods sagely. 'All the more reason for Mitchell to move with care.'

'Elias, there is a struggle for land out there. It has been going on for over a century. When people deliberately allow their cattle onto your field while it is resuscitating, just in order to disrupt your farming, you do not come to an agreement with them over a beer. When people out of sheer spite cut down the fences you have just built, you do not solve the matter by showing you are a nice guy.'

'So what do you do then?'

'I am not sure. I am not sure that there is any easy solution. But I want you to see that Mitchell's rules were not the rules of a maniac. They were about defending his business, every one of them. When your neighbours are deliberately sabotaging your farming operation, you need to control them. When your tomatoes are pinched every night, when your fields are being set alight, there is a limit to the logic of give and take. It's not as if there was a clear, easy space for compromise here. There was a war of attrition. He had to defend the boundaries of his farm.'

Elias looks at me closely. He did not expect me to defend Mitchell. The cautiousness of his body language, which had begun to ease during the course of the afternoon, returns quite suddenly.

'I see we are set for a battle this afternoon. So let me begin by conceding the first round. Yes, this is not a matter that can be resolved over a crate of beer. You're right. Every inch he gave they would have taken, and then some more. Mitchell's problem is that he approached the matter as if we are still living under apartheid. He pretended to himself that he could think up some rules, march onto the tenants' land, shout them out, go home and then everything would be all right.'

'He was a fool to think that. He dug his son's grave.'

'Dug his son's grave? Are you saying that when tenants don't like their landlord's rules, they can be expected to kill his son?'

'They would not have killed him if this had happened in the 1980s,' Elias says. He smiles at me again, but curtly this time, humourlessly. 'Same families, same farmer, same rules. Nobody would have died. Do you know why that is, my friend? Do you know what was different then?'

'They were afraid then? They were afraid of the white state?'

'No.' Elias is getting into his stride now. He is less alienated by the strange surroundings. He motions to the bartender and points at his empty beer bottle. The bartender nods. 'In the 1980s there was hope. Change was around the corner. The ugly things would soon be leaving. Then democracy came. Mandela's government.

Then another election. Mbeki's government. And the white farmers still run the countryside. Things are getting worse, in fact. The farmers are building these game reserves and taking over miles of land they have never used before. They don't trust the police any longer so they create their own private police forces. These men in their uniforms stand on the hilltops watching your every move with their binoculars and their night-vision glasses, defending the law of their land.

'There is nowhere to escape to. You can't go to the cities because there is no work there. You will starve to death. You are a prisoner in the white man's countryside, and now there is no prospect of anything different. It is you against him for the rest of time. So when he marches onto your land and tells you he is going to inter-view your future son-in-law and decide whether he can live in your house, you take matters into your own hands, because nobody else is going to.'

'You kill his son?'

'Yes. It has come to that.'

I try to hide my shock but I am exasperated, and as I begin speaking I am surprised by the aggression in my voice.

'Elias, the last time I saw you, you spoke bitterly about the anarchy in Izita. You complained that the place was run by thugs who kill people to get their own way. What is different here?'

'The difference is a feeling in my gut. I would not want the man who pulled the trigger to go to jail.'

'It was a just killing?'

'That is a big question. Let me answer it in a small way. If I was a tenant living on that farm, and I knew that my neighbour was planning to kill the farmer's son …' He shrugs and thinks for a while. 'As I think about it, it becomes more complicated. I would have advised against it, but not out of sympathy for the farmer. Only because my home would have become a war zone. The police would come in and out, with their fists and their guns. A crazy farmer might come in the night and shoot all of us. I am not a warrior. I don't want to live in the middle of that hatred. But if my neighbour had refused to listen to me and gone ahead with his plans, I would not have stood in his way. I would have held my tongue. After he killed the young man, and the police came to ask me questions, I would have looked the white policeman in the eye and told him I know nothing.'

246

'And if your neighbour had asked you to help plan the murder?'

The bartender arrives with Elias's beer, and we wait in silence until he has gone. Elias watches him all the way back to the counter, then pours his beer slowly into his glass, puts it down and continues speaking.

'I would have said to him: "I cannot help, my friend. But I implore you to take care."'

'I thought only bad people commit murder. The sort of person who kills a white landlord because of his rules will also kill a black neighbour for his cattle. You are giving these people the green light. But you claim they are your enemies.'

The old man is genuinely moved by my comment. He thinks a long time before answering. 'You're right,' he says eventually. 'If the tenants had been my family, and eight other families just like us, nobody would have died. There must be some evil in you to solve the matter the way it was solved. And your second point is also right. I would not sleep easy at night if I knew that my neighbour had killed the landlord. I would wonder when my turn would come. I would move. Find somewhere else to live.'

The small victory has given me confidence and I go for another.

'You still think that if Mitchell had presented his rules differently, his son would be alive today?'

'Who can say for sure? I don't know the people who killed him. I hear everything from you. What is it you want from me? Do you want me to tell you I mourn the death of the white man? Will that put you at ease?'

'I just want you to finish a train of thought you started earlier.'

'Okay. Okay, I will finish it. I suspect that if Mitchell had gone down to the tenants with his crate of beer and showed them he was a human being who understood them as human beings ...' He sees the end of his thought process, disbelieves it and starts again. 'Two different things might have happened. The first is that Mitchell makes a few compromises. The tenants can walk on his land to fetch firewood. They will steal a couple of his tomatoes while they are there. Every now and again, they will even pick up a newborn calf and put it in their herd. Mitchell will curse them that night, but he'll get over it. They'll live together. He will regard the small thefts as a necessary part of his business.'

I interject and finish Elias's thought in my own words. 'And the second option is that they regard his flexibility as weakness. He

247

allows them onto Normandale to collect firewood, and they use the opportunity to steal all his cattle and shoot all his game. He allows them to build a road to Langeni, and they drive in a truck and harvest his crop in the middle of the night.

'Maybe they decided the farm was theirs as soon as Steyn left. Maybe any new landlord who tried to defend his farm would have died.'

'Perhaps,' Elias replies. 'Perhaps. That is a very grave situation. It means someone like Mitchell has a choice to make. Either fight a war or pack up and leave.'

'So you admit that Mitchell may have had to fight a war in order to farm, but you still see no tragedy in his son's death.'

'Well, if running a farm means behaving like a dictator, if it means going to take photographs of people's homes and counting them like goats, maybe he had no business farming there.'

'That is a very heavy thing to say.'

'It's not so heavy. He is white. He has money. He can set up a farm in a quieter district.'

'So Mitchell leaves, and the peasants move onto what used to be his land, and the border between the farms and the peasants recedes, and then the farmer behind Mitchell is on the border and he must leave too, and soon the peasants own the whole country-side and the whites barricade themselves into the cities.'

Elias chuckles malevolently. He has tired of the conversation. He sees no reason to maintain its civility and he goes for my jugu-lar. I arrived at the pub about half an hour before him and there is a well-read copy of *Business Day* – the financial daily consumed by South Africa's business elite – lying on the table between us. Elias points at my newspaper scornfully.

'What do you read there? The price of your shares? The value of the rand against the dollar? To you, these are important things. They tell you about the future of your country. Where I come from, these things have fuck all to do with the future.'

This is the first time he has sworn in front of me. It is way out of character.

'Maybe next year the economy will grow at four per cent, maybe one per cent, maybe even minus four per cent. It means nothing in the countryside. There are no decent jobs for people who don't speak English, who don't read and write well. The economy could explode and it would still leave these people behind. There is nothing for them. Whatever happens, it is the white farmers and their rules. To escape from that you would have to go and live in a slum in KwaMashu, where you will get your throat slit for the shirt on your back. So what if the countryside is returned to the peasants. For you it is horrible. For them ...' He opens his shoulders rhetorically, and allows his body to finish his sentence.

'In the union movement I was taught about Karl Marx. I was told that the age of the white bosses is good because it will lead to the age of the workers. Maybe that was nonsense. Maybe we should go back to our cattle and our goats. Maybe my great-grand-father's life was quite good.'

'You're not talking sense, Elias.'

'No, my friend. The problem is that your imagination is not big enough to put you in somebody else's shoes. You come here to the midlands to write about the murder of a white farmer. The farming community opens their arms to you because they want the world to know about their outrage. And you write their book for them. Yes, you go to the other side, with your informers and your old friends from Cosatu. And you try to do the blacks justice. But no matter what you say, your book is still about the white man being chased off the land. And people in the cities read it and get upset, and politicians put pressure on the police to solve this murder so they can tell the country they are still in control. And so you send a man to jail.

'It would be better if you did not come. Just let things sort themselves out quietly. If it is the destiny of the place to become a peasant society again, then so be it. Get on with your own life in Johannesburg.'

Elias's soliloquy seduces me. I feel exhilarated as he sweeps across history, painting the last century as a brief interlude, an interruption. He seduces me and I hate myself for it. When I rose to Mitchell's defence, I did so as a journalist. I wanted my subject to work for his prejudices. But a part of me listened to myself defending Mitchell, and as I heard my voice, I knew it was for real. I was not a journalist, but a white man, like Mitchell, and I was in his corner. I needed Elias to lose his argument because he scared me. And as he dug in his heels, and spoke to me as a racist, I slipped out of this primordial whiteness, became a journalist again, listened to my subject sweep across time, was excited in the most abstract and unsatisfying of ways, as if I was observing a foreign country, and would send a dispatch home, to be read by other disinterested observers. I feel cramped and inhibited, miles away from myself. I would rather be Elias or Mitchell, a protagonist, full of fire and conviction, ready to fight to the death.

Elias leaves the pub before me. I watch his back, and the back of his head, and he is a humble old worker again, slouched slightly, his instinctive deference waiting should a stranger cross his path. He wanted to hurt me, but I feel no animosity toward him. I would like myself more for hating him. I even try for a moment, but it is no use. I am marvelling at the situation from far away, as if there is nothing personal at stake.

SEVENTEEN

Some time after his son's murder case was struck off the court roll, Arthur Mitchell sold Derbytin, the farm on which Peter was killed, as well as Normandale, where the nine tenant families live. Eleanor, the land on which Mitchell's farmhouse stood, was also on the market. Once that was sold, Mitchell would abandon the Sarahdale/Izita border and go back to the northern suburbs of Durban, from whence he came.

Mitchell swung like a pendulum during the last six months of 2000. Listening to his phone ring, I would not know what to anticipate. There were times when his soft voice barely rose above a murmur, and I would have to strain against the distant traffic of downtown Johannesburg to hear him.

'Selling Derbytin was the hardest thing I ever did,' he told me. 'That last drive down to the irrigation fields ... I am not a tearful man, but ... It was all for him. All for him.'

It was during one of his darkest periods that I first stumbled on the story Mitchell's tenants told – the threats of a game farm, the five-cattle rule, the personal supervision of building renovations.

'Arthur,' I said. 'I have been in touch with your tenants, and they have a story to tell. I am going to tell it and you are not going to like it.'

'Are you warning me, Jonny?' Mitchell replied. There was a chuckle in his voice, but it was devoid of humour. Or malice. I felt I was talking to a man who was physically ill, his body frail, the simple process of forming words too cumbersome to bother with.

'How long is your book?'

'I guess it will end up being about 250 pages.'

'That's a lot of reading, Jonny. Maybe you should highlight the parts you feel I should read.'

I am not sure how long moods like that lingered, but when he said it he meant it. He really did not care. He was watching the world from the depths of depression, and it was all too far away to mean anything to him.

Other times, Mitchell was as bubbly as a toddler with a new tricycle.

'Have you found anyone interested in buying Eleanor yet?' I asked him once.

'Hell, no,' he replied, all perky and jovial. 'No, it's mine for the moment, and I'm going to have fun. I've been toying with the idea of bringing beef back to Eleanor. A big herd. Up to 300 head, like it was before. If it wasn't for the foot-and-mouth epidemic, I swear I'd do it.'

'Is the epidemic that bad?'

'You'd be crazy to farm beef for the next three years. A disease like that; you don't mess around with it.'

The disease was first detected in October on a farm near Camperdown, outside Pietermaritzburg. A crate of contaminated feed had been off-loaded from Durban harbour a week or two earlier, and a lax and incompetent port authority had let it through. Despite the fact that the provincial veterinary authority picked up the disease early, it spread south, racing towards towns like Alanview within a matter of days.

A myriad legends about the spread of the disease soon circulated among the white farmers of the southern midlands. They all spoke of the irresponsibility of black peasants. Some said that peasant farmers surreptitiously transported their tiny herds out of the quarantine zone as soon as they heard that the veterinary authority was to cull their animals. 'The fucking coons,' one of Mitchell's neighbours cursed. 'They're prepared to bring down the whole province to save six malnourished bulls.' Other farmers used the occasion to nurture their feelings of cultural fascination and tolerance. 'We must be big and imaginative about these things,' the former president of the KwaZulu-Natal Agricultural Union, Graham MacIntosh, told me. 'For you and me, cattle are commodities. Beyond that, they mean nothing. For the Zulus they are a store of value, like a piece of antique furniture. Of course they'll push their cattle out of the culling zone. So would you if you shared their culture.'

As the days wore on, the stories told by white farmers grew more detailed. I read an intelligence report which claimed that a truck driver heard news of the quarantine on the radio while driving on the N3 motorway between Pietermaritzburg and Ladysmith in the early hours of the morning. He turned his truck around, drove straight to Camperdown and offered to transport peasant herds out of the zone for an exorbitant fee. Others said that a local Camperdown induna, anxious to shore up his waning support, offered to smuggle cattle out of the zone free of charge.

The truth is that foot-and-mouth is a notoriously contagious disease and almost impossible to contain. It is spread by wind, by human breath and by milk. There are a thousand ways in which it might have broken free of its Camperdown confines before the quarantine was enforced, from the smuggling of black-owned cattle to the breath of a white farmer. But, of course, farmers sifted prejudicially through the possibilities and chose the ones they liked best. No matter what the occasion, the inhabitants of the midlands will always tell the same stories about each other. If there is no evidence, it will be spun, automatically, from the sure and certain wells of collective prejudice. No one will know quite where the facts came from, but everyone will know that they are true.

In my imagination, I see Mitchell rebuilding his herd – hundreds of beef cattle chomping Eleanor's fields. I imagine the Cubes, the Mashabanas and the Mabidas watching the changes on Eleanor, and I smile to myself as I think of the things that cross their minds. White beef farmers go insane when they find peasant cattle on their fields. Their primary fear is disease. Their cattle are dipped and inoculated. Peasant cattle may carry diseases in their urine to which the commercial herds have long lost their immunity. With foot-and-mouth, the ante is raised that much higher. A stray cow could destroy one's entire herd. I imagine Mitchell's tenants thinking these things. They cut a hole in his fence and drive a sickly-looking cow onto his grazing pastures, and that night over dinner, they chuckle to themselves. They have four generations of knowledge of these games at their disposal. And they are far more imaginative than their forebears; they could happily drive Mitchell insane.

'I am itching to replenish my herd,' Mitchell told me. 'But it would be so imprudent. So I am turning my attention to game. My boys tell me they have counted 60 head on Eleanor alone. Zebra, warthog, a whole assortment of buck.

'Jonny, I am thinking of fencing. The whole farm. It's a huge undertaking. It will cost me about twenty grand, but I'm going to do it. Damn it, I'm going to do it.'

'Your black neighbours will be delighted,' I remarked.

'The bastards,' Mitchell replied. There was no anger in his voice. He was too high on his plans to harbour unpleasant thoughts. 'They love to eat those warthogs. They go mad for them.'

I puzzled through Mitchell's excitement and his motivations for sinking R20 000 into a fence. He must surely know that his new fence would not be uncontroversial, that his neighbours would delight in tampering with it, in eroding its integrity over a long, patient and invisible campaign.

Sometimes I think Mitchell had chosen to forget what it means to put a fence around Eleanor. He had imagined himself in a world where there were no Cubes or Mashabanas; no peasants, just game farms. Other times, I wonder whether he was not acutely aware of what he was doing. He was giving them the finger on his way out, ensuring that his legacy on that border would be their pain. I think that farming and revenge had become inextricable in Mitchell's head. There was no separating the two.

*

A man by the name of Anton Benfield bought Derbytin and Normandale from Arthur Mitchell. The reputations of newcomers always travel the district's gossip circuits long before they arrive in the flesh, and I heard a lot about Benfield before I spoke with him. He was a very wealthy man from Cape Town, I was told. Made his money in the retail sector, supermarkets in particular. He had two sons, young adventurers in their late twenties with a passion for farming, and he had bought the land for them.

'Lots of money,' I was told. 'He's into irrigation. Interested in the river bank. Doesn't care about the rest of the land. And he is sinking more capital into his operation every day. Bought his own bulldozers and machines. No hiring or renting. This man is very serious.'

Mike Glossop began talking about Benfield on one of our tours around the district. This was before Glossop's unfortunate adventure into the locations. We were sitting in his car, at dawn, on the edge of one of his client's cabbage fields.

'He's a liberal,' Glossop told me. 'He has some imagination

when it comes to dealing with the blacks. He reckons Arthur Mitchell might have sunk himself by being too confrontational, too hard-arsed. He reckons he can accommodate. Find out what these people want and meet them halfway.

'I'm impressed. I'm interested. You see, he has a lot going for him. He's going to start a massive irrigation operation in the area, so he's going to employ tons of people. Which means he's already got something to bargain with. He's bringing money into the area and it's going to be spread around. The other thing is that if he is only going to irrigate, he doesn't need most of his land. A bit of imagination and there is a lot of room to accommodate. Plenty land. Plenty labour. Add that to the right disposition, the right psychology, and you have something going.'

'Are you sceptical?' I asked.

'The powers that be are sceptical.' Glossop was no doubt talking about Waugh and the board of directors at Farm Watch. 'But they're trying to have their cake and eat it. On the one hand, they want to turn that area into a tourist trap; game farms, natural beauty, tranquillity. And yet they're also telling people that there is a civil war raging on that border. They can't have it both ways. Either there is war, or there are tourists. What you need out there is some level-headedness. Somebody who sits down and says, "Okay, let's talk. What do you want? I'll do my damnedest to give it to you."'

It was vintage Glossop, but it spoke to all the parts of me that were listening. When I told Elias in the Pietermaritzburg bar that Mitchell's political disposition was irrelevant, that the son of a liberal might also have been killed, I really hoped that I was talking nonsense. I had asked myself so many times whether a different white man might have reached a compromise with Normandale's tenants. Everyone wants to write a redemptive story. Leading your reader into a heart of darkness is a pretty bleak vocation. So if the problem begins and ends with one man, the rest of the world is inoculated against evil. Everything is fixable. And then Anton Benfield arrives on the scene. The escape route beckons.

When I told Mitchell I would be contacting Anton Benfield, he laughed nervously. 'Whatever you do, Jonny, don't scare him. The money isn't in the bank yet.'

I laughed as well. 'Don't worry, Arthur. I won't talk, I'll just listen.'

'He's an interesting man,' Mitchell said. 'Brings a different perspective to the area. He's recently divorced. And one of his sons is married to a black woman. So you can see he has a very different perspective on things.

'But his sons are very serious about farming. Nice boys. I've met them.'

I called Benfield on his cellphone and told him my business. It was clear from the start that he did not want to speak to me. His choice of words was amicable and polite, his tone guarded and vaguely hostile.

'My family wasn't in the district when Peter Mitchell was killed,' he said. 'What could I possibly tell you?'

'You can understand why I want to speak to you,' I replied. 'I've written a book on a murder and you've bought the land on which it took place. You can understand that I'm interested in your thoughts on the matter.'

'I'm in Cape Town,' he replied. 'I'm not sure when I'll be on the farm next.'

'I can meet you wherever you like. Cape Town, Sarahdale. Wherever is convenient.'

'Okay. I plan to spend the weekend at the farm. I'll meet you there. Friday morning, ten o'clock.'

*

I spent Thursday night in Durban and set out for Sarahdale shortly after dawn the following morning. There was something urgent and irrational about my desire to meet Benfield, and I imagined that if I left any later I would get stranded in gridlock on one of the arteries that runs from Durban into the countryside. So I found myself at the gate of the Benfields' farm more than an hour early. It was late spring again – like the first time I drove along that dust road past Langeni. The sun had just scaled the steep banks of the ravine, and the countryside was bathed in harsh light. I remembered my first trip down that road well – the ravine, the mountains, the beauty of Langeni and of Izita itself. It had all been new and indecipherable then. I wondered what it would look like now. So I did the whole journey, from the junction where the Ndunge road meets the regional road, past Langeni and Eleanor on the right, the Kriek farms and Izita on the left, through the forestry plantations and into the tiny town centre of Sarahdale.

It was a confusing journey. There were two, maybe three countrysides beyond the bubble of my car, and they all clamoured for attention. The first was the scene I had witnessed a year before, a tourist's scene, the one the game hunters would one day take in on their journey to Eleanor and its new owner. It was stupendously beautiful, and I realised for the first time why it was so moving. The secret was in the sudden play between confinement and expansiveness. Down at the bottom of the ravine, the hilltops were so tall and so close, they threatened to fold over and touch one another, closing the ravine and my tiny car into an interminable cavern. And yet, every now and again, the dust road would climb a short hill, and with that delicate elevation the hills would open into the suggestion of a vista, and it seemed as if they rolled on forever, growing wider and wider apart, opening up the whole world. Everything about the countryside that invokes the spiritual in city people was there, exaggerated and overbearing. The sense of the natural as an infinite and unreadable being, moody and callous.

Another countryside began to intrude. It was as hazy and ephemeral as the first, but it sprang unmistakably from the knowledge I had absorbed during the past year. The roadside was almost entirely deserted for the duration of my drive. I must have passed five or six souls on the 50-kilometre journey to Sarahdale and back. And yet the anger of those who had grown up in that district was there. The emptiness echoed with the people who trod that road every day, and in the silence I saw their ghosts; generation upon generation steeped in bile and hatred and disappointment. The social history in my head mingled with the landscape outside, invaded it, came to own it, and soon all I could see was an ancient and silent battle.

The scars themselves became visible. Each place I passed opened up its history to me. The untamed bush and invisible dagga plantations of the Kriek farm; an undelivered gift handed to an influential Afrikaans family by the young apartheid state; the unwritten quid pro quo of dagga harvesting for tenancy; the bulldozers and private security guards as the quid pro quo was broken and a new landowner came to claim his farm. Izita and its succession of priest-landowners, each one spiked on the uselessness of his ideals; their successors – the fat-bellied bandits and their lean, armed children, swaggering down the streets, their stolen guns on their hips. And then, on the outskirts of Sarahdale, the commercial timber plantations and the ghosts of the animals and the people cleared to put them there, the defeated watching the rows of tall trees from the new boundary, their identities shaped by the memory of when that land was theirs.

The countryside clattered with the noise of its cruel politics, each new scene a micro-world of stubborn memories and pernicious games. I remembered my trip through the plantations with Jude Fowler. I had remarked on their beauty, he on their ugliness. I was looking at the blend of colours, as an outsider does; he understood things by their history and their function. For a brief moment as I drove back to the Benfield farm, I imbibed the landscape as a native does; everything marked by a thousand particulars; the history of power and people engraved in every mutation.

*

You can see the green roof of the Benfields' farmhouse from the district road, but you must travel a good 200 metres down a hastily built gravel path before you get there. As the path opens out onto the front of the homestead, you see that there are actually two structures which make a courtyard of the space between them. The yard was a playpen for grown men. It was littered with motorcycle parts and tractor parts and toolboxes, and the messy, haphazard arrangement of these things suggested playful recreation rather than a serious craft.

Two young men went about their business in the courtyard. The first sat astride a motocross bike. He was strong, dark and very good-looking; several days of thick growth covered his cheeks, and his thick black hair was pulled back into an unfashionable ponytail. There was swagger and arrogance in his eyes and he nodded at me coolly. The other man was clearly his brother. Also strong and dark, also unshaven, his black hair as thick as his brother's, but cropped short at the back of his neck. He crouched over a piece of machinery and worked expertly with blackened and greasy hands.

The second brother looked up as I got out of my car, and then continued fiddling with the machinery in his lap. I walked up to him and introduced myself and began to explain my business. I realised that I had forgotten Benfield's first name.

'I have a 10 o'clock appointment with Mr Benfield,' I said.

'We're all Benfields,' he replied, smiling at me a little haughtily. 'Which one?'

I looked at his brother and then back at him. 'Your father, I guess.'

'He's in Cape Town. He'll be here on Sunday.'

'Are you sure?' I replied. 'We set up this appointment a couple of days ago.'

The young Benfield shook his head. 'I spoke to him this morning. He said nothing about a meeting with a man writing a book.'

'I guess I'll have to phone him and reschedule.'

'I guess.'

There was an uncomfortable silence, and then I said: 'Well, I clearly have some time to kill. Do you mind if we chat for a bit?'

'I have nothing to say, really.' He looked at me warily. 'We weren't living here when Peter was killed. And besides, I'm going out in a few minutes.'

'Of course. I see you're busy. I'll phone your dad and make another time.'

As I began walking back to my car, he called after me. 'A whole book, just about the murder of Peter Mitchell?'

'It's a complicated story,' I replied.

'Why was he killed?'

'You'd think that's the one question I should be able to answer. But it's a long, difficult story. I guess the short answer is what everyone says. It was one of the tenants at Langeni.'

'That's what I've been told.'

'Have you had any contact with them?' I asked. 'The tenants, I mean.'

'Ja. They came to us and asked if they could build a road through our farm. We said no.'

'I hope you don't mind my asking, but why?'

He shrugged. 'I guess you need to set up an appointment with my dad.'

I started to say something and then stopped. I wanted to tell him that he had just begun to answer his own question; he had started at the beginning of the story about the young white man who was killed.